# WOMEN AND CRIMINAL JUSTICE

## From the Corston Report to Transforming Rehabilitation

Edited by

Jill Annison, Jo Brayford and John Deering

D1613200

First published in Great Britain in 2015 by

Policy Press
University of Bristol
1-9 Old Park Hill
Bristol
BS2 8BB
UK
t: +44 (0)117 954 5940
pp-info@bristol.ac.uk
www.policypress.co.uk

North America office:
Policy Press
c/o The University of Chicago Press
1427 East 60th Street
Chicago, IL 60637, USA
t: +1 773 702 7700
f: +1 773-702-9756
sales@press.uchicago.edu
www.press.uchicago.edu

British Library Cataloguing in Publication Data
A catalogue record for this book is available from the British Library

Library of Congress Cataloging-in-Publication Data
A catalog record for this book has been requested

ISBN 978 1 44731 931 3 paperback
ISBN 978 1 44731 930 6 hardcover

Cover design by Andrew Corbett
Front cover image: www.alamy.com

# Contents

# Notes on the contributors

**Jill Annison** is associate professor (senior lecturer) in criminal justice studies at Plymouth University. In the early part of her career she worked as a probation officer and social worker.

**Kate Asher** works in probation and was runner up in the National Probation Awards (2012) for her work with women offenders and short-listed for the women's category, Howard League awards (2013).

**Gemma Birkett** is a lecturer in criminology at the University of Winchester. Prior to commencing her PhD, Gemma was a parliamentary researcher in the House of Commons and also worked for a criminal justice charity.

**Jo Brayford** is senior lecturer in criminology and criminal justice at the University of South Wales. She previously worked as research officer (effective practice) for the Probation Service (Gwent Area).

**Gillian Buck** is a PhD student at Keele University and lecturer in criminal justice at Liverpool John Moores University. She is the (co-) author of articles on mentoring in criminal justice.

**Michele Burman** is professor of criminology and deputy head of the School of Social and Political Sciences at the University of Glasgow and co-director of the Scottish Centre for Crime and Justice Research.

**Mary Corcoran** is senior lecturer in criminology at Keele University. She has written extensively about women and criminal justice, especially in relation to the role of the voluntary sector.

**John Deering** is senior lecturer in criminology and criminal justice at the University of South Wales. He previously worked as a probation officer.

**Anita Dockley** is research director at the Howard League for Penal Reform. Her research interests include suicide and self-harm; women; and, order and control in the prison environment.

**Martina Feilzer** is a senior lecturer in criminology and criminal justice at Bangor University. She is involved in several research projects including the ESRC-funded Wiserd/Civil Society Centre; and research on the changing nature of probation.

**Loraine Gelsthorpe** is professor of criminology and criminal justice, Institute of Criminology, University of Cambridge. She has written widely on women, crime and criminal justice, community penalties, and youth justice.

**Alma Hageman** is the RECOOP (Resettlement and Care of Older Ex-Offenders and Prisoners) project worker responsible for running The Rubies group for older women offenders at Eastwood Park Prison. She has current and past experience of working and mentoring in other relevant areas.

**Margaret Malloch** is reader in criminology at the University of Stirling and a member of the Scottish Centre for Crime and Justice Research.

**Gill McIvor** is professor of criminology at the University of Stirling and co-director of the Scottish Centre for Crime and Justice Research.

**Leeanne Plechowicz** has worked in the National Probation Service for ten years. She became a Griffins Society fellow in 2009, applying attachment theory to practice in women's centres and resettlement.

**Becky Shepherd** is a probation officer, currently seconded to the Beth women's centre in Lambeth. She has a BA Hons in women's studies and is undertaking a criminology MSc.

**Alisa Stevens** is lecturer in criminology at the University of Southampton and the author of *Offender rehabilitation and therapeutic communities* (Routledge, 2013).

**Julie Trebilcock** is a senior lecturer at Middlesex University. Julie's main research interests relate to imprisonment, forensic mental health and legal decision-making.

**Kate Williams** is senior lecturer in criminology at Aberystwyth University and director of the Welsh Centre for Crime and Social Justice. She is presently involved in research with Leverhulme, YJB Cymru and police.

**Anne Worrall** is professor emerita of criminology at Keele University and honorary professorial fellow at the University of Western Australia. She has written extensively about women and criminal justice.

**Serena Wright** is a research associate in the Prisons Research Centre, Institute of Criminology, University of Cambridge. She has recently completed her doctorate on women offenders, persistence, and 'frustrated desistance'.

# Acknowledgements

The data in Chapter Thirteen, 'The role of the media in women's penal reform' by Gemma Birkett, were previously published in:
Birkett, G. (2014) Penal reform discourse for women offenders: Campaigners, policy strategies and 'issue reframing', *Crime, Media, Culture: An International Journal*, 10 (2): 115-32, Sage.

The editors would like to thank Sage Journals for permission to publish these data.

The original idea for this book came from one of the annual one-day conferences organised by the Newport Centre for Criminal and Community Justice which ran between 2005 and 2013 at the former University of Wales, Newport (now part of the University of South Wales). The 'Women and Justice' conference was held on 21 May 2013. Nine of the chapters in the book have been written by conference attendees. We would like to thank colleagues for their support in running the conference during those years.

We would also like to thank staff at Policy Press who supported the idea for the book from the outset and gave us every assistance, thus allowing its publication to run as smoothly as possible.

*Jill Annison, Plymouth University*
*Jo Brayford, University of South Wales*
*John Deering, University of South Wales*
*October 2015*

# Acknowledgements

# ONE

# Corston and beyond

*Jill Annison and Jo Brayford*

## Introduction

This chapter provides an overview and discussion of the central theme of the book – women and criminal justice. In particular, it focuses on the publication of the 2007 Report *A Review of Women with Particular Vulnerabilities in the Criminal Justice System*, undertaken by Baroness Jean Corston; it places this review within its wider context and considers key developments that followed. Of crucial importance was the central message underpinning the recommendations of the Report:

> It is timely to bring about a radical change in the way we treat women throughout the whole of the criminal justice system and this must include not just those who offend but also those at risk of offending. This will require a radical new approach, treating women both holistically and individually – a women-centred approach. (Corston, 2007: 2)

In the Foreword to the Report, Baroness Corston highlighted the inappropriateness and disproportionality of remands in custody and prison sentences for women who had committed minor or non-violent crimes.[1] The thrust of the report was that women's vulnerabilities should be identified and worked with to reduce their offending behaviour, and that 'community solutions for non-violent women offenders should be the norm' (Corston, 2007: 9). Most of all, the Corston Report endeavoured to kick-start 'a new approach to women in the criminal justice system, with central drive and direction at the highest level' (Corston, 2007: 13). This stance acknowledged the wider social problems and personal issues that many women offenders faced, endeavouring to situate interventions at a much earlier, more accessible and less stigmatising level within local communities.

The importance of the overall rationale underpinning the recommendations of the Corston Report cannot be overstated. The ethos of this review endeavoured to generate a seismic change in the way that women were dealt with by the criminal justice system, with fundamental implications for social justice and for society's response to women offenders in England and Wales.

This chapter commences with a discussion of the main findings of the Corston Report (2007) and then moves on to explore the situation since the Report was published. In summary, while there have been some reformist accomplishments since Corston, it can be described, at best, as a mixed picture of developments since 2007, with increasing concerns in the face of the 'Transforming Rehabilitation' agenda (Gelsthorpe and Hedderman, 2012 and Chapter Two in this book). In this respect, Carlen's portrayal of 'carceral clawback' provides an apt, if somewhat dispiriting, characterisation 'of the unexpected and retrogressively oppressive consequences of the best-intentioned reforms' (Carlen, 2002a: 220). This concept is drawn on in this chapter to ask a central question: why have Corston's recommendations not maintained the anticipated scope and impact, given their positive reception at the time?

The central stance taken in this chapter, and indeed throughout the book, is that while it is relatively easy to identify women's vulnerabilities and needs (and many have done so since the burgeoning of feminist criminology from the 1970s onwards), we support the injunctions that flow from the Corston Report (2007) that a more radical approach has to be adopted and, in particular, that the centrality of prison as an appropriate response for dealing with women offenders needs to be challenged and displaced.

## The 2007 Corston Report

Baroness Jean Corston's Report *A Review of Women with Particular Vulnerabilities in the Criminal Justice System* was an independent review commissioned by the Home Secretary in November 2005, partly as a result of the high number of women's self-inflicted deaths while in custody. There were no less than 14 self-inflicted deaths of women in prison in 2003 and there were 13 in 2004 (Corston, 2007: 2); six of those deaths occurred over a period of one year in relation to women in custody at HM Prison Styal.[2] Charles Clarke, the then Home Secretary, subsequently asked Baroness Corston to conduct a review of vulnerable women in the criminal justice system.

While the six suicides at Styal triggered the review, it was envisaged that a broad investigation would go beyond prisons and offenders to include ways in which issues such as mental health problems impact on the lives of women (Roberts, 2010). The review was to be 'focused on the group of women offenders who have multiple needs, particularly those women whose risk factors could lead them to harm themselves in prison' (Corston, 2007: Terms of Reference, Appendix B).[3] Thus throughout 2006, Baroness Corston and her team visited women's jails, local women's centres and alternatives to custody for women across the UK. Baroness Corston's final review was published in March 2007 and outlined the need for a 'distinct, radically different, visibly-led, strategic, proportionate, holistic, woman-centred, integrated approach' for female offenders (Corston, 2007: 9). The report made 43 recommendations for improving the approaches, services and interventions for women in the criminal justice system and women who were at risk of offending.

In welcoming the report, Juliet Lyon, Director of the Prison Reform Trust, said:

> The Corston review gives government the chance at long last to join up its social policy with its criminal justice policy. Most women in prison have committed petty offences. Very many have been victims of serious crime and sustained abuse. A new commission for women, with a sensible blueprint for reform across government departments, will largely do away with big prisons that operate as social dustbins for vulnerable women and introduce instead a network of small units and effective local services coupled with proper supervision and support. Many women who offend will have their first real opportunity to beat drugs, drink, mental illness and crime and to take responsibility for their lives, and those of their children, and most will take it. (Prison Reform Trust, 2007)

In this respect Corston (2007) identified three broad categories of vulnerabilities:

- domestic circumstances and problems such as domestic violence, childcare issues, being a single parent;
- personal circumstances such as mental illness, low self-esteem, eating disorders, substance misuse;
- socioeconomic factors such as poverty, isolation and employment.

The report written by Corston was not the first to identify these vulnerabilities or women's particular needs (see Hedderman, 2011); for example, a number of campaigning organisations, such as the Prison

Reform Trust (2000) and the Fawcett Society (2004), had earlier conducted a rigorous body of research. However, taken together, these findings had been consistent in identifying ways in which women could be provided with help more appropriate to their needs, for instance through women-centred provision (Roberts, 2010).

Furthermore, several official investigations and reports had addressed issues and problems relating to women and their vulnerabilities in the years leading up to the Corston Review. Of particular note was the suspension of an inspection at Holloway in 1995 by HM Inspectorate of Prisons due to the appalling conditions found there (Ramsbotham, 2005) and the subsequent thematic review on *Women in Prison* (HM Inspectorate of Prisons, 1997). This report had highlighted the 'urgent need for a thorough analysis of the needs of women prisoners, and a national strategy for implementing and managing policies appropriate to satisfying them' (HM Inspectorate of Prisons, 1997: Preface). The Labour government subsequently published *The Government's Strategy for Women Offenders* (Home Office, 2001), which in turn led to the Women's Offending Reduction Programme, which was intended to coordinate: 'work across departments and agencies to ensure that policies, services, programmes and other interventions respond more appropriately to the particular needs and characteristics of women offenders' (Home Office, 2004: 3).

It can thus be seen that concern about the personal, social and structural problems experienced by women offenders was on the agenda ahead of Corston. For instance, the 1997 thematic review had recommended that:

> a thorough needs analysis across the whole of the female prisoner population is necessary so that relevant strategic policies can be formulated for health care, education, employment, physical education, food, contacts with families, security, tackling offending behaviour, tackling drug and alcohol misuse, childcare, counselling and resettlement. (HM Inspectorate of Prisons, 1997: 20)

Moreover, the impetus to provide more holistic community provision was already in operation via the Labour government's injection of funds into the Together Women demonstration projects in five centres across the North West of England and the Yorkshire and Humberside regions (see Hedderman et al, 2008).[4]

It is therefore interesting to observe that while the push towards coordinated community interventions preceded the Corston Report, it was reinforced by the wide-ranging recommendations contained therein. Nevertheless, Corston raised the key question of why, given the weight of evidence, criminal justice policy did not flow logically from research:

> I have been dismayed at the high prevalence of institutional misunderstanding within the criminal justice system of the things that matter to women and at the shocking level of unmet need. Yet the compelling body of research which has accumulated over many years consistently points to remedies. Much of this research was commissioned by government. There can be few topics that have been so exhaustively researched to such little practical effect as the plight of women in the criminal justice system. The volume of material might lead one to suppose that this is a highly controversial area, which might account in some way for the lack of progress and insight in the way women continue to be treated. This is not the case. (Corston, 2007: 16)

In this respect the zeitgeist of that period needs to be noted: New Labour had come into government promising to be 'tough on crime and tough on the causes of crime', with the concomitant parameters of 'What Works' and of 'evidence-based' policy and practice firmly in place. Critiques of these approaches have been made in relation to the criminal justice system more generally (see, for example, McLaughlin et al, 2001; Raynor, 2004; Hope, 2008), but are of particular pertinence in relation to women offenders, where there were intermingled and often contradictory messages over this period of time. Carlen and Worrall noted these strains as follows:

> Most of the academic books and campaigning and semi-official reports of the last decades of the twentieth century implicitly challenged the legitimacy of continuing to imprison so many women with such appalling histories of poverty and abuse ... The solution of the New Official Criminology for Women in Prison was simple. Change women prisoners' beliefs about the world, the problem is in their heads, not their social circumstances. (Carlen and Worrall, 2004: 23)

This clearly chimed with the Labour government's focus on the responsibilisation of offenders via cognitive-behavioural accredited programmes within the 'What Works' agenda (Kendall, 2002; Shaw and Hannah-Moffat, 2004)[5] – and indeed within the climate of punitiveness that existed then and that still persists as a populist ideological retort at government level.[6] The persistence of these conflicting strands has significant implications for the way women offenders are dealt with in and by the criminal justice system; we will return to these issues later in this chapter.

## Responses to the Corston Report

In the immediate aftermath of the publication of the Corston Review there were indications that the government welcomed the Report, with acceptance of most of the recommendations in full or in part (Ministry of Justice (MoJ), 2007). In the Foreword to the government's response, David Hanson, the then Minister of State at the Ministry of Justice, announced:

> I am therefore very pleased that we are able to set out in the Government's Response the action that will now be taken to improve governance arrangements. An Inter-Ministerial Group will provide the governance for this work, we will establish a cross-departmental Unit within the Ministry of Justice to coordinate and monitor work on taking forward Baroness Corston's recommendations, and we have identified a ministerial Champion – my colleague Maria Eagle MP in the Ministry of Justice – who will be responsible for women and criminal justice matters. (MoJ, 2007: 4)

In the subsequent *Short Study on Women Offenders*, carried out by the Social Exclusion Task Force within the Cabinet Office, there was a stated commitment to deliver systemic change and to complement 'existing provision with earlier, intensive and tailored support' (Cabinet Office, 2009: 3). Momentum for such change was maintained with funding from central government and from charities, and by 2010 there was a network of approximately 40 women's community centres across England and Wales (Hunter and Radcliffe, 2013). There was also activity from the centre, with the National Offender Management Service (NOMS) issuing a National Service Framework for Women Offenders, which set out the kinds of services that were to be provided for women[7] (NOMS, 2008a). In addition, a guide was written to support the implementation of the government's strategic aims and objectives as set out in the National Service Framework for Women (NOMS, 2008b). HM Prison Service (2008) also issued related guidance on regimes and standards of care.

However, the *Second Report on Women with Particular Vulnerabilities in the Criminal Justice System* (Howard League for Penal Reform, 2011), conducted by an All Party Parliamentary Group under the chairmanship of Baroness Corston, revealed that while many of the original recommendations had been implemented, there were outstanding concerns. Most importantly, the recommendation to replace the existing women's prisons with a number of small, multifunctional custodial centres had not been taken forwards. The significance of this was indicated in a detailed analysis, *Corston Report 5 Years On,* conducted by the Women in Prison campaigning group; the summary of this review celebrated the progress that had been made, but called for renewed efforts to bring about the implementation of the remaining recommendations. In particular, they welcomed the end to mandatory strip searching of women in prison and acknowledged the support for additional community support and diversion services for women. Nevertheless they made some salutary observations in terms of overall impact:

> The Report is worth more than its individual recommendations and part of their importance lies in their outlining a coherent road to reform, rather than a collection of piecemeal changes. Five years and two governments later too little distance has been travelled. (Women in Prison, 2012)

## Progress made: policy and practice developments

In terms of the force of its evidence and informed argument, the Corston Report carried moral weight and influence and, as noted above, it did impact on both policy and practice over the following years in England and Wales. The Labour government then in power accepted outright 25 of the recommendations and a further 14 in principle or in part, and the rhetoric was of a coordinated and cross-departmental response to women's offending (MoJ, 2007). However, Hedderman (2011) noted four critical aspects, which cut across Corston's wish for radical reform: first, 'the Government persisted with the line that sentencing was a matter for the courts'; second – and in contrast to the foregoing emphasis on judicial independence – sentencers' discretion was curtailed in the Criminal Justice Act 2003, thus making imprisonment more likely for a breach of a community sentence; third, 'the Government rejected the idea that women who were unlikely to receive a custodial sentence should not be remanded in custody'; and fourth, there was complete rejection of Corston's recommendation for large women's prisons to be closed and replaced by small, more geographically dispersed custodial units (Hedderman, 2011: 36).

These embargoes effectively 'holed below the waterline' the potential for radical change, as they left unchallenged imprisonment as a means of dealing with women offenders and, moreover, kept the prison estate as currently constituted. The importance of prison remaining in place as a sentencing disposal for women offenders can be seen as a critical decision by central government, taken despite acknowledgement that women generally commit low-level offences and that they represent a small percentage of offenders overall (Wahidin, 2013).

Concern had been expressed about the rising level of imprisonment of women offenders in England and Wales from the mid-1990s onwards (Hedderman, 2004), with Gelsthorpe noting 'the "punitive turn" towards women' (Gelsthorpe, 2007: 48). The overall pattern of imprisonment with regard to women offenders over the past 50 years is clearly demonstrated by the statistics (see Heidensohn and Silvestri, 2012). Figure 1.1 shows the steep upward trend that took place from the 1990s (annual average figures).

Meanwhile, Figure 1.2 indicates that while the numbers have dropped a little over the recent past,[8] the number of women being sent to prison still remains at a historically high level.

**Figure 1.1:** Average female prison population in England and Wales, 1960-2010

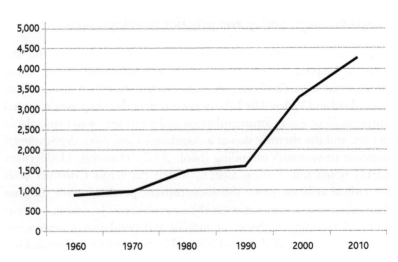

**Figure 1.2:** Number of women prisoners 2004-2014

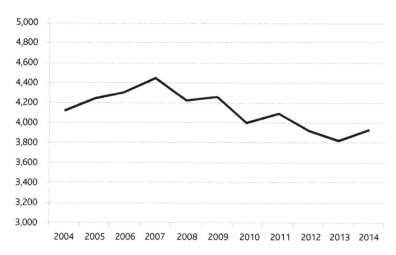

Note: End-of-year figures (except 2014, which is end of July)

Source: Howard League for Penal Reform, 2014

These findings of the persistence of custodial sentencing give rise to considerable concern, not least because of the longstanding acknowledgement that many women prisoners were receiving prison sentences for relatively low-level crimes and were posing low risk to others (Gelsthorpe and Morris, 2002). Moreover, they were disproportionately experiencing the 'pains of imprisonment' (Carlen, 2012).

In this respect it seems likely that these women are at the sharp end of 'an absurd and ironic impasse' (Snider, 2003) of two contradictory developments: on the one hand, feminist criminologists and progressive managers and practitioners have endeavoured to 'make prison programmes more "effective", overcome programme failure, and "meet women's needs"' (Snider, 2003: 371). This approach is understandable, given the troubled situations that many women offenders experience, but is extremely problematic given Corston's imperative that: 'The practice of sending a woman to prison as a "place of safety" or "for her own good" is appalling and must stop' (Corston, 2007: 9).

On the other hand, responses come from an 'opposite corner' where 'critical and Foucauldian academics are deconstructing the knowledge claims, agendas, rationalities and techniques of the first group' (Snider, 2003: 371), which may lead to fragmentation and a lack of constructive engagement. This is important for, as Player articulates:

resilience to change cannot be attributed to a single cause but is arguably best understood as a consequence of a political process in which different policies compete for implementation and where the outcome of the context is already weighted in favour of certain ideas, values and beliefs rather than others. (Player, 2014: 281)

Carlen has provided valuable theoretical insights about the situation and the 'carceral clawback' that has ensued (Carlen, 2002b). She has raised the interesting question about why 'myths' about the possibilities of a benign prison persist. Of particular relevance in this current critique is her argument that campaigners for penal reform have become disillusioned by their own lack of impact on imprisonment and thus reluctantly accept the invitation to join prison administrators to help shape in-prison initiatives that are designed to reduce both the pain and the damaging effects of imprisonment (Carlen, 2002c: 160). She points to an ironic outcome where:

> Oppositional discourses supposed to be championing a reduction in the women's prison population unwittingly helped fashion a new policy discourse on women and crime, an official discourse which will justify more and more women being locked up in the future – so that their 'criminogenic needs can be met' – not somehow, but legitimately! (Carlen, 2002c: 170)

The intransigence of structural change, affected not least by atrophy by encroachment (Hannah-Moffat, 2002), has been noted by Nick Hardwick, HM Chief Inspector of Prisons. In a lecture in 2012 he reflected on developments in the UK since the 2007 Corston Report; while he talked about inspections finding some significant change in the experience of women in prison, he also claimed that:

> despite these changes and despite the hard work of those involved, the structural problems to which Baroness Corston points remain almost untouched. The different needs and circumstances of men and women prisoners remain as stark today as they did when Baroness Corston wrote her report – little has changed. The number of women in prison has remained almost constant and too little has yet been done to fully utilise community alternatives to custody – and what

has been done is not secure. There are too many women in prison who do not need to be there. (Hardwick, 2012)

Despite these gloomy conclusions in relation to the situation for women in prison, the Corston Report and subsequent developments can be seen as supporting the positive steps that had already been made in developing holistic, one-stop-shop interventions in the community for women offenders (Gelsthorpe, 2011). Recognition of the progress made during the latter years of the Labour government was summarised by Hedderman as follows:

> There is no question that in the last few years of its administration, the Labour government made important progress in supporting and fostering the development of community-based programmes for women offenders; and that support was not just rhetorical but financial. While £26 million is not a huge sum compared to £3 billion spent on prison each year, it bought a significant amount of support for some of the most socially disadvantaged women in England and Wales. (Hedderman, 2010: 495)

However, the problems associated with countervailing tendencies also arose in respect of community sentencing of women. First, sentencers were informed, encouraged and exhorted to use such sentences, but their powers were not restricted in any judicial way; Hedderman (2011) noted that this strategy had not worked in the past and did not seem to be working in the present. Second, Hedderman voiced concerns about the potential for net-widening and up-tariffing of troubled women, given the access route to 'help', particularly within a climate of punitiveness. While curtailment of magistrates' powers to remand in custody and to pass short prison sentences for minor offences could address some of these issues, she commented that:

> Perhaps the real issue at stake is not judicial independence, but the continuing preference for being seen to be 'tough on crime' rather than genuinely seeking to reduce offending and reoffending by being 'tough on the causes of crime'. (Hedderman, 2011: 40)

## Conclusion

This chapter has outlined the scope and intentions of the Corston Report (2007) and critically reviewed the ultimately unfulfilled promise that it held. The complexities of well-intentioned developments, which nevertheless failed to bring about the hoped-for level of change, particularly in relation to radical alternatives to custody for women offenders, have been subjected to theoretical critique and in-depth analysis. While the change of government in 2010 undoubtedly stalled some of the initiatives, not least because of the loss of the 'champion' as advocated by Corston[9] (and enacted by the Labour government), many of the community interventions did persist, albeit with uncertain funding.

The chapters that now follow engage with policy and practice developments over the period from 2007 to the current situation, where the Coalition government's 'Transforming Rehabilitation' revolution (MoJ, 2014) is being operationalised. Yet again, the parameters for 'effective practice' have been shifted, this time within a climate of political ideology that has prioritised contestability and payment by results (see Gelsthorpe and Hedderman, 2012).

Chapter Two, 'Transforming Rehabilitation: implications for women', leads Part One of the book: this chapter outlines recent developments and critically analyses the pathway to the current position regarding penal responses to women offenders. The subsequent chapters within this section in turn examine wider contexts.

Part Two and the chapters therein contribute a range of perspectives, by reviewing the implementation of practice, both in the community and in prisons, thus providing insights into the direction of policy and the delivery of interventions.

Meanwhile, the chapters in Part Three turn to consider issues relating to best practice and possible ways forward. Finally, Chapter Fourteen draws together some of the key issues in this area, endeavouring to maintain the impetus for change and to support the vision for innovative policy and practice that the Corston Report inspired.

### Notes

[1] In stating her personal standpoint, Baroness Corston said: 'I do not believe, like some campaigners, that no women should be held in custody. There are some crimes for which custody is the only resort in the interests of justice and public protection, but I was dismayed to see so many women frequently sentenced for short periods of time for very minor offences,

causing chaos and disruption to their lives and families, without any realistic chance of addressing the causes of their criminality' (Corston 2007: i).

[2]   The Safety in Custody statistics for the period 1978-2013 concerning self-inflicted deaths in prison custody are as follows: www.gov.uk/government/statistics/safety-in-custody-statistics-quarterly-update-to-december-2013. For women these are as follows: 1978 – 1; 1979 – 0; 1980 – 0; 1981 – 1; 1982 – 0; 1983 – 0; 1984 – 0; 1985 – 1; 1986 – 1; 1987 – 1; 1988 – 0; 1989 – 2; 1990 – 1; 1991 – 0; 1992 – 2; 1993 – 1; 1994 – 1; 1995 – 2; 1996 – 3; 1997 – 3; 1998 – 3; 1999 – 5; 2000 – 8; 2001 – 6; 2002 – 9; 2003 – 14; 2004 – 13; 2005 – 4; 2006 – 3; 2007 – 8; 2008 – 1; 2009 – 3; 2010 – 1; 2011 – 2; 2012 – 1; 2013 – 2.

[3]   It is salutary to see the numbers of individual women prisoners who are noted as self-harming each year (figures only available from 2004 at www.gov.uk/government/statistics/safety-in-custody-statistics-quarterly-update-to-december-2013): 2004 – 1,240; 2005 – 1,345; 2006 – 1,316; 2007 – 1,337; 2008 – 1,389; 2009 – 1,327; 2010 – 1,247; 2011 – 1,301; 2012 – 1,094; 2013 – 1,037.

[4]   Hedderman et al (2008) note that 'Together Women builds on best practice developed by other smaller-scale initiatives such as the 218 Centre in Scotland and the Calderdale and Asha Centres in England and Wales. Key features of these projects and Together Women include the fact that they offer a tailored response to individual needs rather than being a "one-size fits all" programme' (Hedderman et al, 2008: 1). See also Gelsthorpe et al, 2007.

[5]   This response was demonstrated most explicitly in the comments made in the Government's Strategy for Female Offenders (Home Office, 2001: 7), when it was stated that: 'This Government promised to be tough on crime and its causes. There is no excuse for crime, whatever a person's background or experience. However, the characteristics of women prisoners suggest that experiences such as poverty, abuse and drug addiction lead some women to believe that their options are limited. Many offending behaviour programmes are designed to help offenders see that there are always positive choices open to them that do not involve crime. At the same time, across Government, we are tackling the aspects of social exclusion that make some women believe their options are limited. Our work with women offenders should therefore be seen in the context of our wider programme to tackle social exclusion.'

[6]   This is exemplified by Chris Grayling's pronouncement in June 2014, in response to concerns about the current increase in the size of the prison population expressed by Nick Hardwick, Chief Inspector of Prisons, that 'overcrowding would mean that "a few hundred prisoners more will have to share a cell over the next few weeks"' (BBC News, www.bbc.co.uk/news/uk-27847007). Grayling's words overlook wider issues of safety,

interpersonal relations and the operation of day-to-day activities within such closed institutions.

[7]   This was subsequently replaced by the guide *A Distinct Approach: A Guide to Working with Women Offenders*, published by NOMS Women and Equalities Group in March 2012.

[8]   A peak of 4,671 was reached on 23 April 2004 (Howard League for Penal Reform, 2014).

[9]   A discussion of this issue in the Justice Committee Oral Evidence of the Women Offenders follow-up meeting took place on Wednesday, 16 July 2014 – see www.parliament.uk/business/committees/committees-a-z/commons-select/justice-committee/inquiries/parliament-2010/women-offenders-follow-up/

## References

Berman, G. and Dar, A. (2013) *Prison population statistics*, www.parliament.uk/business/publications/research/briefing-papers/SN04334/prison-population-statistics

Cabinet Office (2009) *Short study on women offenders, Report conducted by the Social Exclusion Task Force 2009*, London: Cabinet Office and MoJ.

Carlen, P. (2002a) New discourses of justification and reform for women's imprisonment in England, in P. Carlen (ed.) *Women and punishment: The struggle for justice*, Cullompton: Willan.

Carlen, P. (2002b) Carceral clawback: The case of women's imprisonment in Canada, *Punishment & Society*, 4, (1):, 115-21.

Carlen, P. (2002c) Controlling measures: The repackaging of common-sense opposition to women's imprisonment in England and Canada, *Criminal Justice*, 2 (2):, 155-72.

Carlen, P. (2012) 'Women's imprisonment: An introduction to the Bangkok Rules', Lecture at the University of Barcelona, May 2012, http://revistes.ub.edu/index.php/CriticaPenalPoder/article/viewFile/5058/6756

Carlen, P. and Worrall, A. (2004) *Analysing women's imprisonment*, Cullompton: Willan.

Corston, J. (2007) *The Corston report: A report by Baroness Jean Corston of a review of women with particular vulnerabilities in the criminal justice system*, London: Home Office.

Fawcett Society (2004) *Women and the criminal justice system*, London: Fawcett Society.

Gelsthorpe, L. (2007) Sentencing and gender, in R. Sheehan, G. McIvor and C. Trotter (eds) *What works with women offenders* , Cullompton: Willan.

Gelsthorpe, L. (2011) Working with women offenders in the community: A view from England and Wales, in R. Sheehan, G. McIvor and C. Trotter (eds) *Working with women offenders in the community*, Abingdon: Willan.

Gelsthorpe, L. and Hedderman, C. (2012) Providing for women offenders: The risks of adopting a Payment by Results approach, *Probation Journal*, 59 (4):, 374-90.

Gelsthorpe, L. and Morris, A. (2002) Women's imprisonment in England and Wales: A penal paradox, *Criminal Justice*, 2 (3):, 277-301.

Gelsthorpe, L., Sharpe, G. and Roberts, J. (2007) *Provision for women offenders in the community*, London: Fawcett Society.

Hannah-Moffat, H. (2002) Creating choices: Reflecting on choices, in P. Carlen (ed.) *Women and punishment: The struggle for justice* , Cullompton: Willan.

Hardwick, N. (2012) 'Women in prison: Corston five years on', Lecture at the University of Sussex, 29 February 2012, www.justice.gov.uk/downloads/about/hmipris/women-in-prison.pdf

Hedderman, C. (2004) Why are more women being sentenced to custody?, in G. McIvor (ed.) *Women who offend*, London: Jessica Kingsley.

Hedderman, C. (2010) Government policy on women offenders: Labour's legacy and the Coalition's challenge, *Punishment & Society*, 12 (4),: 485-500.

Hedderman, C. (2011) Policy developments in England and Wales, in R. Sheehan, G. McIvor and C. Trotter (eds) *Working with women offenders in the community*, Abingdon: Willan.

Hedderman, C., Palmer, E. and Hollin, C., with Gunby, C., Shelton, N. and Askari, M. (2008) *Implementing services for women offenders and those 'at risk' of offending: Action research with Together Women*, Ministry of Justice Research Series 12/08. London: MoJ.

Heidensohn, F. and Silvestri, M. (2012) Gender and crime, in M. Maguire, R. Morgan and R. Reiner (eds) *The Oxford handbook of criminology* (5th edn), Oxford: Oxford University Press.

HM Inspectorate of Prisons (1997) *Women in prison: A thematic review*, London: Home Office.

HM Prison Service (2008) *Women prisoners, Prison Service Order Number 4800*, www.justice.gov.uk/offenders/types-of-offender/women

Home Office (2001) *The government's strategy for women offenders*, London: Home Office.

Home Office (2004) *Women's Offending Reduction Programme (WORP) action plan*, London: Home Office.

Hope, T. (2008) The first casualty: Evidence and governance in a war against crime, in P. Carlen (ed.), *Imaginary penalties*, Cullompton: Willan.

Howard League for Penal Reform (2011) *Women in the penal system: Second report on women with particular vulnerabilities in the criminal justice system*, London: Howard League for Penal Reform.

Howard League for Penal Reform (2014) *Week by week prison population breakdown*, www.howardleague.org/weekly-prison-watch/

Hunter, G. and Radcliffe, P. (2013) Are magistrates doing justice to women?, *Criminal Justice Matters*, 92, 34-5.

Kendall, K. (2002) Time to think again about cognitive behavioural programmes, in P. Carlen (ed.) *Women and punishment: The struggle for justice*, Cullompton: Willan.

McLaughlin, E., Muncie, J. and Hughes, G. (2001) The permanent revolution: New Labour, new public management and the modernization of criminal justice, *Criminology and Criminal Justice*, 1 (3):, 301-18.

MoJ (2007) *The Government's response to the report by Baroness Corston of a review of women with particular vulnerabilities in the criminal justice system*, Cm 7261, London: HMSO.

MoJ (2014) *Transforming Rehabilitation*, www.justice.gov.uk/transforming-rehabilitation

NOMS (2008a) *National Service Framework improving services to women offenders 2008*, London: MoJ.

NOMS (2008b) *The offender management guide to working with women offenders*, London: MoJ.

NOMS Women and Equalities Group (2012) *A distinct approach: A guide to working with women offenders*, London: MoJ.

Player, E. (2014) Women in the criminal justice system: The triumph of inertia, *Criminology and Criminal Justice*, 14 (3):, 276-97.

Prison Reform Trust (2000) *Justice for women: The need for reform. The Wedderburn Report of the Committee on Women's Imprisonment*, London: Prison Reform Trust.

Prison Reform Trust (2007) Corston Report, quote from Juliet Lyon, Director of the Prison Reform Trust, www.prisonreformtrust.org.uk/ProjectsResearch/Women/Corstonreport

Ramsbotham, D. (2005) *Prison-gate: The shocking state of Britain's prisons and the need for visionary change*, London: The Free Press.

Raynor, P. (2004) The Probation Service 'Pathfinders': Finding the path and losing the way?, *Criminology and Criminal Justice*, 4 (3):, 309-25.

Roberts, J. (2010) Women offenders: More troubled than troublesome?, in J. Brayford, F. Cowe and J. Deering (eds) *What else works? Creative work with offenders*, Cullompton: Willan.

Shaw, M. and Hannah-Moffat, K. (2004) How cognitive skills forgot about gender and diversity, in G. Mair (ed) *What matters in probation*, Cullompton: Willan.

Snider, L. (2003) Constituting the punishable woman: Atavistic man incarcerates postmodern Woman, *British Journal of Criminology*, 43 (2):, 1-39.

Wahidin, A. (2013) Gender and crime, in C. Hale, K. Hayward, A. Wahidin and E. Wincup (eds) *Criminology* (3rd edn), Oxford: Oxford University Press.

Women in Prison (2012) *Corston report 5 years on*, www.no-offence. org/pdfs/7.pdf

# Part One
# Context

TWO

# *Transforming Rehabilitation*: implications for women

*Jill Annison, Jo Brayford and John Deering*

This chapter looks at changes to the criminal justice system brought in by the previous Coalition Government, following proposals made in the Ministry of Justice's (MoJ's) *Transforming Rehabilitation* (MoJ, 2013a), referred to here as 'TR'. The particular needs of women – and what might 'work' with them – are covered elsewhere in this book, and this chapter will not include these discussions. However, the criminal justice system has long been regarded as being designed for men; the overriding view of critics is that the stance of successive governments that only minor modifications were needed to accommodate women has been an inadequate response (see, for example, Worrall and Gelsthorpe, 2009).

In the recent past, policy has been dominated by the Corston Report (Corston, 2007) and government reactions to it. Overall, the consensus of critical opinion has been that while certain elements have improved, these have been somewhat piecemeal and that a paradigm shift has not occurred. Moreover, this is unlikely to take place unless the government accepts the central argument that most offending by women can – and should – be dealt with in the community, and that sentencers' powers should be limited in that direction (see Chapter One and Chapter Fourteen).

## The background to *Transforming Rehabilitation*

The New Labour government laid the ground for TR and the privatisation and marketisation of the probation service with the creation of the National Offender Management Service (NOMS) in 2004 (Hough et al, 2006). The impetus for this was the Carter Report (*Managing Offenders, Reducing Crime – the Correctional Services Review*, Carter, 2003), which proposed breaking up the National Probation Service for England and Wales, which itself was only created in 2001, and putting out to tender some of its services. NOMS was initially an administrative entity, until the Offender Management Act 2007 allowed the Secretary of State to commission 'any other person' to undertake probation roles except for the supervision of the highest 'risk of harm' individuals and advice to courts (MoJ, 2011a). It is this Act that the Coalition government relied on as the legal basis for the break-up of the probation service under TR.

After the election of 2010, the Coalition government introduced proposals to address what it argued were high rates of reoffending within the criminal justice system, particularly by those prisoners sentenced to fewer than 12 months' custody; this includes the majority of women sentenced to imprisonment. The then Justice Minister, Kenneth Clarke, announced a 'Rehabilitation Revolution' (Clarke, 2010) that would be driven by marketisation and competition, which Clarke saw as necessary to increase innovation and flexibility in the supervision of offenders. In a series of documents, including a Green Paper *Breaking the Cycle* (MoJ, 2010), the government consulted on its proposals (see MoJ, 2011a; 2011b; 2012a; 2012b), eventually arriving at the proposals contained within TR.

These proposals included a system of Payment by Results (PbR). Initially, it was envisaged that any new provider of 'probation services' under PbR would only receive payment if reduced reoffending targets were achieved. The organisation would then receive payment for providing the service, plus a 'bonus' apparently to be paid from the overall reduction in costs to the public purse brought about by the reduction of reoffending (MoJ, 2012b). The efficacy and processes involved in PbR within the criminal justice system have been controversial (Fox and Albertson, 2011) and, at the time of writing (winter 2014), the percentage of income linked to results remains unknown (Clinks, 2013a), although it seems to have been reduced to a proportion small enough to attract private sector bidders. In any event, the government announced, in October 2014, that PbR payments (or deductions) would be linked to percentage changes in the predicted reoffending rate, but gave no indication of the percentage of the contract value that this would involve (MoJ, 2014a).

The proposals within TR became possible with the passing of the Offender Rehabilitation Act in March 2014.[1] This allowed for 12 months' compulsory supervision on release of all offenders sentenced to short-term custody. Under the Act, the supervisor must be an 'officer of a provider of probation services'[2] or an officer of a youth offending team. In addition, the supervising organisation needs to 'identify anything in the arrangements that is intended to meet the particular needs of female offenders'.[3] This supervision is mandatory under the

Act and subject to enforcement and breach proceedings, with custody a possibility on conviction.

## Transforming rehabilitation

Probation trusts ceased to exist on 1 June 2014. The National Probation Service for England and Wales, set up in 2001, had therefore passed into history, to be replaced by a new National Probation Service (NPS), which is part of the civil service, and 21 new community rehabilitation companies (CRCs)[4] covering England and Wales, the latter passing into private hands on 1 February 2015. The NPS is responsible for supervising 'high risk of harm' cases, providing advice to courts and processing breach proceedings on all offenders, including those supervised by the CRCs.

When considering the detail of the initial TR document (MoJ, 2013a), it is apparent that its tone and language largely ignored women as a separate group. In a more general sense it did discuss the root causes of all offending and to 'overcoming barriers that prevent them [all offenders] from turning their lives around' (MoJ, 2013a: 7). It also encouraged flexibility and innovation in delivery of rehabilitation services, which potentially could provide more appropriately for women. Women were mentioned specifically in only one paragraph (MoJ, 2013a: 17), which stated that future provision should meet the 'specific needs and priorities' relating to women. In short, it was clear that the reforms were largely about saving money and about cost-effectiveness (MoJ, 2013a: 9). This runs counter to Corston's proposals for a more individualised, intensive (if needed), needs-based approach more suited to women. Furthermore, at this point it became evident that the government had significantly moved away from its original level of commitment to PbR, as the idea of the entire contract being subject to PbR had been replaced by a split between a 'fee for services' and the PbR element.

Following formal public consultation, revised plans were issued in May 2013. The final document *Transforming Rehabilitation: A Strategy for Reform* (MoJ, 2013b) gave details of provision under community orders and the new compulsory 12 months' supervision arrangements. Much was made of the need to reduce reoffending, arguing that rates for both custodial and community sentences were too high. It noted the £3 billion a year spent on prisons and the £1 billion spent on community sentences, arguing that for such large sums outcomes should be improved for both sectors. However, despite noting the higher rate of reoffending following a custodial sentence, no comment was made about the principle or (in)effectiveness of the continued high use of custody in the criminal justice system (MoJ, 2013b: 6). Thus it is clear that perhaps one of the best measures to reduce levels of reoffending and to save considerable amounts of money – the reduction in the rates of custodial sentencing – did not enter into the Coalition government's thinking. It was clearly committed to the high use of custody and had no intention of limiting sentencers' powers in this regard.[5] Despite this, the language was one of rehabilitation, rather than retribution, although this lack of a critique on the continued use of custody shows something of an apparent philosophical confusion.[6] For example, the document discussed rehabilitation and the 'emphasis on responding to the broader life management issues that often lead offenders back to crime' (MoJ, 2013b: 6) and mentioned high levels of unemployment, anxiety and depression, homelessness and substance misuse as associated with offending and thus matters to be addressed via supervision on community orders and licences.

The overall strategy for future provision was divided into the following sections.

### Reducing reoffending

The large increase in numbers being supervised as a result of post-custody supervision for short-term prisoners would be within existing expenditure. This would be achieved by 'competing the majority of services' and a 'more efficient public sector service' and achieved 'within allocated budgets' (Ministry of Justice, 2013b: 11). These proposals and claims seem to have been based on little more evidence than the savings on the Serco/London Probation Trust Unpaid Work contract awarded in 2012, which was used as a pathfinder for privatisation. However, it is of note that this was cancelled by the MoJ in February 2014 due to poor performance (Watts, 2014). Rehabilitation was intended to be tailored to individual needs but, at the same time, the document noted the introduction of the compulsory punitive Requirement into all Community Orders under the Crime and Courts Act 2013.

There was only one short section on 'responding to women's needs' (MoJ, 2013b: 15-16). This noted that women make up 15% of the probation caseload and 5% in custody. Awareness was shown of many women's previous experience of abuse and neglect, of them having complex needs and that some two thirds of women enter custody having dependent children. However, despite this, the document had little to say other than that CRC providers should be able to 'articulate and respond to the particular needs of women' (MoJ, 2013b: 16). Finally, the document outlined the aim of promoting the involvement of small, local organisations as subcontractors to the major CRC contractors.[7] For the detail on reducing reoffending, see MoJ, 2013b: 9-19.

## Protecting the public

All risk assessments would be carried out by the NPS, initially for court reports and thereafter to decide whether individuals would be supervised by the NPS or the CRC. All 'high risk of harm' offenders are now supervised by the NPS. It is thus clear that the majority of women, because they are low/medium risk or serving short custodial sentences, are now to be supervised by CRCs. Moreover, it seems likely that the new post-custody supervision arrangements will increase likelihood of breach, as they will involve ex-prisoners in mandatory reporting, with the majority of women who receive custody being in this category. For the detail on protecting the public, see MoJ, 2013b: 20-23.

## Making the system work

NOMS and commissioning structures are intended to provide a mix of providers responsive to local needs. As most probation trust employees have transferred to CRCs, in the short term at least skills and expertise will remain, but no guarantees of this for the future were given in the document. Moreover, while the NPS will retain the ability to train staff professionally, CRCs will only be required to provide a workforce with 'appropriate levels of training and competence' (MoJ, 2013b: 26).

The CRCs cover large geographical areas and it is therefore open to question how local and flexible these will be in terms of service provision for women. There was also an expectation of future co-commissioning of services, so there will be the possibility of a CRC being funded by NOMS and, for example, the NHS to provide more joined-up services, around substance misuse and mental health services. For the detail on making the system work, see MoJ, 2013b: 24-32.

For now, these proposals present a range of challenges and concerns: indeed, as Gomm (2013) argues:

> The impact of good quality service provision on women with complex and diverse needs must be considered within a more sophisticated framework and commissioners from Prime providers and the MoJ should be held accountable for ensuring this. (Gomm, 2013: 153)

## Other concurrent developments

At the same time as the consultation and finalisation of TR, other official reports and processes were recognising, in theory at least, the different needs of women offenders. However, these also tended to talk of needing to accommodate women's rehabilitation, while also declaring the need for community penalties to be robust and primarily about punishment. For example, the NOMS Women and Equalities Group report *A Distinct Approach: A guide to working with women offenders* (MoJ, 2012c) can be seen to fit within well-worn government mantras of punishment, as it initially lists the following principles and practices (MoJ, 2012c: 4):

- 'Punishment' – all punishments must be 'robust and demanding' on the assumption that this will make women 'confront the consequences of their crimes';
- 'Payback' – women must pay their victims back for their crimes, either directly or indirectly;
- 'Progression' – assistance is needed for women, to help them stop abusing drugs/alcohol, to help them resolve relationship issues, address mental health problems and 'get into work';
- 'Protection' – women's risk of harm and reoffending must be assessed and managed and thereby reduced.

Presumably, these are listed in order of priority and reveal the continuity of the increased importance and persistence of more punitive philosophies over recent decades among many Western governments (irrespective of political hue) within late modernity (Garland, 2001; Pratt et al, 2005; Snacken and Dumortier, 2012). At the same time, there is a tacit acceptance of (at least some of) the underlying reasons behind women's offending; the remainder of the document looks at statistics about offending rates, offence types, sentencing trends, and so on, and identifies what has been noted elsewhere in terms of the differential way in which women and men are regarded and treated within the criminal justice system. In this way, little (if any) of the content relates to issues of punishment, although there is mention of punishment linked to deprivation of liberty (MoJ, 2012c: 17), and the document contains a list of 'top tips' for probation trusts and practitioners in terms of policy and practice related to women. These include accommodation, education and training, financial management, relationships, lifestyle and associates, drug and alcohol misuse, thinking and behaviour, attitudes and health and emotional well-being.

Shortly afterwards, the MoJ published its *Strategic Objectives for Female Offenders* (MoJ, 2013c). It announced the setting up of an Advisory Board under the Minister of State, Helen Grant, and set out the following priorities:

1. 'Ensuring the provision of credible, robust sentencing options in the community that will enable female offenders to be punished and rehabilitated in the community where appropriate.
2. 'Ensuring the provision of services in the community that recognise and address the specific needs of female offenders, where these are different from those of male offenders.
3. 'Tailoring the women's custodial estate and regimes so that they reform and rehabilitate offenders effectively, punish properly, protect the public fully, and meet gender specific standards, and locate women in prisons as near to their families as possible; and
4. 'Through the transforming rehabilitation programme, supporting better life management by female offenders ensuring all criminal justice system partners work together to enable women to stop reoffending.' (MoJ, 2013c: 4)

Again, talk of punishment existed alongside priorities with a largely different focus. The work of the Advisory Board was to be within four 'work streams' (MoJ, 2013c: 5-6): to promote enhanced provision in the community for women, while retaining the 'punitive' element; to ensure that the TR proposals made proper provision for women; to review the prison estate for women; and to take a whole-systems approach working with partners within and outside the criminal justice system, to ensure appropriate provision for women.

A year after the publication of the strategic objectives, the government published an update on progress (MoJ, 2014b). This stated that a review of women-specific provision in the community had been completed that showed an increase, and it gave examples of work within particular probation trusts of women-only provision. In terms of the prison estate, all female prisons were to be designated resettlement prisons under the TR proposals, and the large majority of women prisoners would have resettlement needs handled by their home CRC. The document makes specific mention of TR, arguing that it has been amended to ensure that the contractual arrangement for CRCs will reflect the need to provide for women, particularly those short-term prisoners who will be subject to post-custody supervision. Specifically, it will provide for women to: (i) have a female supervisor/responsible officer; (ii) attend meetings or appointments in a female-only environment; and (iii) not be placed in a male-only environment for unpaid work or attendance requirements (MoJ, 2014b: 4).

In addition, following consultation with the Advisory Board, all CRCs will receive information about the range and type of women's needs and existence of women-only provision that can address these. In terms of funding, existing community services for women were due to be funded centrally until March 2015. However, at that point, CRCs were able to review these in terms of 'concerns about performance or ... *insufficient demand*' (MoJ, 2014b: 4 – emphasis added).

Of course, these reports were produced at central government level and might be expected to be couched in positive terms. In contrast, a cross-party report was produced by the House of Commons Justice Committee: *Women Offenders – after the Corston Report* (House of Commons Justice Committee, 2013). It noted that the government had created a ministerial position for women offenders (House of Commons Justice Committee, 2013: 3), although it doubted whether the Advisory Board also created would have sufficient authority (House of Commons Justice Committee, 2013: 82). While this development was to be welcomed, the Committee was of the view that while government recognised the need for a 'whole systems' approach to women that included preventive measures, little had emerged in terms of concrete thinking about what this actually meant, and that neither the MoJ nor NOMS had fully reflected on what was known about women in their policies and practices (House of Commons Justice Committee, 2013: 81).

Similarly, the report bemoaned the lack of evidence of effectiveness concerning interventions with women, and it urged NOMS to consider a more proactive preventive approach, given what is known about the causes of women's offending (House of Commons Justice Committee, 2013: 4). It also argued that the growth of suitable, community-based provision had been uneven and, linked to this, the committee took the government to task for its male-centrism in terms of criminal justice (House of Commons Justice Committee, 2013: 4). One of the consequences of this, it was argued, was the over-concentration of reducing reoffending to the exclusion of prevention and a more holistic approach. This would be 'likely to reinforce the loss' of generic funding for community provision for women. The report reached a number of conclusions and made recommendations, including what it called a 'compelling' case for the separate commissioning of services for women which, among other things, would include incentives to encourage diversion from prosecution for less serious offences. Most radically perhaps, it also argued that the use of custody should be reduced for women, stating that over half of women sentenced to custody received 'ineffective short-term sentences' (House of Commons Justice Committee, 2013: 4) and that community provision should be bolstered, including services for mental health and drug/alcohol misuse, as there remained widespread 'gaps' in provision (House of Commons Justice Committee, 2013: 84).

The government's response to the Justice Committee's report (MoJ, 2013d) acknowledged the need to treat women differently to men but, somewhat contradictorily, also argued that there should be one criminal justice system for all offenders (MoJ, 2013d: 5) and that the system proposed under TR would be able to accommodate those needs via NOMS producing 'guidance' for CRCs (MoJ, 2013d: 16). It also rejected the significant call from the Justice Committee for the reduction in the use of custody for women, claiming that prison is not ineffective and that, in any event, sentencing is the province of the courts, rather than government (MoJ, 2013d: 5). This ignores the fundamental point that court powers are the result of legislation and thus subject to change. More generally, the government also argued that NOMS was making continuing progress in identifying the needs of women and on pursuing effective practice. It claimed that this would be enhanced by the Crime and Courts Act 2013, which provided for a punitive element in every community order, although how this would 'improve' provision was not explained. It further stated that the provisions within TR would improve services for women and that, more recently, NOMS had provided targeted funds to probation trusts (£3.78 million in 2013-14) for this purpose (MoJ, 2013d: 10-13). Finally, the government rejected the view that TR has been designed for men, arguing that CRCs, the NPS and the new post-custody supervision arrangements would allow suitable provision for all (MoJ, 2013d: 15-17).

## Discussion

From its outset, TR has been controversial and bitterly opposed by Napo, the probation trade union and professional organisation, which has argued against the changes on the grounds that punishment (in whatever form) be carried out only by agencies of the state and that profit should not be made from it; and also that the breaking up of a unified probation service would be an organisational and operational disaster (Napo, 2013). Other critics argued that the TR proposals are ideologically based, with no empirical evidence to support them and that the government used the provisions of the Offender Management Act 2007 to avoid proper parliamentary scrutiny and debate about the break-up of the probation service (Burke, 2013).

Indeed, it may be seen that even before TR was fully implemented, two of the main ideological reasons behind it had been seriously undermined. First, the idea of an open, competitive market in corrections, that would 'drive up' standards may be regarded as compromised, given that there were only a small number of CRC bidders left by mid-2014 (Rogers, 2014); in December 2014, the government announced the 'successful bidder' status for only eight companies/consortia covering the 21 CRCs (MoJ, 2014c). This small number was perhaps due to the complexity of contracts and allegations of poor performance by private sector organisations in the sector (*The Guardian*, 2013; Howard League for Penal Reform, 2014). Second, it is apparent that, presumably following private sector lobbying, the percentage of any contract dependent on PbR has shrunk, to the point where it had still to be finalised where the awarding of a PbR element would be on relatively small reductions on predicted reoffending rates (MoJ, 2014a). Thus, it may be the case that TR became a 'simple' privatisation, subject to a very limited tendering process, while the possibility of contracts lasting as long as 10 years (*The Guardian*, 2014) reinforces the lack of competition and may result in complacency in terms of practice development.

These questions and issues, while central to the question of quality and provision overall, do not deal directly with provision for women. According to Burke (2013), the government ignored the growing effectiveness of probation supervision and the lessons of the Offender Engagement Programme employed within NOMS (NOMS, 2013) based, as these were, on the effective professional relationship between practitioner and supervisee. Burke pointed out (2013: 378) that under TR, the CRCs would only have to provide 'appropriate levels of training and competence' for staff, and argued further that supervision under TR would be inevitably fragmented, with individuals possibly receiving intervention from a number of individuals and/ or agencies. This was pointed out as a possibility under the NOMS Offender Management Model as inimical to a good relationship and good supervision (Raynor and Maguire, 2006), and supplements the emerging evidence of recent years about the importance of good supervision and continuity with both female and male offenders (NOMS, 2010; Gelsthorpe, 2013; Raynor et al, 2013).

One of the aims of TR is to make changes cost-neutral. This is clearly a challenge, as the changes to post-custody supervision alone are said to involve a further 50,000 cases (Burke, 2013: 378) and TR itself makes only a passing reference to the issues, claiming that this can be achieved by 'competing the majority of services' and a 'more efficient public sector service' (MoJ, 2013b: 11). However, no detailed costings or explanations are included. At the very least, then, funding arrangements are open to considerable question and, as we know, the majority of women are likely to be supervised by more generic, community-based organisations that will be most at risk of budgetary uncertainty. The House of Commons Justice Committee (2013) expressed concern about the provision of suitable services for women, and a report, *Run Ragged*, by Clinks, an organisation which supports the third sector within the criminal justice system, outlined widespread concern about recent funding under NOMS and probation trusts (Clinks, 2013b).

*Run Ragged* reported on a study carried out with a number of voluntary agencies in 2013 and had three main findings (Clinks, 2013b: 2):

- 89% of projects felt that their service was less secure or as insecure as it was 12 months previously;
- the sustainability of gender-specific services for female offenders was often not embedded in local strategies;
- there was an emergent crisis among service users as a result of current austerity measures, most significantly welfare changes including rising debt, an inability to purchase food, increased anxiety, self-harm and depression.

The report noted the proposals within TR that require specific provision to be made for women by the CRCs, but set this against their experience of inconsistent support from local commissioners to date. Some of their respondents were said to be perplexed that 'statutory commissioners did not seem to want to protect their investment in a bespoke service for women, which had been developed with their support' (Clinks, 2013b: 12). Such uncertainty had made it hard for projects to retain experienced and skilled staff, and this had had a negative impact on the women using their services. The coming of TR was also the cause of more specific anxiety, as there was the belief that the need for targeted services for women did not have enough emphasis within the document, partly perhaps as these had also never formed a core part of the work of probation trusts. The lack of detail of contractual arrangements within TR existing at the time was also a source of concern.

For Gelsthorpe and Hedderman (2012), security of funding for the type of projects best suited to working with women is crucial to good practice. They argue that the *Together Women* pilots were able to show reductions in offending (Gelsthorpe and Hedderman, 2012: 380), by improving women's overall functioning and empowering them to take greater control over their lives. This process (rather than more interventionist approaches) is seen as vital to success. They acknowledge that the whole area is under-theorised and that the disparate nature of service provision makes evaluation difficult. They emphasise the general level of agreement about the most likely successful forms of intervention (Joliffe et al, 2011, cited in Gelsthorpe and Hedderman, 2012: 385) and suggest there is evidence of community-based approaches being as effective as more formal probation interventions.

Furthermore, criminal justice interventions notably bring about small levels of change of behaviour and functioning, and the direct source of any change is difficult to establish. Relating this to a possible PbR approach, Gelsthorpe and Hedderman (2012: 386) question whether CRCs would bid for contracts on the basis of providing such specific, targeted services for women, thus placing such services' long-term future in doubt. Moreover, positive outcomes for women are often in non-criminal areas such as reduced dependency on benefits or fewer admissions of children into care (Gelsthorpe and Hedderman, 2012: 386); such services are often provided creatively by agencies with a strong moral purpose and it is questioned whether such phenomena could survive a PbR approach concentrating on harder outcomes such as reduced reoffending (Gelsthorpe and Hedderman, 2012: 387).

Finally, sentencing patterns, the views of sentencers (Hedderman and Gunby, 2013) and the attitude of government are of central importance in this debate. One of the fundamental conclusions of the Corston Report drew attention to the impact of the Equality Act 2006 and noted the lack:

> [o]f any real [government] understanding that treating men and women the same results in inequality of outcome. Equality does not mean treating everyone the same. The new gender equality duty means that men and women should be treated with equivalent respect, according to need. Equality must embrace not just fairness but also inclusivity. This will result in some different services and policies for men and women. There are fundamental

differences between male and female offenders and those
at risk of offending that indicate a different and distinct
approach is needed for women. (Corston, 2007: 3)

Corston was clearly arguing that, in this sense, there needed to be
'two' criminal justice systems, in terms of the powers of the courts,
sentencing guidelines, and so on, to differentiate the sentencing of
women. However, the previous Coalition government specifically
rejected this argument in TR and in its response to the Justice
Committee report (MoJ, 2013d). Although it set up the Advisory
Board regarding women offenders and took forward a number of
policies (as outlined above), it seems reasonable to assume that unless
the fundamental issue of sentencing and the associated entrenchment
of prison are addressed in the near future one of the main aims of the
Corston Report is unlikely to be realised.

## Conclusions

Clearly, trying to consider the implications for women of the TR
proposals requires a certain amount of crystal-ball gazing. However,
sufficient questions have been posed about the nature of women's
offending, its causes and how responses might best be constructed, to
give cause for concern about future developments. Overall, we feel
that the concerns can be summarised as follows.

1. The criminal justice system remains dominated by male offenders
   and its responses are conditioned by this fact. Although it is now
   generally recognised that women need to be treated differently
   within the system, this recognition has not extended to the
   development of clearly differentiated services, commissioning or
   ring-fenced funding. This seems unlikely as the previous Coalition
   government asserted the need for 'one criminal justice system'
   (MoJ, 2013b).
2. In the light of this and recent experience, planning and funding
   of services for women may well remain inconsistent. The most
   appropriate provision is provided by smaller, community-based
   groups and these may well continue to face uncertain funding,
   quite apart from any difficulties that they may experience in being
   contracted to large, private prime contractors, in terms of issues
   that may arise from their different ethical and moral approaches to
   practice (Annison et al, 2014).

3. This calls into question the future of services for all, particularly lower 'risk of harm' individuals (but with high needs and likely higher risk of reoffending) within the privatised CRCs, unless strict conditions are written into contracts with government. Will CRCs be prepared to allow community-based projects the freedom to act in more flexible, coordinated and holistic ways, when outcomes are linked to a PbR element and the possible renewal of a contract? As mentioned, the commitment to such open-ended, needs-based approaches is far from certain. Indeed, the record of the private sector in a range of criminal justice activities has been called into question in terms of its quality and ethics (Howard League for Penal Reform, 2014).

4. The provisions for compulsory post-custody supervision for short-term sentenced prisoners will include the majority of women prisoners. While on the face of it, this may give women access to appropriate help, the use of breach for failures to comply may well bring women into additional conflict with the justice system. -

It is perhaps in considering this final point that the problem can be scrutinised more clearly. The previous Coalition government used the language of toughness and punishment alongside that of rehabilitation for both women and men offenders, perhaps based, as we have suggested, on a bifurcatory approach (Player, 2014) and it seems likely that the new Conservative government will continue in this manner. There seems little to indicate that in the end, the Coalition government, in common with previous recent administrations, was not committed to populist, punitive sentencing. If this continues, the improvements to services for women will probably take place in terms of the 'quality' of existing provision, rather than in anything more fundamental that changes the balance between high levels of custody and the use of community sentences. Statutory limits on the use of custody are perfectly possible and effective, as shown with young offenders in the 1982 and 1988 Criminal Justice Acts and with adults in the Criminal Justice Act 1991. There is no reason, other than ideological opposition, why such changes cannot again be introduced for women who do not pose a real risk of harm to the public.

## Notes

[1]  At this point, it is worth considering the changing nature of 'rehabilitation' from a perhaps ill-defined notion of helping individuals improve their lives for its own sake, to one which is now more or less synonymous with a more instrumental meaning of the reduction of reoffending (for example, see Robinson and McNeill, 2004; Deering, 2011).

[2]  Ch. 11, Section 2 Offender Rehabilitation Act 2014.

[3]  Ch. 11, Section 10 Offender Rehabilitation Act 2014.

[4]  There is an approximate 30:70 split in existing staff allocation between the new organisations, with the largest share going to the CRCs, reflecting the assessment that the highest-risk offenders constitute around 30% of the existing probation caseload.

[5]  This is, of course, perfectly feasible and possible, as shown by the drop in the adult numbers imprisoned following the Criminal Justice Act 1991.

[6]  This might be explained by considering a bifurcatory approach. In this way, the support for different types of punishment is consistent with a punitive view that sees the use of custody as appropriate and proportionate for a wide range of offences, due to their alleged 'seriousness' or 'persistence'. At the same time, non-custodial 'rehabilitation' (or measures to reduce reoffending) can also be promoted but only for those women committing offences not deemed 'deserving' of custody. In a continuing climate of populist punitiveness (Bottoms, 1995), we would argue that the balance is set far too often in favour of custody for women (and indeed for men).

[7]  It is worth noting that concerns about the involvement of voluntary third sector organisations in a privatised system have been expressed by a number of organisations, see Russell, 2013; Clinks, 2013b.

## References

Annison, J., Burke, L. and Senior, P. (2014) Transforming Rehabilitation: Another example of English 'exceptionalism' or a blueprint for the rest of Europe?, *European Journal of Probation*, 6 (1): 6-23.

Burke, L. (2013) Editorial: Grayling's hubris, *Probation Journal*, 60 (4): 377-82.

Carter, P. (2003) *Managing offenders, reducing crime – the Correctional Services review*, London: Home Office Strategy Unit.

Clarke, K. (2010) *Revolving door of crime and reoffending to stop says Clarke*, www.justice.gov.uk/news/newsrelease300610a.htm

Clinks (2013a) *Transforming Rehabilitation* [Homepage of Clinks], www.clinks.org/criminal-justice/transforming-rehabilitation

Clinks (2013b) *Run ragged: The current experience of projects providing community based female offender support services, Interim Headlines*, London: Clinks.

Corston, J. (2007) *The Corston report: A report by Baroness Jean Corston of a review of women with particular vulnerabilities in the criminal justice system*, London: Home Office.

Deering, J. (2011) *Probation practice and the new penology: Practitioner reflections*, Aldershot: Ashgate.

Fox, C. and Albertson, K. (2011) Payment by results and social impact bonds in the criminal justice sector: New challenges for the concept of evidence based policy?, *Criminology and Criminal Justice*, 11 (5): 395-413.

Garland, D. (2001) *The culture of control*, Oxford: Oxford University Press.

Gelsthorpe, L. (2013) Legitimacy, law and locality: Making the case for change, in M. Malloch and G. McIvor (eds) *Women, punishment and social justice: Human rights and penal practices*, Abingdon: Routledge.

Gelsthorpe, L. and Hedderman, C. (2012) Providing for women offenders: The risks of adopting a Payment by Results approach, *Probation Journal*, 59 (4): 374-90.

Gomm, R. (2013) What will 'count' and be transformed for women in the criminal justice system?, *British Journal of Community Justice*, 11 (2/3): 153-8.

*The Guardian* (2013) G4S and Serco stripped of offender tagging contracts ov er fraud claims [Homepage of *The Guardian*], www.G4S and Serco stripped of offender tagging contracts over fraud claims _ UK news _ theguardian.com.htm

*The Guardian* (2014) Two companies to run more than half of privatised probation services, *The Guardian*, 29 October 2014, www.theguardian.com/uk-news/2014/oct/29/justice-probation-contracts-private-companies

Hedderman, C. and Gunby, C. (2013) Diverting women from custody: The importance of understanding sentencers' perspectives, *Probation Journal*, 60 (4): 425-38.

Hough, M., Allen, R. and Padel, U. (eds) (2006) *Reshaping probation and prisons: The new offender management framework*, Bristol: Policy Press.

House of Commons Justice Committee (2013) *Women offenders – after the Corston Report, 2nd Report 2013-14*, Vol. 1, London: TSO.

Howard League for Penal Reform (2014) *Corporate crime? A dossier of the failure of privatisation in the criminal justice system*, London: Howard League for Penal Reform.

Ministry of Justice (MoJ) (2010) *Breaking the cycle. A Green Paper*, London: MoJ.

MoJ (2011a) *Competition strategy for offender services*, London: MoJ.

MoJ (2011b) *Government response to the Justice Committee's Report: The role of the probation service*, London: MoJ.

MoJ (2012a) *Punishment and reform: Effective probation services. Consultation Paper CP7/2012*, London: MoJ.

MoJ (2012b) *Punishment and reform. Effective community sentences. Consultation Paper CP8/2012*, London: MoJ.

MoJ (2012c) *A distinct approach: A guide to working with women offenders*, March edn, London: NOMS Women and Equalities Group.

MoJ (2013a) *Transforming Rehabilitation: A revolution in the way we manage offenders*, January 2013, London: MoJ.

MoJ (2013b) *Transforming Rehabilitation: A strategy for reform*, May 2013, London: TSO.

MoJ (2013c) *Strategic objectives for female offenders*, March 2013, London: MoJ.

MoJ (2013d) *Government response to the Justice Committee's 2nd Report of Session 2013-14. Female Offenders*, London: TSO.

MoJ (2014a) *PbR payment mechanism baselines and thresholds by CPA*, October 2014, London: MoJ.

MoJ (2014b) *Update on the delivery of the Government's strategic objectives for female offenders*, March 2014, London: MoJ.

MoJ (2014c) *The Transforming Rehabilitation Programme: The bidders awarded contracts to run the community rehabilitation companies*, December 2014, London: MoJ.

Napo (2013) Justice not for sale: Time for action! *Napo News,* Issue 248, London: Napo.

National Offender Management Service (NOMS) (2013) *Offender Engagement Programme news – Final edition*, March, London: NOMS.

Player, E. (2014) Women in the Criminal Justice System: The triumph of inertia, *Criminology and Criminal Justice*, 14 (3): 276-97.

Pratt, J., Brown, D., Brown, M., Hallsworth, S. and Morrison, W. (eds) (2005) *The new punitiveness: Trends, theories, perspectives*, Cullompton: Willan.

Raynor, P. and Maguire, M. (2006) End-to-end or end in tears? Prospects for the effectiveness of the National Offender Management model, in M. Hough, R. Allen and U. Padel (eds) *Reshaping probation and prisons: The new offender management framework*, Bristol: Policy Press.

Raynor, P., Ugwudike, P. and Vanstone, M. (2013) The impact of skills in probation work: A reconviction study, *Criminology and Criminal Justice*, 14 (2): 235-49.

Robinson, G. and McNeill, F. (2004) Purposes matter: Examining the 'ends' of probation, in G. Mair (ed.) *What matters in probation?*, Cullompton: Willan.

Rogers, D. (2014) Why TR bidders are getting nervous, *Napo News*, 256, London: Napo.

Russell, J. (2013) *Evidence to House of Commons Justice Committee report: 'Women offenders – after the Corston Report'*, www.publications. parliament.uk/pa/cm201314/cmselect/cmjust/92/9207.htm

Snacken, S. and Dumortier, E. (eds) (2012) *Resisting punitiveness in Europe*, London: Routledge.

Watts, J. (2014) Serco's 'disastrous' £37m probation deal cut short [Homepage of *London Evening Standard*], www.standard.co.uk/news/ uk/sercos-disastrous-37m-probation-deal-cut-short-9119524.html

Worrall, A. and Gelsthorpe, L. (2009) 'What works' with women offenders: The past thirty years, *Probation Journal*, 56 (4): 329-45.

# THREE

# The context:
# women as lawbreakers

*Loraine Gelsthorpe and Serena Wright*

Baroness Corston's report, *A review of women with particular vulnerabilities in the criminal justice system*, made a series of recommendations to bring about improvements in relation to the treatment of women in the criminal justice system. Now, some six years after her report, we found that it is well recognised that women face very different hurdles from men in their journey towards a law abiding life, and that responding appropriately and effectively to the problems that bring women into the criminal justice system requires a distinct approach. (House of Commons Justice Select Committee, 2013: 3)

## Introduction

In this chapter, we review not only the profile of female lawbreakers in terms of the range of offences committed, but also what we know about such women: about their backgrounds, needs and problems, with a particular focus on any changes in relation to this since the Corston Report was published in 2007. We also examine what we know of women offenders in relation to who persists and who desists, and point to some policy and practice developments post-Corston.

Responses to women lawbreakers have been a focus of interest and controversy for some considerable time, as Lucia Zedner (1991) vividly describes in an analysis of Victorian responses to them. At that time, a prison matron wrote of her charges:

> As a class, they are desperately wicked ... deceitful, crafty, malicious, lewd and devoid of common feeling ... in the penal classes of the male prisons there is not one man to match the worst inmate of our female prisons. There are some women less easy to tame than the creatures of the

jungle, and one is almost sceptical of believing that there
was ever an innocent childhood or better life belonging to
them. (A prison matron, 1862: 46)

There was particular interest in the issues affecting women lawbeakers
following the publication of *Women in prison*, in which Ann Smith
(1962) painted a clear picture of the sorry lives of the women within,
and an article by Frances Heidensohn (1968), which challenged the
invisibility of women in the study of crime and deviance. The 1970s
saw the publication of Carol Smart's (1976) book *Women, crime and
criminology*, in which she not only questioned why so many women
were being imprisoned for relatively small crimes, but also heavily
critiqued the possibility that there might be a functional equivalent
between prisons for men and psychiatric hospitals for women. These
early texts set in motion important critical thinking regarding the
treatment of women as lawbreakers.

On a related issue, we wish to note from the outset what we view
as a crucial point: in many ways, the study of 'deviant' or 'delinquent'
women and 'women lawbreakers' cannot (and indeed *should* not)
be separated off from the study of how *all* women are defined and
controlled in society. Ideas and stereotypes about women abound in
regard to sexuality, motherhood, prostitution, abortion, alcoholism
and retirement, for instance, in all societies. Women and girls are
disciplined, managed, corrected and punished as prisoners, partners,
patients, mothers and victims, through imprisonment, medicalisation,
secure care and cultural stereotypes (Hutter and Williams, 1981;
Cain, 1989; Balfour and Comack, 2006). Thus what behaviours are
*criminalised*, and how this process is demarcated along gendered lines,
is as much an issue as what we 'know' about women lawbreakers. This
is a guiding theme in this chapter.

## Women as lawbreakers: who, what and why?

Historically, the study of crime has been male-centred and the criminal
justice system's treatment of women has been imbued with assumptions
about men. When the female offender has not been ignored, she has
been pathologised and treated as abnormal. It is only recently that we
have begun to recognise more nuanced accounts of women's pathways
into crime, with acknowledgment that women do not offend as much
as men and that their offending behaviour is primarily of a less serious
nature. There have been periodic moral panics about women's crime,
particularly in relation to violent crime and 'girl gangs', but it is hard

to sustain the arguments in this direction in light of the research evidence (Sharpe, 2012; Chesney-Lind and Pasko, 2013). Poverty features highly in women offenders' lives (Carlen, 1988; Wacquant, 2009; Gelsthorpe, 2011), and there have been consistent messages from the research literature on women offenders and from experienced service providers and service users (Sheehan et al, 2007) that women offenders tend to have a history of unmet needs in relation to sexual and violent victimisation, physical and mental health, housing and income, and training and employment. Substance misuse and childcare responsibilities often compound these problems. Indeed, 31% of women offenders interviewed for a Surveying Crime Reduction study reported having spent time in local authority care, while 53% of female offenders reported having experienced emotional, physical or sexual abuse as a child (Ministry of Justice (MoJ), 2012).

Desistance studies relating to pathways out of crime serve to highlight the complexity of factors relating to women's pathways *into* crime, while pointing to the need for broadly based provision that can be individually tailored. Service providers in prisons and probation/community corrections, as well as academic research, support claims that there may well be indirect relationships between women's abuse and mental health, labour market participation, and substance abuse, all of which are associated with risk of reoffending. In other words, 'victimization' creates psychological sequelae[1] that can lead to offending behaviour (Sheehan et al, 2011).

## Women lawbreakers: an offending profile

While there is perhaps 'no such thing as the "typical" criminal woman' (Carlen et al, 1985: 10), it is fair to say that some offence types are *more* typical of women's offending than others. Thus while women appear as offenders in all categories of offence (from the most serious to the least serious), offence statistics consistently demonstrate that women's lawbreaking is more often than not related to property crime, and that men's lawbreaking is more often violent, and more serious, than that committed by women. In this way, what we know about the characteristics of all known offending is structured by gender.

Jean Corston highlighted the fact that the profile of female offending was different from that of men. In her eponymous review of the 'particular vulnerabilities' of women in prison, she drew attention to the most obvious difference between men and women in the criminal justice system: that women commit far less crime than men, and in a manner disproportionate to their relative presence within the general population:

> Women represent *half* the general population but [within the offending population] ... there were 1,120,200 (83%) men arrested for recorded crime offences compared with 233,600 (17%) women. (Corston, 2007: 17)

Corston (2007: 18) observed that women's offending profile was more likely to feature acquisitive crime (more than a third of all women sentenced had been convicted for theft and handling offences) and a 'lower involvement in serious violence, criminal damage and professional crime'. A further observation was that women coming before the courts in England and Wales were first-time offenders (or rather, were experiencing their first conviction), with over a third of adult women in court in 2002 having no previous convictions (this was more than double the rate for men). Finally, addressing concerns regarding comparatively minor increases in (some) violent and drugs offences by women, Corston concluded that 'the nature and seriousness of women's offending [was] not, on the whole, ... getting worse' (Corston, 2007: 16).

Almost a decade on from the statistics reported in the Corston Report, there appears to have been little change in relation to the nature of women's criminal convictions. In 2013, for example, men continued to make up the vast majority of offenders in the criminal justice system, with women representing just 23% of those given out-of-court disposals (such as Penalty Notices for Disorder, Cautions, and Conditional Cautions), 18% of arrests and 25% of convictions (MoJ, 2014). Women continue to commit less serious crimes than men, and they are dealt with primarily in the magistrates' court rather than the Crown Court. Theft accounted for nearly a quarter of female indictable convictions in 2013 and within this category shoplifting accounted for 45% (MoJ, 2014: 63). We should also note the high proportion of women who are prosecuted for TV licence evasion, and for summary offences (85% in 2013) (MoJ, 2014: 42). Prosecution seems a remarkably unimaginative (and inappropriate) way to achieve compliance, especially when sanctions may include fines, which – for women who are poor – may result in *further* sanctions when there is inability to pay the fines.

Women continue to represent around 5% of the total prison population in England and Wales (MoJ, 2014), and despite Baroness Corston expressing particular concern about the number of women receiving short sentences of imprisonment (under 12 months), 77% of all female offenders were given custodial sentences in 2013, compared with 63% of male offenders' short sentences. This is of continuing concern, especially when we consider that women's offending continues to be property-related in the main.

The gendered picture of *reoffending* also appears to have changed little. In the most recent data period (2012), females reoffended at a rate of 18.5%, compared with rates of 27.7% for both male adults and juveniles (MoJ, 2014: 83). However, this perhaps masks some concerns. In light of a general reduction in the use of cautions and other out-of-court disposals, it now seems increasingly likely that women being processed through the court system are *repeat* (rather than first-time) offenders, with 86% of women receiving a sentence in 2013 for an indictable offence having at least one previous caution or conviction. In fact, just under a third of all such women were recorded as having *15 or more* previous sanctions (MoJ, 2014: 53), perhaps bringing to bear the prediction by Soothill et al (2003) that women's *persistent* offending would continue to rise. We turn to this issue in the next section.

To conclude this profile of women's offending, we want to mention specifically both drugs and violence, since these are offences which have generated considerable media attention. As indicated earlier, theft offences account for the highest proportion of women's crimes. Violence Against the Person features as the second largest (mainly Actual Bodily Harm (ABH)), an offence category which accounted for approximately half of all convictions for both men and women until 2010, but by 2013 had fallen to a third (MoJ, 2014: 65). Anecdotal evidence from senior police officers suggests that in the case of women, such cases of ABH frequently concern *minor* violence centred around the pubs and clubs scene, and are not indicative of a rise in serious violent offending for women.

With regard to drugs offences, from 2008 onwards minor drugs offences have been increasingly likely to be dealt with via a Penalty Notice for Disorder (introduced for the possession of cannabis in 2009). However, a higher proportion of male drugs offenders continue to be dealt with through conviction at court compared with female offenders; the number of whom sentenced to immediate custody for drugs offences in 2013 was *less than half* the number sentenced in 2003, reflecting a sharp fall in the number of women convicted of importation of Class A drugs (a drop from 5% in 2003 to 1% in 2013).

We also want to mention benefit fraud which, since 2014 (MoJ, 2014), features a new section in analyses of offending in government s.95 statistics (a biennial publication specifically designed to focus on gender and race issues). Interestingly, in the MoJ's 2014 version of the statistics, women feature largely in the two main categories that specifically address benefit fraud: dishonest representation and false representation (MoJ, 2014: Figure 7.09).[2] However, such figures may well reflect what is well known about the majority of women who find themselves on the wrong side of the law, in respect of poverty, lack of education and employment opportunities, and so on. For instance, a Cabinet Office Social Exclusion Task Force (2009) study on female offenders found 28% of women's crimes to have been financially motivated, for instance, while a survey of prisoners (Light et al, 2013) found that nearly half of all women (48%) reported having committed offences to support someone else's drug use, compared to just over one fifth of men surveyed. Here, then, Corston's (2007) characterisation of criminalised women still applies.

## Women lawbreakers: who persists, and who desists?

With this picture of the deeds and needs of women in mind, and notwithstanding the fact that it is a truism of criminological knowledge that women who offend are far less likely to become 'recidivists and professional criminals' than their male counterparts (Silvestri and Crowther-Dowey, 2008: 26), we think that it is worth exploring a little further the issue of women who persist in offending, particularly as this was not something that the Corston Report focused on.

That the majority of women are 'infrequently repeat offenders' (Kong and AuCoin, 2008) has meant that they have remained largely absent from debates relating to the persistent offender (for example DeLisi, 2002; Soothill et al, 2003; Pavlich, 2010), as well as being overlooked by Baroness Corston. While 'persistent offending' has been defined as remaining 'criminally active' over a period of 10 years or more (Hopkins and Wickson, 2013), such discourses have more frequently been informed by Moffitt's (1993) formulation of the 'life-course persistent' offender. Such individuals – who exhibit an early onset of anti-social behaviour, which develops into repeat offending across the lifespan – are so 'very rarely female' (Piquero and Chung, 2001: 192) that the very *existence* of lifecourse persistent women offenders has been called into question (DeLisi, 2002).

It is perhaps the tendency of the persistent offender debate to focus on Moffit's (1993) formulation, which centres on *early* onset, that is partially responsible for the exclusion of women, who are more typically *late* onset offenders (Eggleston and Laub, 2002; Simpson et al, 2008; Blokland and van Os, 2010). Also of importance here is the tendency to use arrest and conviction data in the majority of such studies in identifying 'early' onset, which can provide only so much detail. Self-report data, however, provides a different picture, indicating that age of onset is remarkably *similar* between young male and young female offenders (Moffitt et al, 2001; Budd et al, 2005). When moving away from reliance on official statistics – and what Pavlich (2010) has identified as the 'sexist, patriarchal formulations of the habitual criminal' of core criminological studies on the matter – one can begin to acknowledge the abundance of 'chronic low-level female offenders' on our streets and in our prisons (Rockell, 2008: 5).

The small body of literature which *does* exist specifically in relation to women who persistently come to the attention of the criminal justice system has, in recent years, attempted to identify not only the potential size of this population (for example DeLisi, 2002), but also their pathways to 'long-term' offending across the lifecourse (for example Block et al, 2010) and the key factors associated with this (for example Brennan et al, 2012). Using data from the Criminal Career and Life-Course Study, for instance, Block et al described the 'criminal careers' of women in the United States (*n*=432), identifying a pattern whereby the onset of offending for the majority of women occurred not in adolescence but in adulthood and continued through middle-age (Block et al, 2010: 96). Such women were markedly different from lifecourse persistent male offenders, in that the former were *less* likely to have engaged in violent crime but *more* likely to have experienced violence committed against them. In terms of understanding why some women persistently reoffend, Brennan et al (2012) found 'housing problems' to be statistically 'diagnostic' in predicting persistence in the offending pathways of their sample of women awaiting release from the Central California Women's Facility and the Valley State Prison for Women in the United States (n=718). Brennan et al (2012) also identified the complexities associated with 're-entry' as playing a major part in the persistence of the sample's offending. In particular, 'substance abuse' emerged as '[s]ignificantly linked to the success or failure of the prisoner reentry process' for the majority of women in the study, appearing in six out of the eight pathways to women's 'serious habitual criminal behavior' identified by Brennan et al (2012). Based on these findings, then, it is not sensible to talk how and why women *persist* without looking to the related issue of how and why women do, or do not – or *cannot* even – *desist* from offending.

However, studies acknowledging the link between persistence and desistance are rare (Bushway et al, 2004), just as there exist similarly few studies focusing specifically on desistance among female offenders

(Farrall et al, 2007, 353; Farrall et al, 2010), although Brown and Ross (2010) and Baldry (2010) represent important exceptions. This is problematic, since it is likely that women's experience of desistance differs from men's experience, and thus theories that are androcentric in nature cannot be straightforwardly applied to the lives of women. For example, romantic relationships (Sampson and Laub, 1995), 'fatherhood' (Moloney, Mackenzie, Hunt and Joe-Laidler, 2009) and considering oneself to be a 'family man' (LeBel et al, 2008) are important narratives in the desistance literature concerning men. This appears to be *less* so for women, since it is comparatively less likely for female offenders to find prosocial 'romantic' partners to support desistance (Leverentz, 2006), while the 'practical difficulties' associated with maintaining desistance from crime for women may limit the degree to which being a mother can actually contribute to this process (Michalsen, 2013).

Farrall et al (2007) argue (correctly in our view) that little work exists in regard to theorising processes of desistance for women within the central canon of the desistance literature. This is perhaps evidence of the continued disjuncture between 'masculinist' critiques of modern penality (which more effectively engage in 'new theorisations' of punishment regimes) and 'feminist' critiques (which focus more often on the 'impact of disciplinary power on female bodies') (Howe, 1994: 2). Much of the work relating to female desistance, then, has not traditionally engaged with 'desistance theory', although Baldry (2010) has argued that a 'generalised' theoretical framework of desistance is unhelpful in attempting to understand the interaction between women, criminogenic need, the criminal justice system and recidivism. This is particularly the case, she argues, with respect to women serving very short sentences, female remand prisoners, and those with 'combined and multiple mental health and substance abuse disorders' (Baldry, 2010: 253). Crucially, Baldry accuses desistance theory of failing to account for 'the marginal space from which most [female offenders] come and to which most return' (p.253).

This is perhaps why scholars working with female offenders and re-entry have worked hard to document the *structural* barriers (such as a lack of social capital, or the tendency to stigmatise mothers who commit crime) and the *personal* barriers (for example absence of a prosocial identity) that have negative impacts on women's processes of desistance (compared with Reisig et al, 2006; Rumgay, 2004). Such barriers are often discussed in terms of *criminogenic needs*; that is, dynamic factors in offenders' lives that are 'functionally related to criminal behavior', and that – when changed – are 'associated within changes in the chances of recidivism' (Andrews and Bonta, 2010, 45; Andrews et al, 1990, 31). The traditional 'Big 4' needs – criminal history, criminal personality (that is, impulsivity, grandiosity and egocentricity), criminal thinking, and criminal associates (Andrews and Bonta, 2010) – are not considered to be 'relevant' to female offenders (Buell et al, 2011: 57) (see also Hubbard and Matthews, 2008). However, a wide range of other criminogenic needs have been identified, as *specifically* linked to women's offending. For example, experience of both physical and sexual violent victimisation in both childhood and adulthood is high among criminalised women (Shaw et al, 1991, cited in Comack, 2006). While traditionally regarded as a 'non-criminogenic' factor (that is, not functionally related to offending behaviour), Moloney, van den Bergh and Moller (2009) argue that the prevalence of 'trauma histories'[3] among criminalised and incarcerated women is not spurious; that is, they have been found to have a 'strong influence on [women's] offending behaviour' (p.426), with the number of childhood traumatic events experienced by criminalised women 'positively correlated with lifetime number of arrests' (Messina and Grella, 2006).

Of course, the desistance process is not solely associated with the effective management of criminogenic needs – there is also the phenomenon of *natural* desistance to consider. In such instances, 'external expert supervision may be complementary, but is not necessary for reform' (Rumgay, 2004: 405), and – as the following quote from a police officer working with Prolific and other Priority Offenders (PPOs) illustrates – is acknowledged among practitioners as more concomitant with any decrease in offending than any input they might have had:

> [O]ut of the nine [prolifically offending] females that I looked at on our spread-sheet this morning, there are one or two that have completely stopped all offending which is, you know, which is ideal. Whether that's been through, as a result of the PPO Scheme and the monitoring, or just as a result of – that they have decided and they've made the choice that they want to stop offending, which is more likely, really. (Wright, 2015b: 160)

The concept of natural desistance, and the importance of working towards a model of offender engagement that acknowledges and encourages this process with female offenders, is discussed in the following section.

## Implications and challenges

Women's low share of recorded criminality has significant consequences for those women who do offend. They are often seen to be 'doubly deviant', for example, for having transgressed not only social norms but gender norms too. As a result, they may feel that they are doubly punished, especially when informal sanctions and stigmatising processes are taken into account. There is double jeopardy in women offenders being seen as worse than men, then; they are both failing individuals and failed women.

One particular concern relates to the conflation of 'risk' and 'needs' in dealing with women offenders. Correctional authorities have become increasingly concerned with assessing the risks and needs of offenders in recent years. This move towards risk/needs assessment can be seen as a contemporary manifestation of two residual concerns: predicting future offending; and determining 'what works'. However, as Canadian researchers Hannah-Moffat and Shaw (2003) have highlighted – with international reverberations – the research behind these assessment tools rarely considers the gendered, racialised or otherwise stratified characteristics of risk and need. One concern is the tendency for sentencers to conflate women's 'risk' levels (often low) with their 'needs' (often many, and varied). This can result in 'up-tariffing', that is, an increase in sentence severity, which is then disproportionate to the risk of harm and potential future recidivism actually posed by women. The time is therefore ripe for empirical research to test whether or not there are risk/need confusions in practice in the UK. In addition, in light of what we know about persistence and desistance, there is perhaps need for sentencers and practitioners to adopt a different perspective in responding to patterns of criminalisation over the life course. This should include consideration of ways in which criminal justice system sanctions can militate *against* their purpose. That is, that rather than reduce crime and promote desistance, current criminal justice sanctions might instead be working to *perpetuate* persistence and further entrench individuals in an offending lifestyle (Wright, 2015a, 2015b).

## Positive post-Corston developments

We also want to refer to some of the positive developments in relation to the provision of services for women since the Corston Report, although these are amplified and scrutinised in later chapters.

Notwithstanding various developments in programmes designed to address offending behaviour in the 1990s, there were controversies regarding their suitability for all offenders (women, black and ethnic minorities, young offenders, offenders with mental health problems, and very high risk and psychopathic offenders). Offender treatment programmes were typically designed for white, male, adult offenders, with only minor adaptations for other groups of offenders. Indeed, the criminogenic needs that have emerged from research on men have typically been applied to women offenders.

The research base (particularly the meta-analyses) developed since the early 1990s in the UK and other parts of Europe (drawing especially on work in Canada) now strongly supports the position that effective work with offenders is possible. Moreover, as indicated earlier, it has been argued that the concepts of 'risk' and 'need' are themselves 'gendered', and that differences between men and women should be taken into account in devising intervention programmes. But there had hardly been any attention to 'what works with women offenders' among policy makers in different countries until the 1980s, leading to the claim that women are 'correctional afterthoughts' (Ross and Fabiano, 1986). While the focus of campaigns has commonly been on the high numbers of women in prison, on the lack of gender sensitivity in prisons, and on the lack of attention to women's specific needs, in the Western world in particular there have been recent attempts to focus more directly on what we know about women offenders and their needs and, based on this, to divert them from crime in general – and from prison in particular.

One post-Corston study in England and Wales tried to take things forward, by exploring women's lower rate of completion on the community-based General Offending Behaviour Programme, which focused on developing behavioural habits more compliant with prosocial and non-offending norms (Martin et al, 2009). The study indicates that despite some similarities, the predictors of programme completion not only vary for men and women, but also operate differently between them, particularly in relation to the concept of *compliance*. The findings support the 'gender-responsiveness' position that men and women should be approached differently. They suggest, moreover, that men are more likely to engage in *instrumental* compliance (where people comply because of perceived benefits, or because they believe that the costs of non-compliance outweigh its benefits) and women are more likely to achieve *normative* compliance (the product of internalised mechanisms through social bonds or attachments or through perception of the legitimacy of the authority) (Martin et al, 2009; see also Gelsthorpe, 2013).

Attempts to facilitate gender-responsiveness in programmes and interventions have been limited, because criminological research and programme development for women generally lag behind that for men, but we are able to deduce what is likely to 'work' with women from educational and other areas of research as well as from emerging research findings. From educational research we learn that most women prefer to learn in collaborative, rather than competitive, settings (Belenky et al, 1986). On the basis of analysis of work in Canada, Taylor and Blanchette (2009) take us further, in advocating the integration of a number of gender-informed theories and methodologies in responses to women offenders. Specifically, they recommend gendered pathways, the use of relational theory, strengths-based approaches, and the use of positive psychology. All of these are critical frameworks for intervention with women (but which are perhaps not yet fully integrated into offence-focused programmes within prisons and the community/probation domain). We might add to this the need for such interventions to be sensitive to 'trauma', the centrality of which was discussed earlier. In other words, provision for women – either in prison or in the community – should reflect these lessons.

In the US, the National Institute of Corrections (NIC) in cooperation with the University of Cincinnati (UC) (National Institute of Corrections, 2013) has created a series of new gender-specific risk/need assessments for adult women offenders. The assessments include:

- the Women's Risk/Needs Assessment, a full instrument that assesses both gender-neutral and gender-responsive factors, creating separate versions for probation, prison and pre-release;
- the Women's Supplemental Risk/Needs Assessment, which is designed to supplement existing risk/needs assessments, such as the Level of Service Inventory.

The NIC/UC project was developed from two perspectives on offender rehabilitation: research by Canadian scholars which stresses the importance of treating 'dynamic' (rather than static) risk factors; and work by feminist criminologists stressing the importance of women's unique 'pathways to crime'. Both paradigms identify dynamic risk factors as central to offending-focused programmes, and while the pathways model asserts that women's unique needs are not adequately tapped by currently used risk/needs assessments, the new women's assessments created by NIC/UC do identify such needs, including: trauma and abuse; unhealthy relationships; parental stress; depression; self-efficacy; and current mental health symptoms.

Elsewhere in the US there are developments relating to gender responsive programming in prisons (Lawston, 2013); and in Victoria, Australia, developments regarding diversion from prison and better community provision in relation to drug and alcohol support, family reunification, debt management and independent living skills (Sheehan, 2013) have been identified through research.

There have also been attempts to summarise evidence on what offers the most potential for fruitful work with women, drawing on a range of evidence, concluding that women-only (or women-focused) environments best facilitate personal development. We can see that the evidence adds up to a need to work with women in non-authoritarian, cooperative settings, where women are empowered to engage in social and personal change. In addition, 'women-specific' factors such as healthcare, childcare and mental health (together with factors relating to race and gender combined) need to be addressed (Gelsthorpe, 2010).

Of course, some of the pre-Corston developments reflect this kind of thinking. In Scotland, we can turn to 218 Centre, which has its origins in reviews following a series of suicides in HMP Corton Vale – Scotland's women-only prison facility. The centre is based on the idea that female offenders should be able to get 'time out' of their normal (and perhaps chaotic and stressful) environment without resorting to 'time in' custody. 218 Centre thus serves as a diversion from prosecution and as an alternative to custody, and also offers access to provision specifically shown as relevant to women lawbreakers, such as detoxification, and support and outreach to health, social work or housing services. The ethos is therapeutic in intention and there is much emphasis on providing a safe environment for the women (Beglan, 2013). In England and Wales, some pre-Corston initiatives, most notably the introduction of the Together Women initiative, piloting women's centres in different parts of the country (Hedderman, 2010), captured the essence of the need to respond to women's vulnerabilities and their varied needs and problems (Gelsthorpe, 2010).

Importantly, a number of new centres for women have been set up post-Corston in the form of community holistic services based, for example, in women's centres in the community. There is now a national network of over fifty such centres (Women's Breakout: www.womensbreakout.org.uk/).[4] Of course, there are questions to ask: do the developments reflect a new sense of responsibility towards disadvantaged women, or might they be interpreted as an extension in the network of control and regulation (Wacquant, 2009)? What is perhaps at issue now is how the centres can be sustained in a market economy of justice, and how they can provide hard evidence of positive impact beyond consumer views (Gelsthorpe and Hedderman, 2012), which relates to increasing involvement of the private and commercial sector in running the criminal justice system in England and Wales. There are also concerns about the geographical distribution of women's centres (with some notable gaps), in addition to perennial problems of gathering data relating to impact and reoffending rates. Further, there are serious questions about sentencers' awareness of such centres, since there has been no discernible impact on the use of custody attributable to the work of these centres with women offenders (or at least, no hard evidence to support a causal link).

## Concluding reflections

Altogether, while it is obviously impossible to provide illustration of all the new developments across different jurisdictions following Corston (2007), there is now strong emerging evidence that provision for women offenders should:

- be women-only, to foster safety and a sense of community;
- enable staff to develop expertise in work with women;
- integrate offenders with non-offenders, so as to normalise women offenders' experiences;
- facilitate a supportive environment for learning;
- foster women's empowerment, so they gain sufficient self-esteem to directly engage in problem-solving themselves, and feel motivated to seek appropriate employment.

Thus the following provision is required:

- the utilisation and integration of what is known about effective learning styles with women;
- a holistic and practical stance to helping women to address social problems that may be linked to their offending;
- links with mainstream agencies, especially health, debt advice and counselling;
- capacity and flexibility to allow women to return for 'top-ups' or continued support and development where required;
- arrangements for women to have a supportive milieu or mentor to whom they can turn when they have completed any offender-related programmes, since personal care is likely to be as important as any direct input addressing offending behaviour.

In addition, it is important to provide women with practical help with transport and childcare, so that they can maintain their involvement in the centre or programme (Gelsthorpe, 2010). This is of particular importance in a post-Corston world where women are being increasingly recriminalised, and while some current methods for dealing with women's 'persistence' may paradoxically diminish opportunities for pathways to desistance (Wright, 2015b). Jean Corston's signposts to what is needed have thus been important, but it is a journey not yet ended.

## Notes

[1] 'Psychological sequelae' here include the after effects and consequences of victimisation which may reduce confidence and individual 'agency'.

[2] It is hard to discern benefit offences, since those who have committed benefit fraud may be convicted for a more general offence relating to fraud, forgery, identity or serious organised crime.

[3] Defined as 'any form of interpersonal or domestic physical, sexual or emotional abuse or neglect which is sufficiently detrimental to cause prolonged physical, psychological or social distress to the individual' (Moloney, van den Bergh and Moller, 2009: 427).

[4] Women's Breakout is recognised as the representative body for a national network of women-centred services offering gender specific community alternatives to custody as well as a range of other services and possibilities for women, including the 'specified activity' requirement of a Community Order (Criminal Justice Act 2003). Women's Breakout also provides a point of contact for consultation for a wide range of statutory and voluntary sector organisations interested in researching and evaluating the integrated, women's community solutions.

## References

Andrews, D. and Bonta, J. (2010) Rehabilitating criminal justice policy and practice, *Psychology, Public Policy, and Law*, 16 (1): 39-55.
Andrews, D., Bonta, J. and Hoge, R. (1990) Classification for effective rehabilitation: Rediscovering psychology, *Criminal Justice and Behavior*, 17 (1): 19-52.
Baldry, E. (2010) Women in transition: From prison to..., *Current Issues in Criminal Justice*, 22 (2): 253-67.
Balfour, G. and Comack, E. (eds) (2006) *Criminalizing women: Gender and (in)justice in neo-liberal times*, Nova Scotia: Fernwood Publishing.

Beglan, M. (2013) The 218 Experience, in M. Malloch and G. McIvor (eds) *Women, punishment and social justice: Human rights and penal practices*, Oxon: Routledge, 152-66.

Belenky, M., Clinchy, B., Goldberger, N. and Tarule, J. (1986) *Women's ways of knowing*, NY: Basic Books.

Block, C., Blokland, A., Van der Werff, C., van Os, R. and Nieuwbeerta, P. (2010) Long-term patterns of offending in women, *Feminist Criminology*, 5 (1): 73-107.

Blokland, A. and van Os, R. (2010) Life span offending trajectories of convicted Dutch women, *International Criminal Justice Review*, 20 (2): 169-87.

Brennan, T., Breitenbach, M., Dieterich, W., Salisbury, E. and van Voorhis, P. (2012) Women's pathways to serious and habitual crime: A person-centered analysis incorporating gender responsive factors, *Criminal Justice & Behavior*, 39 (11): 1481-1508.

Brown, M. and Ross, S. (2010) Mentoring, social capital and desistance: A study of women released from prison, *The Australian and New Zealand Journal of Criminology*, 43 (1): 31-50.

Budd, T., Sharp, C. and Mayhew, P. (2005) *Offending in England and Wales: First results from the 2003 Crime and Justice Survey. Home Office Research Study No. 275*, London: Home Office.

Buell, M., Modley, P. and Van Voorhis, P. (2011) Policy developments in the USA, in R. Sheehan, G. McIvor and C. Trotter (eds) *Working with women in the community*, Cullompton: Willan Publishing, 45-71.

Bushway, S.D., Brame, R. and Paternoster, R. (2004) Connecting desistance and recidivism: Measuring changes in criminality over the lifespan, in S. Maruna and R. Immarigeon (eds) *After crime and punishment: Pathways to offender reintegration*, Cullompton: Willan Publishing, 85-101.

Cabinet Office Social Exclusion Task Force (2009) *Short study on women offenders*, London: Cabinet Office.

Cain, M. (1989) (ed.) *Growing up good. Policing the behaviour of girls in Europe*, London: Sage.

Carlen, P. (1988) *Women, crime and poverty*, Buckingham: Open University Press.

Carlen, P., Hicks, J., O'Dwyer, J., Christina, D. and Tchaikovsky, C. (1985) *Criminal women: Autobiographical accounts*, Cambridge: Polity Press.

Chesney-Lind, M. and Pasko, L. (eds) (2013) *The female offender: Girls, women, and crime* (3rd ed.), London: Sage Publications.

Comack, E. (2006) The feminist engagement with criminology, in G. Balfour and E. Comack (eds) *Criminalizing women: Gender and (in) justice in neo-liberal times*, Nova Scotia: Fernwood Publishing, 22-55.

Corston, J. (2007) *The Corston report: A report by Baroness Jean Corston of a review of women with particular vulnerabilities in the criminal justice system*, London: Home Office.

DeLisi, M. (2002) Not just a boy's club: An empirical assessment of female career criminals, *Women & Criminal Justice*, 13 (4): 27-45.

Eggleston, E. and Laub, J. (2002) The onset of adult offending: A neglected dimension of the criminal career, *Journal of Criminal Justice*, 30 (6): 603-22.

Farrall, S., Bottoms, A. and Shapland, J. (2010) Social structures and desistance from crime, *European Journal of Criminology*, 7 (6): 546-70.

Farrall, S., Mawby, R.C. and Worrall, A. (2007) Prolific/persistent offenders and desistance, in L. Gelsthorpe and R. Morgan (eds) *Handbook of probation*, Cullompton: Willan Publishing, 352–81.

Gelsthorpe, L. (2010) What works with women offenders? in M. Herzog-Evans (ed.) *Transnational criminology manual*, Vol 3, Nijmegen, The Netherlands: Wolf Legal Publishers, 223-40.

Gelsthorpe, L. (2011) Women, crime and control: A response to 'Punishing the Poor: The Neoliberal Government of Social Insecurity and Prisons of Poverty' by Loïc Wacquant, Special Issue of *Criminology and Criminal Justice: An International Journal*, 10 (4): 375-86.

Gelsthorpe, L. (2013) Working with women in probation: 'Will you, won't you, will you, won't you, won't you join the dance?', in P. Ugwudike and P. Raynor (eds) *What works in offender compliance: International perspectives and evidence-based practice*, Basingstoke: Palgrave Macmillan, 279-94.

Gelsthorpe, L. and Hedderman, C. (2012) Providing for women offenders the risks of adopting a payment by results approach, *Probation Journal*, 59 (4): 374-90.

Hannah-Moffat, K. and Shaw, M. (2003) The meaning of 'risk' in women's prisons: A critique, in B. Bloom (ed.) *Gendered justice: Addressing female offenders*, Durham, NC: Carolina Academic Press, 69-96.

Hedderman, C. (2010) Government policy on women offenders: Labour's legacy and the Coalition's challenge, *Punishment & Society*, 12 (4): 485-500.

Heidensohn, F. (1968) The deviance of women: A critique and an enquiry, *British Journal of Sociology*, 61(Issue Sup. s1), 160-75.

Hopkins, M. and Wickson, J. (2013) Targeting prolific and other priority offenders and promoting pathways to desistance: Some reflections on the PPO programme using a theory of change framework, *Criminology and Criminal Justice*, 13 (5): 594-614.

House of Commons Justice Select Committee (2013) *Second report – Women offenders: After the Corston Report* [HC 92]. London: House of Commons Justice Committee.

Howe, A. (1994) *Punish and critique: Towards a feminist analysis of penality*. London: Routledge.

Hubbard, D. and Matthews, B. (2008) Reconciling the differences between the 'gender-responsive' and the 'what works' literature to improve services for girls, *Crime & Delinquency*, 54 (2): 225-58.

Hutter, B. and Williams, G. (eds) (1981) *Controlling women*, London: Croom Helm in association with the Oxford University Women's Studies Committee.

Kong, R. and AuCoin, K. (2008) Female offenders in Canada, *Juristat*, 28 (1): 1-23.

Lawston, J. (2013) Prisons, gender responsive strategies and community sanctions: The expansion of punishment in the United States, in M. Malloch and G. McIvor (eds) *Women, punishment and social justice: Human rights and penal practices*, Oxon: Routledge, 109-20.

LeBel, T., Burnett, R., Maruna, S. and Bushway, S. (2008) The 'chicken and egg' of subjective and social factors in desistance from crime, *European Journal of Criminology*, 5 (2): 131-59.

Leverentz, A. (2006) The love of a good man? Romantic relationships as a source of support or hindrance for female ex-offenders, *Journal of Research in Crime and Delinquency*, 43 (4): 459-88.

Light, M., Grant, E. and Hopkins, K. (2013) *Gender differences in substance misuse and mental health amongst prisoners – Results from the Surveying Prisoner Crime Reduction (SPCR) longitudinal cohort study of prisoners*, London: MoJ.

Martin, J., Kautt, P. and Gelsthorpe, L. (2009) What works for women? A comparison of community-based general offending programme completion, *British Journal of Criminology*, 49 (6): 879-99.

Messina, N. and Grella, C. (2006) Childhood trauma and women's health outcomes: A California prison population, *The American Journal of Public Health*, 96 (10): 1842-8.

Michalsen, V. (2013) A cell of one's own? Incarceration and other turning points in women's journeys to desistance, *International Journal of Offender Therapy and Comparative Criminology*. OnlineFirst edn, 1 September 2013, DOI: 10.1177/0306624X13498211.

Ministry of Justice (MoJ) (2012) *Prisoners' childhood and family backgrounds*, London: MoJ.

Ministry of Justice (2014) *Statistics on women and the criminal justice system 2013*, London: MoJ.

Moffitt, T. E. (1993) Adolescence-limited and life-course-persistent antisocial behavior: A developmental taxonomy, *Psychological Review*, 100 (4): 674-701.

Moffitt, T. E., Caspi, A., Rutter, M. and Silva, P. A. (2001) *Sex differences in antisocial behaviour: Conduct disorder, delinquency, and violence in the Dunedin Longitudinal Study*, Cambridge: Cambridge University Press.

Moloney, M., MacKenzie, K., Hunt, G. and Joe-Laidler, K. (2009) The path and promise of fatherhood for gang members, *British Journal of Criminology*, 49 (3): 305-25.

Moloney, K., van den Bergh, B. and Moller, L. (2009) Women in prison: The central issues of gender characteristics and trauma history, *Public Health*, 12 (3): 426-30.

National Institute of Corrections (2013) *Women risk needs assessment*, www.uc.edu/womenoffenders.html

Pavlich, G. (2010) The emergence of habitual criminals in 19th-century Britain: Implications for criminology, *Journal of Theoretical and Philosophical Criminology*, 2 (1): 1-62.

Piquero, A. and Chung, H. (2001) On the relationships between gender, early onset, and the seriousness of offending, *Journal of Criminal Justice*, 29 (3): 189-206.

A Prison Matron (1862) *Female life in prison* (2 vols). London: Hurst & Blackett. (Published anonymously, but later attributed to Frederick William Robinson.)

Reisig, M., Holtfreter, K. and Morash, M. (2006) Assessing recidivism risk across female pathways to crime, *Justice Quarterly*, 23 (3): 384-405.

Rockell, B. A. (2008) *Women street hustlers: Who they are and how they survive*, Washington, DC: American Psychological Association.

Ross, R. and Fabiano, E. (1986) *Female offenders: Correctional afterthoughts*, Jefferson, NC: McFarland.

Rumgay, J. (2004) Scripts for safer survival: Pathways out of female crime, *The Howard Journal*, 43 (4): 405-19.

Sampson, R. and Laub, J. (1995) *Crime in the making: Pathways and turning points through life*, MA: Harvard University Press.

Sharpe, G. (2012) *Offending girls: Young women and youth justice*, Oxon, Routledge.

Sheehan, R. (2013) Justice and community for women in transition in Victoria, Australia, in M. Malloch and G. McIvor (eds) *Women, punishment and social justice: Human rights and penal practices*, London: Routledge, 121-35.

Sheehan, R., McIvor G. and Trotter, C. (eds) (2007) *What works with women offenders*, Cullompton: Willan Publishing.

Sheehan, R., McIvor, G. and Trotter, C. (eds) (2011) *Working with women offenders in the community*, Cullompton: Willan Publishing.

Silvestri, M. and Crowther-Dowey, C. (2008) *Gender and crime*, London: Sage Publications Ltd.

Simpson, S., Yahner, J. and Dugan, L. (2008) Understanding women's pathways to jail: Analysing the lives of incarcerated women, *Australian & New Zealand Journal of Criminology*, 41 (1): 84-108.

Smart, C. (1976) *Women, crime and criminology: A feminist critique*, London: Routledge and Kegan Paul.

Smith, A. (1962) *Women in prison: A study in penal methods*, 6, London: Stevens.

Soothill, K., Ackerley, E. and Francis, B. (2003) The persistent offenders debate: A focus on temporal changes, *Criminal Justice*, 3 (4): 389-412.

Taylor, K. and Blanchette, K. (2009) The women are not wrong: It is the approach that is debatable, *Criminology & Public Policy*, 8 (1): 221-9.

Wacquant, L. (2009) *Punishing the poor: The neoliberal government of social insecurity*, US: Duke University Press.

Wright, S. (2015a) *Narratives of 'punishment' and 'desistance' in the lives of repeatedly criminalised women*, Unpublished paper presented 20 May 2015 at the Punishment and Desistance conference, Liverpool Hope University.

Wright, S. (2015b) *'Persistent' and 'prolific' offending across the life-course as experienced by women: Chronic recidivism and frustrated desistance*, Unpublished PhD thesis, University of Surrey, UK.

Zedner, L. (1991) *Women, crime, and custody in Victorian England*, Oxford: Clarendon Press.

FOUR

# A comparison: criminalised women in Scotland

*Michele Burman, Margaret Malloch and Gill McIvor*

## Introduction

Between 1995 and 2002, a total of 11 women killed themselves in what was then Scotland's only prison for women, HMP and YOI Cornton Vale. The deaths, and the seeming frequency with which one followed another (seven women died within a 30-month period between 1995 and 1997; and two women died in one week in 2001), sent shock waves through the Scottish criminal justice system and wider Scottish society. Although the subsequent fatal accident inquiries failed to identify any single reason for the suicides, it was acknowledged that a history of drug use and withdrawal problems following imprisonment were common experiences among the women who died. As Scotland is traditionally distinct from England and Wales, with its emphasis on a more welfarist approach to criminal justice (via criminal justice social work rather than probation), the deaths of these women called for drastic action and led academics, practitioners and policy makers to question the appropriateness of existing sentences and associated interventions for women.

As with England and Wales, where the deaths of six women prisoners between 2002 and 2003 led ultimately to the Corston Inquiry and Report (Corston, 2007), these tragic events in Scotland were the catalyst for a far-ranging examination of women in prison, and in the criminal justice system more broadly. Yet despite the plethora of reports, inspections and practice initiatives that were undertaken and introduced, the female population in Scotland continued to rise, resulting most recently in the establishment of the Commission for Women Offenders which, under the leadership of Eilish Angiolini, former Lord [*sic*] Advocate of Scotland, reported in 2012. The aim of this chapter is to provide a critical analysis of the work of the Commission, its recommendations and Scottish government responses.

## Responding to criminalised women in Scotland: a brief historical account

The social and economic circumstances of women drawn into the criminal justice system in Scotland, and internationally, has historically been a cause for concern. While women have traditionally featured in every category of crime, they predominate in the realms of low-level offending, often linked to adverse social and personal circumstances. Since the advent of the prison reform movement, women have traditionally constituted a small proportion of the overall prison system in the UK.

However, during the 1990s the number of women imprisoned, both in Scotland (Scottish Executive, 1999) and in England and Wales (Home Office, 1999) increased rapidly. Despite the simultaneous increase in the use of community sanctions such as probation and community service (although the latter was underresourced and underutilised for women (McIvor, 1998)), this had a negligible effect on the number of women being sent to prison. This rising prison population was marked by a growing number of women imprisoned for offences such as theft (shoplifting) and fraud, or for the non-payment of fines, accrued from these offences and others, notably soliciting for prostitution (an offence which did not in itself entail a custodial sentence). Many women were admitted to prison for failing to comply with a non-custodial penalty, including non-payment of fines, and while women could be found in all offence categories, they formed a majority in only two: offences relating to prostitution; and failure to have a television licence (Gelsthorpe, 2004).

Hedderman and Dowds (1997) pointed out that while sentencers in England and Wales were often reluctant to fine women, it was noticeable that a high proportion of women in prison in Scotland were there due to fine default. In 1995, some 70% of women appearing in court in Scotland were fined (Social Work Services and Prisons Inspectorate for Scotland, 1998), with up to 52% of female prison-sentenced admissions in Scotland being for fine default, reflecting the high incidence of fines as a non-custodial sentence for women. Furthermore, in Scotland, this brought women into prison who had not been sentenced previously: over two thirds of women serving sentences at HMP Cornton Vale had never been in prison, under sentence or on remand, and almost half were first offenders (Social Work Services and Prisons Inspectorate for Scotland, 1998).

The deaths of seven women at HMP Cornton Vale between June 1995 and December 1997 (the oldest, Sandra Brown, was only 28 years of age and five of the women were on remand at the time of their deaths), required a drastic response. Henry McLeish MP, then Scottish Office Minister for Home Affairs, commissioned an urgent review to be carried out by the Social Work Services and Prisons Inspectorate for Scotland. Its purpose was to 'review, and make recommendations about, community disposals and the use of custody for women offenders in Scotland' (Social Work Services and Prisons Inspectorate for Scotland, 1998: iii). This resulted in the production of the report *Women offenders: A safer way* in May 1998. The title of the report was itself indicative of the recognition that for many women prisoners, custody was an 'unsafe' environment. Like the 1997 report for England and Wales by HM Inspectorate of Prisons, which provided a thematic review of the imprisonment of women, the Scottish report concluded that many women were imprisoned for relatively minor offences. A significant number of women who came to the attention of the courts had experienced a range of social, economic and emotional problems that contributed to their 'vulnerability' (HM Inspectorate of Prisons, 1997; Loucks, 1998; Loucks et al, 2000; Prison Reform Trust, 2000).

Research, commissioned as part of the Social Work Services and Prisons Inspectorate for Scotland review, into the background and experiences of women prisoners drew attention to a number of factors that characterised the lives of many women in prison in Scotland. While women were imprisoned for minor offences related to poverty or drug use, the lives of many of them were characterised by high rates of past and/or current abuse, drug and/or alcohol addiction, inadequate housing and employment opportunities, and a general lack of relevant support services in the community (Loucks, 1998; Social Work Services and Prisons Inspectorate for Scotland, 1998). Women's experiences prior to imprisonment meant that custody could have a significant impact on them in a way that differed to men's experiences (Carlen, 1983 and 1998; Dobash et al, 1986; Howe, 1994). For many women prisoners, issues of childcare caused them serious concerns throughout their sentence (Dobash et al, 1986).

Without the availability of credible community-based treatments (particularly for drug users), the courts tended to continue the trend of increased custodial sentencing for women. Few identifiably distinct resources existed for women, despite attempts by workers in the field and women's organisations to highlight the need for such services. The lack of woman-oriented resources was particularly noticeable in the statutory sector. The Social Work Services and Prisons Inspectorate for Scotland report (1998) found *none* of the local authorities included in their research to have a defined strategy for women, nor were there any criminal justice hostels specifically for women. Women were often restricted from resources for more general reasons: few residential rehabilitation services existed specifically for women; few accommodated women with dependent children; and local authorities were sometimes reluctant to provide the financial resources for such services. Significantly, the availability of appropriate services could be crucial when sentencing decisions were taken (Scottish Affairs Committee, 1994).

Following the publication of *Women offenders: A safer way*, a number of things happened. One of the report's recommendations was that an inter-agency forum be established to develop services for women in Glasgow since, at the time of the review, the majority of women in prison in Scotland were from Glasgow and the west of Scotland. This inter-agency forum was established in 1998 with representatives from all the key agencies working in this area in Glasgow, including criminal justice, health, housing, employment and drugs rehabilitation services. The forum proceeded to make recommendations aimed at providing women with access to services and support that would address the social and personal problems that were believed to contribute to their offending. Among these recommendations was the creation of 'Time out' centres which, it was anticipated, would provide a range of services for women, including residential support.

The recommendations were taken forward by a Ministerial Group on Women's Offending, established in December 2000 with the remit of translating the forum's proposals into practical objectives. The Ministerial Group produced a report, *A better way* (Scottish Executive, 2002), which elaborated on the measures required to take forward this work. The Ministerial Group also indicated that more emphasis was required on the alleviation of the social circumstances that led some women to offend in order to survive, the need to intervene early to ensure that women's needs could be met, and the promotion of community disposals. The Ministerial Group also recognised that interventions developed for male offenders may not be appropriate for women, and that 'gender specific' programmes should be developed that would be better able to address women's needs in a safe and non-threatening environment more conducive to supporting women's growth and change (Bloom and Covington, 1998).

A key recommendation of the Ministerial Group was that 'Time out' centres should be developed, providing a locus for key services in an accessible and supportive environment. In August 2003, the first (and only) 'Time out' centre (or '218' as it was called after its location in a street in the city centre) was established in Glasgow, opening its doors to women in December 2003. The original emphasis of 218 was on: alleviating the social circumstances that characterise the lives of many women in the criminal justice system; early intervention to meet the needs of women (with drug and/or alcohol problems prominent among these); and promoting the use of the full range of community disposals with the ultimate aim of reducing reoffending and consequently reducing the number of women who ended up in custody. Specifically, its objectives were to:

- provide a specialist facility for women who were subject to the criminal justice system;
- provide a safe environment for women in which to address offending behaviour;
- tackle the underlying causes of offending behaviour;
- help women to avert crises in their lives;
- enable women to move on and reintegrate into society.

As such, 218 was an innovative project in Scotland, responsible for providing services for women involved with the criminal justice system in a relatively unique way (Loucks et al, 2006; Malloch et al, 2008; Easton and Matthews, 2010; Malloch, 2010).

As HM Inspectorate of Prisons for Scotland noted in 2001 (1.10): 'It is now recognised by many that the problems which some women prisoners face are unlikely to be resolved by imprisonment. The realisation of credible and reliable alternatives to custody in communities across Scotland for petty offenders is, therefore, what the prison now needs most.' Despite the publication of *A safer way* (Social Work Services and Prisons Inspectorate for Scotland, 1998) and *A better way* (Scottish Executive, 2002), community-based provision for women remained patchy and the female prison population continued to rise. Successive inspections by Her Majesty's Inspectorate of Prisons for Scotland (HMIP for Scotland) drew attention to the resultant overcrowding in HMP and YOI Cornton Vale. Inspection reports pointed to the impact that high levels of overcrowding were having on the delivery of services within the prison, in particular the inadequate provision of treatment for women with complex needs that relate to their social circumstances, previous histories of abuse and mental health and addiction problems (HMIP for Scotland, 2006, 2007). In 2009, HM Chief Inspector of Prisons declared Cornton Vale to be in a 'state of crisis', citing overcrowding, two-hour waits for the toilet, cold meals, lack of activities and a deep problem of prisoner lack of purpose and activity, which was impeding rehabilitation (Scottish Government, 2010).

In June 2011, HMIP undertook a follow-up inspection of Cornton Vale. The subsequent report raised concerns which, in the opinion of the Inspectorate, required immediate attention (HMIP for Scotland, 2011). It pointed once again to the serious overcrowding problem; the adverse consequences for the women prisoners and young offenders detained in Cornton Vale were highlighted; and the Inspectorate called for a clear national strategy to deal with the problems identified.

Women in the criminal justice system received renewed political attention in 2009, when the Scottish Parliament Equal Opportunities Committee examined the issue, again emphasising the importance of recognising the distinctive needs of women and ensuring that criminal justice responses took gender difference into account (Equal Opportunities Committee, 2009).

## Women and the criminal justice system revisited: the Commission on Women Offenders

Despite these reviews, reports and recommendations, and in common with many other Western jurisdictions (McIvor, 2010), the female prison population in Scotland has continued to rise. While the number of women imprisoned for non-payment of fines has reduced significantly as a result of the introduction of mandatory supervised activities as an alternative to imprisonment for fine default (McIvor et al, 2013), the average daily female sentenced and remand prison population has increased steadily: the former rose from 200 in 2002-03 to 360 in 2011-12; and the latter grew from 81 to 108 over the same period (Scottish Government, 2012a). An analysis of police, prosecution and sentencing data provided no evidence of greater levels of female criminality but indicated, rather, that women's offending was being dealt with more punitively by the courts, with women (and especially older women) more likely to receive prison sentences for a range of offences than they would have done 10 years previously (McIvor and Burman, 2011).

Increasing government concern about the rising rate of female imprisonment resulted in the Scottish National Party including a commitment in its 2011 election manifesto to 'address the explosion in the female prison population, which has doubled in the last decade despite the number of females committing offences staying the same'. This would be achieved by commissioning 'a review of female offending, including the rise in female incarceration' (SNP, 2011: 18).

In June 2011, shortly after the publication of HMIP's follow-up report on Cornton Vale (HMIP for Scotland, 2011), the Scottish Cabinet Secretary for Justice announced the establishment of an independent Commission on Women Offenders, to find a more effective way of responding to women in the criminal justice system. The remit of the Commission was: 'to consider the evidence on how to improve outcomes for women in the criminal justice system; to make recommendations for practical measures in this Parliament to reduce their reoffending and reverse the recent increase in the female prisoner population' (Commission on Women Offenders, 2012).

The Commission consisted of: the former Lord Advocate Dame Eilish Angiolini as Chair; Dr Linda de Caestecker, Director of Public Health for NHS Greater Glasgow and Clyde; and Sheriff Danny Scullion. It met for the first time in late August 2011 and reported in April 2012. During that time it consulted widely, meeting with members of the academic research community, criminal justice practitioners, community justice authorities, the Scottish Prison Service, the police, prison visiting committees and those involved with addiction services, psychiatry, psychology and community care. It took oral evidence and considered written evidence submitted by, or on behalf of, 17 organisations. The Commission also made a number of visits to prisons and prison services in various communities, including police cells and specialist drug courts.

The final report of the Commission was published in April 2012 (Commission on Women Offenders, 2012), and marked a significant shift in a lengthy debate that had been played out in numerous previous reports, commentaries and prison inspections concerning the criminal justice response to women offenders. Based on its observations and on available evidence, the Commission formed the view of service provision for women offenders in the community and upon leaving custody to be 'highly variable and disjointed', such that it was difficult to form a comprehensive picture of the services and programmes offered. It found that: interventions delivered in prison were rarely followed up in the community; performance measures were considered inappropriate; and funding arrangements favoured activity over outcomes, making it difficult to measure the impact or effectiveness of programmes being undertaken.

The Commission took a rather distinctive approach in its provision of a coordinated set of practical recommendations that simultaneously sought to address the needs of women offenders, while placing criminal justice processes in the context of the holistic support for criminalised women to begin to resolve the issues that underpin their offending. As a result of what the Commission heard, saw and learned, it made 37 recommendations across seven broad areas for improving outcomes for women in the criminal justice system and reducing their reoffending. The seven areas were: service redesign, alternatives to prosecution, alternatives to remand, sentencing, prisons, community reintegration, and leadership structures and delivery (Commission on Women Offenders, 2012).

## Service redesign

As part of a set of 11 recommendations proposing service redesign through an interconnected and collaborative framework of support and direction for women offenders, the Commission recommended the establishment of community justice centres (*recommendation 1*). These were envisaged as 'one-stop' centres, based on existing examples of good practice, such as the 218 Centre in Glasgow and the Willow Project in Edinburgh, that would coordinate and deliver a consistent range of services to reduce reoffending. These would include interventions for supervision and management suited to the particular needs of women, which challenge women's offending behaviours and attitudes, which address the root causes of reoffending, and which simultaneously provide practical advice and support on matters such as housing, benefits, employment and childcare. The Commission was convinced of the importance of women-specific programmes and solutions to deal with the particular problems that women offenders face. It was therefore considered important that the community justice centres would be available and involved at every stage of the criminal justice system, and that services would be 'proactive and persistent' in engaging with women, rather than expecting them to access conventional pathways to support.

The Commission made a strong case for the value of coordinated working to ensure a holistic approach to women's needs, and recommended that a multidisciplinary, collaborative approach be taken, with the co-location of multi-agency and multiprofessional services where possible (*recommendation 2*). It was also recommended that a key worker system be in place, acting as a single point of contact for women at risk of offending or custody as they move through the criminal justice system (*recommendation 3*). In the recognition that a strong mentoring relationship can impact positively on offender engagement with criminal justice and support services, the Commission recommended that intensive mentoring, where practical support and monitoring is provided by mentors on a wide range of issues relating to offending behaviour, should be available to women at risk of reoffending or custody, and to support compliance with court orders (*recommendation 4*). A strong view was taken that supporting women in their accommodation can have a positive impact on their likelihood of successfully completing an order or complying with bail conditions, and therefore it was recommended that supported accommodation should be more widely available (*recommendation 5*).

The Commission was particularly struck by the high levels of trauma, anxiety and mental health problems experienced by women in the criminal justice system. It took the position that an integrated multidisciplinary approach to the delivery of services would be a positive step towards helping to address women's mental health and addiction needs, and made several specific recommendations in this regard:

- that a national service level agreement for the provision of psychiatric reports is developed between the NHS and the Scottish Court Service, to increase timeliness of reports to assist sentencing decisions (*recommendation 6*);
- that mental health services and approaches should be developed in such a way that facilitates women with borderline personality disorders to access them (*recommendation 7*);
- that mental health programmes and interventions for short-term prisoners are designed such that they can continue to be seamlessly delivered in the community (*recommendation 8*);
- that the government mental health strategy should place a greater focus on criminalised women, specifically through the provision of services to address trauma, self-harm and borderline personality disorder (*recommendation 9*);
- that mental health training should be available for police, prison officers, criminal justice and social service workers and the third sector with ongoing supervision (*recommendation 11*).

The Commission also recommended an urgent review of the services for women with borderline personality disorder and post-traumatic stress disorder (*recommendation 10*).

## Alternatives to prosecution

The Commission acknowledged the importance of early and meaningful intervention with women and made five recommendations regarding alternatives to prosecution, which included:

- the wider use of fiscal work orders (unpaid work orders of between 10 and 50 hours) to be coordinated through the community justice centres, and involving female-only work teams or individual placements (*recommendation 12*);
- greater powers to procurator fiscals (prosecutors) to impose a diversion order which could include both unpaid work and rehabilitative elements (*recommendation 13*);
- new police powers to divert women from prosecution and direct them to attend community justice centres (*recommendation 14*).

Two further recommendations concerned the wider availability of diversion schemes and more consistent use of diversion, again with services and programmes coordinated by community justice centres (*recommendation 15*); and that the police identify suitable cases for diversion in the police report (*recommendation 16*).

### Alternatives to remand

The report noted concern that only around a third of women who are remanded in custody in the end receive a custodial sentence, yet experience the same increased risk of suicide, mental distress, disintegration of social support and family ties, and disruption to employment as prisoners receiving short sentences. A key recommendation here concerned the wide and consistent availability of bail supervision schemes ('bail supervision plus') to include mentoring, supported accommodation and access to the community justice centres to enable compliance (*recommendation 17*).

Other recommendations were that the government examine the potential for electronic monitoring as a condition of bail (*recommendation 18*), and encourage and ensure provision of information, communication and awareness of alternatives to remand (*recommendation 19*).

### Sentencing

In relation to the sentencing process in court, the Commission was encouraged by research on solution-specific or problem-solving courts (McIvor et al, 2006; Rossman et al, 2011) and recommended that a pilot of a generic problem-solving summary criminal court be established for repeat offenders with multiple and complex needs, irrespective of gender (*recommendation 20*).

While mindful of the professional expertise and effort that inform the preparation of background reports, and of the desirability of ensuring that a full background report will always be available where necessary, the Commission was concerned about cases being continued for up to a month to enable reports to be prepared, and so recommended that a truncated criminal justice social work report (a rapid report) be available in summary criminal courts on the day of conviction, or within two working days, to enable the appropriate sentence to be imposed and implemented as quickly as possible (*recommendation 21*).

The Commission concluded that a significant element in motivating individuals to comply with orders was a consistency of dialogue between court officials and offenders, and so recommended that, where possible, the same sentencing sheriff or judge should conduct any subsequent review hearings (*recommendation 22*).

Two new sentences were also proposed: a composite sentence of imprisonment, which could comprise a custodial element, and a community-based element, including a suspended sentence (*recommendation 23*). There was also a recommendation about the training and education of judicial office holders in relation to the issue of sentence (*recommendation 24*).

### Prisons

The Commission made some fairly radical recommendations regarding the prison estate, primarily that Cornton Vale be demolished and replaced by a small, national specialist prison for women serving long-term sentences (that is four years and over) and those who present a significant risk to the public (*recommendation 25*). This specialist prison would have the capacity for what was described as 'meaningful and consistent work', with an adequate medical centre, a young women's unit, a purpose-built mother and baby unit, an appropriate and family-friendly visitor centre, and a community integration unit to help women to access community services and support networks prior to release (*recommendation 26*).

The use of local prisons for remand and short-term prisoners was also recommended, with the aim of improving reintegration (*recommendation 27*). It was considered important that women imprisoned for short periods should have improved links to services when they leave prison, and that links with families and children are maintained, facilitated through the extension and expansion of video technology in Cornton Vale to allow continued maintenance of family relationships (*recommendation 28*). In recognition that there was no one with an overall strategic remit for criminalised women, the Commission recommended that a non-executive member of the Scottish Prison Service Board be appointed with a specific remit for championing and driving through change for women (*recommendation 29*). Gender-specific training for all those working with women was also proposed (*recommendation 30*).

## Community reintegration

The Commission highlighted that effective throughcare and aftercare arrangements for women leaving custody are of vital importance, and it was exercised about the continuing difficulty that women offenders have about accommodation. It therefore recommended that inter-agency protocols on prison discharge and homelessness are introduced across Scotland with the twin aims of: sustaining tenancies when women are in custody; and securing access to safe accommodation for every woman prisoner upon release (*recommendation 31*).

In order to minimise the effects of gaps in the provision of advice to prisoners regarding benefit entitlements, and delay in accessing benefits, it was recommended to the UK government that arrangements are put in place to ensure that every female prisoner can access benefits immediately on release (*recommendation 32*). In its objective to achieve a seamless transition and the continuity of services for women leaving prisons, the Commission recommended that women are met at the gate by their key worker or mentor (*recommendation 33*).

## Leadership, structures and delivery

Key among the many different agencies and individuals involved in an offender's journey through the criminal justice system are criminal justice social work services within local authorities, who are responsible for managing, supervising and rehabilitating offenders in the community, and the Scottish Prison Service, which deals with offenders in the custodial setting. Community justice authorities are the main partnership responsible for providing a coordinated approach for the local delivery of offender services through planning, managing performance and reporting on the performance of local authority criminal justice services, with a number of designated statutory partner bodies including the police, NHS boards, Scottish Court Service, Crown Office and Procurator Fiscal Service, Victim Support Scotland and other individuals/organisations delivering offender services. But there are also other strategic partnerships, such as alcohol and drugs partnerships, community health partnerships and community planning partnerships, that may also have an involvement in the management of offenders, as well as public, private and third sector bodies. In total around 200 organisations are involved.

The Commission described this as a 'grossly cluttered landscape' (Commission on Women Offenders, 2012: 82) and identified a raft of problems, namely the lack of opportunity for strategic leadership and accountability in the delivery of offender services in the community, short-term funding and difficulties in measuring impact, inconsistent service provision and inconsistent throughcare which, taken together, severely inhibit effective working practices.

Three linked recommendations, in relation to implementation, proposed a radical transformation of the existing structural and funding arrangements and associated working practices for the provision of offender services in the community.

- The establishment of a new national community justice service was recommended (*recommendation 34*).
- The setting up of a national Community Justice and Prison Delivery Board was proposed, with an independent chair to promote integration between the community justice services and the Scottish Prison Service, and to deliver a shared vision for reducing reoffending across community and within custodial settings (*recommendation 35*).
- It was proposed that a senior director in each agency should be identified and given responsibility for women in the criminal justice system (*recommendation 36*).

The final recommendation called for the Cabinet Secretary for Justice to report to the Scottish Parliament within six months of the publication of the report, and annually thereafter, on the steps taken by the government in the implementation of the recommendations (*recommendation 37*).

## The government response

The Scottish government published its response to the report of the Commission on Women Offenders in June 2012, indicating its support for its aims and acceptance of 33 out of its 37 recommendations (Scottish Government, 2012b). The recommendations that were not accepted related to the creation of a new national service to commission and deliver community justice services, the introduction of two new sentences to expand the range of non-custodial (or in one case semi-custodial) sentencing options, and a review of services for women with borderline personality disorder and post-traumatic stress disorder. The Commission's proposals regarding the creation of a single national community justice service were perhaps their most controversial and resulted in the Scottish government undertaking a widespread consultation on the organisation and design of criminal justice social work services in Scotland (Scottish Government, 2012c, 2014).

The Scottish government accepted the recommendation by the Commission that HMP and YOI Cornton Vale should be closed and replaced by a smaller specialist prison for women serving long prison sentences who are deemed to present a significant public risk. It also accepted a number of recommendations aimed at providing a more collaborative and 'holistic' response to criminalised women and reducing the use of imprisonment. However, the government's commitment to 'de-centring the prison' was called into question when, in its response to the Commission's report, it announced that £20 million of additional capital funding would be allocated to the Scottish Prison Service for 2014-15 to be targeted towards the needs of the female prison population, compared with £1 million in that financial year to support projects to demonstrate how proposed changes to community-based service delivery could be put into practice (Scottish Government, 2012b).

Subsequently, proposals were developed for a new prison for women (HMP Inverclyde) in the west of Scotland (MacAskill, 2012) to open in 2017 with a capacity of 350. This development was opposed by a variety of individuals and organisations, notably the Howard League Scotland, who argued that the proposed prison, along with existing provision in HMP Grampian and HMP Edinburgh would increase the overall female prison capacity in Scotland. While the new prison had been designed partly in anticipation of projected prison population, it was noted that there was a real possibility that increased capacity would in itself generate increased numbers of women in prison (Armstrong, 2014). Moreover, as the Howard League Scotland (2014) observed, the plan to accommodate such large numbers of women and to house women of different ages, sentencing status, security category and sentence length appeared to represent 'a clear departure from the recommendation made by the Commission' (Howard League Scotland, 2014: 2). The new 'custom made' prison would have state-of-the-art facilities, including a customised medical centre, a separate unit for young women, a mother and baby unit and a visitor centre (MacAskill, 2013). Nevertheless, opponents of the prison argued that the investment of significant amounts of money in the development of such a state-of-the-art facility would create a somewhat perverse incentive, by making imprisonment an *even more* attractive option to sentencers (Malloch and McIvor, 2012). The growing opposition to plans for HMP Inverclyde eventually led the Justice Secretary, Michael Matheson, to announce on 26 January 2015 that the development would no longer proceed, noting that a 'bolder' and 'more radical and ambitious approach' was needed (Scottish Government, 2015).

In contrast to the funding proposed for the development of HMP Inverclyde, the level of financial commitment to the development of community services has been much more constrained both in amount and in timeframe. In April 2013, the Scottish Government announced that six projects would receive £7.7 million in funding over a period of two years from its Reducing Reoffending Change Fund to support the development of mentoring services for a range of offenders, including women. In June 2014, it was announced that a further £8 million – £6 million from the Scottish government and £2 million from the Robertson Trust – would be made available to extend the existing mentoring schemes for a further period of two years. The women's mentoring service is run by a national voluntary organisation, Sacro, in collaboration with other voluntary organisations. However, mentoring is focused primarily on women *leaving prison* rather than on those at risk of criminalisation at an earlier point in the criminal justice process, so its capacity to reduce the numbers of women in prison is likely to be limited.

More promisingly in this regard, perhaps, has been the funding of a range of community projects across the country, including the creation or expansion of community justice centres for women in four Scottish cities (Edinburgh, Glasgow, Dundee and Aberdeen) and the provision of funds for seven other projects to develop and improve their work with women. However, the scale of the allocation – £3 million from 2013 to 2015 – is small in comparison to the estimated £60 million capital expenditure allocated to the development of the new women's prison and set against the significant annual cost of imprisoning women. The decision to halt the development of the proposed national prison for women may create a space for new initiatives that will hopefully adhere more closely to the recommendations of the Commission for Women Offenders. However, in the absence of specific recommendations by the Commission aimed at bringing about changes in sentencing policy and practice in relation to women, and the persistent allure of the prison for some sentencers, we hope that attention does not simply shift to the development of prison places for women in local prisons, as opposed to making real improvements in the lives of criminalised women.

## Conclusions

As this chapter has shown, there has been formal concern about the rate of female imprisonment and the impact of imprisonment on criminalised women in Scotland for almost twenty years. Despite this, the numbers of women imprisoned in Scotland and the length of prison sentences they receive have continued to grow, with analyses suggesting that the growth in the female prison population can more likely be attributed to the increasing use of custodial sentences by courts than to any changes in the pattern of female offending (McIvor and Burman, 2011).

The sentencing of women poses considerable challenges, yet it is clear that this is a key driver in imprisonment rates and it suggests the need for further investigation. The reason for the increase in more punitive sentencing of women is not immediately obvious. One possibility is that there has been an increase in the number of women sentenced who are repeat offenders and whose previous convictions are resulting in them being dealt with more severely by the courts. As Burman and McIvor (2013) have argued, further research might usefully focus on whether there have, indeed, been changes in criminal histories of women appearing before the courts which might account, at least in part, for this worrying 'punitive turn'.

The establishment of a Commission on Women Offenders in 2011, only three years after the publication of a wide-ranging review of punishment in Scotland (Scottish Prisons Commission, 2008) was the cause for some optimism that a fundamental reorientation in how women's offending was dealt with might be possible. Initial developments to build a new national prison for women were met with disappointment – in particular that the Scottish government had not adopted a more radical approach to addressing women's needs in the community while reducing female prison capacity. As experience in the UK and other jurisdictions has shown, ostensibly well-intended initiatives, such as the introduction of gender-appropriate programmes, services and resources in prison can be subverted by wider institutional imperatives and by overarching preoccupations with security and control (Malloch, 2000; Hannah-Moffat, 2001), resulting in 'carceral clawback' (Carlen, 2002) that limits the ability of prison reforms to achieve meaningful change. Furthermore, as Carlen and Tombs (2006) have argued, interventions that are introduced into prisons, such as anti-addiction programmes, would be much more effective if implemented in a community setting.

With a halt to the expansion of prison places, perhaps attention can now be directed to the ongoing development of community services. The establishment of community justice centres and continued provision of mentoring schemes and innovative provisions such as the 218 Centre in Glasgow have the potential to make a significant difference to the lives of those who access them. Although there has been significant investment in this area, funding that is often provided in two-year cycles can cause considerable uncertainty for workers and service users alike, allowing little time for services to continue beyond a set-up and pilot phase. Short-term interventions are unable to evidence longer-term impact. We know that many women who end up in courts and custody in Scotland, and internationally for that matter, live lives characterised by poverty, addiction, experiences of violence, bereavement and often major physical and mental health problems (and this is not to suggest that poverty causes crime, but that the poor are more likely to be criminalised and punished). We also know that recent increases in the imprisonment of women are the result of more punitive sentencing practices, rather than increases in crime or serious crime by women. As a society, we need to ensure that services are available in local communities to provide support and appropriate assistance to those who need it, preferably long before circumstances result in arrest and criminal justice intervention.

In a letter to the Scottish Parliament Justice Committee on the implementation of recommendations of the Commission on Women Offenders, the Howard League Scotland observed that 'real success in preventing offending behaviour, as well as reducing offending, lies beyond the realms of penal policy' (Howard League Scotland, 2014: 4). Herein, we would argue, lies the crux of the matter: to what extent the criminal justice system could – or should – be expected to bring about the transformative structural change that will be necessary to address the social, economic and personal disadvantages that characterise most criminalised women's lives.

## References

Armstrong, S. (2014) *Prison population forecasts: Using the future to predict the past*, Howard League Scotland, www.howardleaguescotland.org.uk/news/2014/september/problem-prison-population-predictions

Bloom, B. and Covington, S. (1998) *Gender-specific programming for female offenders: What is it and why is it important?*, paper presented at the Annual Meeting of the American Society of Criminology, Washington, DC.

Burman, M. and McIvor, G. (2013) The rise of female imprisonment in Scotland, *Scottish Journal of Criminal Justice Studies*, 19: 28-42.

Carlen, P. (1983) *Women's imprisonment: A study in social control*, London: Routledge and Kegan Paul.

Carlen, P. (1998) *Sledgehammer*, London: Macmillan Press.

Carlen, P. (2002) Carceral clawback: The case of women's imprisonment in Canada, *Punishment and Society*, 4 (1): 115–21.

Carlen, P. and Tombs, J. (2006) Reconfigurations of penality: The ongoing case of the women's imprisonment and reintegration industries, *Theoretical Criminology*, 10 (3): 337-60.

Commission on Women Offenders (2012) *Report of the Commission on Women Offenders*, Edinburgh: Scottish Government.

Corston, J. (2007) *The Corston report: A report by Baroness Jean Corston of a review of women with particular vulnerabilities in the criminal justice system*, London: Home Office.

Dobash, R. P., Dobash, R. E. and Gutteridge, S. (1986) *The imprisonment of women*, Oxford: Basil Blackwell.

Easton, H. and Matthews, R. (2010) *Evaluation of the 218 Centre: Examining implementation and outcomes*, Edinburgh: Scottish Government.

Equal Opportunities Committee (2009) *Female Offenders in the Criminal Justice System*, Edinburgh: Scottish Parliament.

Gelsthorpe, L. (2004) Female offending: A theoretical overview, in G. McIvor (ed.) *Women Who Offend*, London: Jessica Kingsley.

Hannah-Moffat, K. (2001) *Punishment in disguise: Penal governance and Canadian women's imprisonment*, Toronto: University of Toronto Press.

Hedderman, C. and Dowds, L. (1997) *The sentencing of women*, London: Home Office.

HM Inspectorate of Prisons (1997) *Women in prison: A thematic review*, London: Home Office.

HM Inspectorate of Prisons for Scotland (2001) *Report on HMP and YOI Cornton Vale*, Edinburgh: HMIP Scotland.

HM Inspectorate of Prisons for Scotland (2006) *Report on HMP and YOI Cornton Vale: Full inspection report (27 February – 3 March 2006)*, Edinburgh: HMIP Scotland.

HM Inspectorate of Prisons for Scotland (2007) *Report on HMP and YOI Cornton Vale: Full inspection report (19-20 March 2007)*, Edinburgh: HMIP Scotland.

HM Inspectorate of Prisons for Scotland (2010) *Report on HMP and YOI Cornton Vale (Full inspection: 21-29 September 2009)*, Edinburgh: The Scottish Government.

HM Inspectorate of Prisons for Scotland (2011) *HMP and YOI Cornton Vale: Follow up inspection (1-4 February 2011)*, Edinburgh: The Scottish Government.

Home Office (1999) *Statistics on women and the criminal justice system*, London: Home Office Research, Development and Statistics Directorate.

Howe, A. (1994) *Punish and critique: Towards a feminist analysis of penality*, London: Routledge.

Howard League Scotland (2014) *Implementation of the recommendations of the Commission on Women Offenders*, letter to the Scottish Parliament Justice Committee.

Loucks, N. (1998) *HMPI Cornton Vale: Research into drugs and alcohol, violence and bullying, suicides and self-injury and backgrounds of abuse*, Scottish Prison Service Occasional Papers No. 1/98, Edinburgh: Scottish Prison Service.

Loucks, N., Malloch, M., McIvor, G. and Gelsthorpe, L. (2006) *Evaluation of the 218 Centre*, Edinburgh: Scottish Executive.

Loucks, N., Power, K., Swanson, V. and Chambers, J. (2000) *Young people in custody in Scotland*, Scottish Prison Service Occasional Paper Series No. 3/2000, Edinburgh: Scottish Prison Service.

MacAskill, K. (2012) *Cabinet Secretary for Justice's first annual progress report to the Parliament on the steps taken to implement the Commission on Women Offenders' recommendations*, Edinburgh: Scottish Parliament Justice Committee.

MacAskill, K. (2013) *Cabinet Secretary for Justice's second progress report to the Parliament on the steps taken to implement the Commission on Women Offenders' recommendations*, Edinburgh: Scottish Parliament Justice Committee.

Malloch, M. (2000) *Women, drugs and custody*, Winchester: Waterside Press.

Malloch, M. (2010) Time out for women in Scotland, in M. Herzog-Evans (ed.) *Transnational criminology manual (Volume 2)*, Nijmegen: Wolf Publishing.

Malloch, M. and McIvor, G. (eds) (2012) *Women, punishment and social justice: Human rights and penal practices*, London: Routledge.

Malloch, M., McIvor, G. and Loucks, N. (2008) Time out for women: Innovation in Scotland in a context of change, *The Howard Journal*, 47 (4): 383-99.

McIvor, G. (1998) Jobs for the boys? Gender differences in referral to community service, *The Howard Journal*, 37 (3): 280-90.

McIvor, G. (2010) Women and crime: The rise of female imprisonment in western jurisdictions, in M. Herzog-Evans (ed.) *Transnational criminology manual (Volume 2)*, Nijmegen: Wolf Publishing.

McIvor, G., Barnsdale, L., Eley, S., Malloch, M., Yates, R. and Brown, A. (2006) *The operation and effectiveness of the Scottish drug court pilots*, Edinburgh: Scottish Executive.

McIvor, G. and Burman, M. (2011) *Understanding the drivers of female imprisonment in Scotland*, Glasgow: Scottish Centre for Crime and Justice Research.

McIvor, G., Pirnat, C. and Grafl, C. (2013) Unpaid work as an alternative to imprisonment for fine default in Austria and Scotland, *European Journal of Probation*, 5 (2): 3-28.

Prison Reform Trust (2000) *Justice for women: The need for reform*, London: Prison Reform Trust.

Rossman, S., Roman, J.K., Zweig, J., Rempel, M. and Lindquist, C. (2011) *The National Institute of Justice's multi-site adult drug court evaluation*, Washington, DC: The Urban Institute.

Scottish Affairs Committee (1994) *Drug abuse in Scotland: First report, Vol. 1*, London: HMSO.

Scottish Executive (1999) *Tackling drugs in Scotland: Action in partnership*, Edinburgh: The Stationery Office.

Scottish Executive (2002) *A better way: The report of the Ministerial Group on Women's Offending*, Edinburgh: Scottish Executive.

Scottish Government (2012a) *Prison statistics and population projections Scotland: 2011-12*, Edinburgh: Scottish Government.

Scottish Government (2012b) *The Scottish Government response to the Commission on Women Offenders*, Edinburgh: Scottish Government.

Scottish Government (2012c) *Redesigning the community justice system: A consultation on proposals*, Edinburgh: Scottish Government.

Scottish Government (2014) *Future model for community justice in Scotland*, Edinburgh: Scottish Government.

Scottish Government (2015) *News release: Plans for female prison in Inverclyde will not go ahead*, Edinburgh: Scottish Government.

Scottish National Party (SNP) (2011) *Scottish National Party election manifesto 2011*, http://votesnp.com/campaigns/SNP_Manifesto_2011_lowRes.pdf

Scottish Prisons Commission (2008) *Scotland's choice: Report of the Prisons Commission*, Edinburgh: Blackwell.

Social Work Services and Prisons Inspectorate for Scotland (1998) *Women offenders: A safer way*, Edinburgh: The Scottish Office.

# Part Two
# Reviews of current practice

# FIVE

# Probation practice with women offenders in Wales

*Kate Asher and Jill Annison*

## Prologue (Kate Asher)

My experience of working with women offenders began in Bristol in 2002, when my first case as a trainee probation officer was a woman. I can still recall the scene – me sitting really rigidly and nervously at the edge of my chair in the interview room, scared that I wouldn't know what to say. However, if I was anxious, just imagine how petrified the woman concerned must have been, to be sitting there talking to a complete stranger about her most personal and difficult life experiences. Staff should never underestimate how hard it is for a woman offender to expose all of her flaws.

In my first interview, I also thought that I didn't really know what to say or do to make her situation better, as I was new to the job. I remember feeling really uncomfortable, but years down the line, with knowledge and experience behind me, I now know that the journey for her started the moment she was just simply heard by me. Empathetic listening continues to be such an important skill that should always underpin practice with women.[1]

## Introduction

Probation policy and practice with women offenders in Wales was strongly influenced by the recommendations in the Corston Report (Corston, 2007). A groundswell of interest drew on the academic literature (for instance Worrall and Gelsthorpe, 2009) and research findings (for example McIvor, 2004), and prompted staff within Wales Probation to review and re-evaluate practice in this area. This engagement gained momentum over the period following Corston and had an impact on the assessment, treatment and management of women offenders in Wales. Of significance were the widespread acknowledgement and acceptance that women offenders have different needs from their male counterparts, leading to the recognition that effective interventions required a new approach, with women's individual needs being at the centre of new plans and projects. These developments took on board Corston's proposals for a 'radical new approach, treating women both holistically and individually – a woman-centred approach' (Corston, 2007: 2).

This chapter outlines the situation relating to women offenders supervised by Wales Probation: it starts by indicating the scale and scope of these developments and then moves on to discuss and critically review the underpinning ethos and impact of these new approaches. Finally, it concludes with some cautionary thoughts about the changing situation in relation to women offenders within the context of the Transforming Rehabilitation reforms (Ministry of Justice, 2014).

## Probation context

The Wales Probation Trust came into being following the Offender Management Act 2007, which afforded the opportunity for reorganisation (NOMS, 2009).[2] It was formed on 1 April 2010, following the merger of the four previous probation areas/trusts in Wales; at that point it was 'the third largest of the 35 probation trusts in England and Wales, employing around 1,000 staff in 7 Local Delivery Units' (Wales Probation Trust, 2014). The *Wales Probation equality information report 2012/2013* provided the following information regarding the gender of offenders supervised by the Trust:

> A total of 12,545 (87%) males and 1801 (13%) females were registered across Wales. There are no significant changes in figures compared to 2011/12 figures. In comparison to each local authority, Carmarthenshire and Blaenau Gwent registered the highest percentage of females (16% of their caseload) with 112 and 59 respectively. Merthyr Tydfil and Ceredigion registered the lowest percentage of females (8% of their caseload) 36 and 13 respectively. (Wales Probation Trust, 2013: 16)

It can thus be seen that women offenders represented a small proportion of the Wales Probation caseload, although they were more significant in terms of numbers in the urban local delivery units. It is perhaps not surprising that probation policy and practice had tended to overlook women's needs in the past and, as noted by Corston, that it was 'marginalised within a system largely designed by men for men' (Corston, 2007: 2).

Interventions were delivered by Wales Probation (prior to the Transforming Rehabilitation changes in 2014) in relation to female offenders who had been made subject to community orders or were subject to licence periods following custodial sentences of 12 months or more.[3] The scope of developments in relation to women offenders is explored in more depth later in this chapter, but at this point it is important to note the underpinning framework as outlined in the *Wales Probation Trust Equalities Annual Report 2011/2012*:

> An awareness of gender issues is crucial to the achievement of good outcomes for female service users. The assessment and planning stages will be most effective if the offender is fully involved and actively engaged in planning and controlling her own future. Wales Probation has developed a Professional Practice Direction which sets out the aims, priorities and expectations for delivering services to women across Wales. Each Local Delivery Unit has a Women's Champion whose role is to promote awareness and implementation of the Practice Direction, to identify and share practice and monitor performance against key areas indicators (including reoffending rates, reducing custodial remands and short term sentences) and to maintain an up-to-date LDU directory of women's services. (Wales Probation Trust, 2012: 13)

The 'Professional Practice Direction' drew on findings from the literature and research findings concerning desistance (see, for instance, Rex, 1999; Laub and Sampson, 2001; Byrne and Trew, 2008) and also took into consideration the extent and prevalence of trauma experienced by this client group (Bloom et al, 2004). These perspectives informed the design of a number of bespoke services, including a Women's Specified Activity Requirement, which was shortlisted for the Women's Category in the Howard League Community Programme Awards in 2013. The information in the citation for the award stated:

> This Requirement is a focused intervention designed to address specific issues relating to women's offending behaviour. The core purpose of this eleven-week community group work programme is to tackle offending related problems and provide a credible alternative to

custody. Run by female facilitators, it operates within a women-only supportive environment on probation premises. Its holistic approach focuses on empowerment to address complex and multiple needs as well as providing practical help. (Asher, 2013)

Practice developments within Wales Probation thus engaged directly and proactively with the recommendation in the Corston Report that 'every agency within the criminal justice system must prioritise and accelerate preparations to implement the gender equality duty and radically transform the way they deliver services for women' (Corston, 2007: 3). These aspects are now explored further in terms of the organisational and practice developments that took place across Wales.

## Change at organisational level

The scale of change post-Corston within Wales Probation in relation to work with women offenders took place at macro, mezzo and micro levels (May, 1991; Deering, 2011). The Corston Report itself and the government's response (Ministry of Justice, 2007) supported change at the macro level. Change was also enacted at the mezzo level by Wales Probation, particularly in relation to partnership arrangements for the Women's Specified Activity Requirement. There was close collaboration on a multi-agency basis at a local community level, thus facilitating links and ensuring ongoing support beyond the time-limited statutory order (Houghton, 2013). This section now focuses on the macro and mezzo levels of change, while the implications for the micro-level work with the women themselves will be investigated later in the chapter.

Developments within Wales Probation towards the end of the first decade of the new millennium followed up on Corston's recommendation urging 'regional offender managers for Wales ... to take forward the projects outlined in my report' (Corston, 2007: 10). Moreover, change at all levels in Wales embodied the ethos outlined in the Corston Report:

Equality does not mean treating everyone the same. The new gender equality duty means that men and women should be treated with equivalent respect, according to need. Equality must embrace not just fairness but also inclusivity. This will result in some different services and policies for men and women. There are fundamental

differences between male and female offenders and those
at risk of offending that indicate a different and distinct
approach is needed for women. (Corston, 2007: 3)

Thus, within Wales Probation, a review was carried out into all aspects
of the women's journey through the whole criminal justice system, from
the offenders' perspectives as well as internally within probation. This
was achieved via a number of work streams, which included gaining
feedback via service user groups that women offenders attended. This
iterative process, alongside the wider strategic overview, allowed for the
design and implementation of gender-responsive services for women
at local community level across Wales.

This approach also took on board the recommendation from the
Corston Report that 'there must also be an investment in more
rigorous training and on-going support and supervision for all those
charged with meeting the complex needs of women' (Corston, 2007:
13). Relevant information and knowledge were therefore cascaded
to all staff members, with some training carried out by the NOMS
Women Team in connection with WASP – the Women Awareness Staff
Programme (see Howard League for Penal Reform, 2009). This was
further supplemented by training input, that emphasised the importance
of heeding women's experience of harm and trauma, particularly in
relation to intervention plans. Again, this was closely linked with the
Corston Report recommendation that proposed the inclusion of two
additional pathways to resettlement,[4] namely:

- 'Pathway 8: support for women who have been abused,
  raped or who have experienced domestic violence.
- 'Pathway 9: support for women who have been involved
  in prostitution.' (Corston, 2007: 7)

As indicated earlier, the developmental process in Wales was facilitated
by the appointment of dedicated women champions in every local
delivery unit, and plans were proceeding to identify women leads in
every team. The champions' remit was simple: to act as advocates for
better services and provision for this client group. This model had
many strengths, with only limited resource implications. These staff
members became empowered as they attended specialist internal and
external training and were kept up to speed with national and local
developments. They became a source of knowledge and contact for
service users, staff and partnership agencies as they drove forward
the agenda at grass-roots level. Again, feedback was sought from the
service users, with responses from qualitative and quantitative research

indicating that they felt they were getting a much improved level of service.

This approach by Wales Probation enabled a constructive engagement with relevant recommendations from the Corston Report (2007) and facilitated active engagement and 'buy in' at the macro, mezzo and micro levels of the organisation. The next sections consider the micro-level change in experience for women in their direct contact with probation.

## The experience of probation for women offenders in Wales

The review within Wales Probation considered all aspects of the experience for women offenders in their contact with the organisation. The scope and extent of this review signified the intention to implement more inventive, gender-specific and holistic practice approaches with women offenders. Thus all aspects of the women offenders' experiences of probation were revisited – from their first impressions of contact with the organisation, through to the more micro level of contact with probation staff.

In terms of first impressions and the impact this can have on offenders' responses in the probation setting, the architecture of probation offices has received little attention (Bauwens, 2013; Phillips, 2014). Phillips has drawn attention to compelling reasons for attending to the physical spaces for such contact, particularly given recent organisational and research emphasis on the importance of offender–officer relationships and offender engagement (Phillips, 2014: 118). Indeed, as Armstrong and McAra (2006: 23-4) have emphasised, these environments 'are the places where penality takes shape, containing and conferring meaning on the objects that are necessary to translate policy into practice'.

It is thus heartening to note that such considerations were central to the policy and practice concerns in relation to working with women offenders in Wales. Given the situations of trauma experienced by many women offenders, issues of personal safety and reduction of psychological anxiety were viewed as crucial elements for women coming to probation offices. Attention was therefore paid to the layout of the waiting rooms, albeit with tensions arising from the current focus on 'health and safety, managerialism and specialization as well as a desire to "rationalize" the service's estate' (Phillips, 2014: 118). Nevertheless, where possible, the waiting rooms avoided the use of bench-style seating (to provide flexibility in terms of personal space), and tried to ensure natural lighting for the waiting area, thus endeavouring to avoid an institutional feel which might recall memories of prison incarceration (see Jewkes and Johnston, 2007).

In addition, women-only reporting sessions were introduced across Wales Probation to reassure women that they could await their individual or group sessions in a place of safety,[5] without any potential triggers that might induce a trauma flashback.[6] In such settings, relevant literature and contact details for advisory services were also made available: for instance, creative ideas were adopted by voluntary organisations such as the All Wales Domestic Abuse and Sexual Violence Helpline, where phone numbers were printed on lip balm or other small items, which could be handed over quickly or picked up discreetly.

These environmental considerations brought about both practical and symbolic changes for the women offenders, which garnered positive responses at service user engagement forums. This is not to ignore the challenges of implementing these women-only spaces in logistical terms[7] and in getting 'buy in' from all staff, which became key aspects to be tackled by the 'local champions'.

## Engagement with women offenders

The Offender Management Act 2007 set out the role and purpose of probation as:

- the protection of the public;
- the reduction of reoffending;
- the proper punishment of offenders;
- ensuring offender awareness of the effects of crime on victims and public;
- the rehabilitation of offenders.

It is within this wider context that staff in Wales Probation incorporated many of the recommendations from the Corston Report into their work with women offenders in the community. In terms of practice, this meant working collaboratively with other statutory and third sector agencies to apply a holistic approach.

In particular, many of the women offenders' involvement with crime was economically motivated – often driven by poverty and/or substance misuse (Chesney-Lind and Pasko, 2013). This made liaison with other services (such as debt advice and substance abuse support services) important elements of the overall contact, not least because this support was then available on an ongoing basis, whereas probation's work was time-limited by the community order or licence period. In line with the desistance research, there was acknowledgement that women offenders needed to be able to take up support when they were ready to do so: for some, this might be during the present contact; for others, the problems were deeply embedded and needed to be revisited; for yet others, achieving and sustaining change was still some way ahead of them (see McIvor et al, 2004).

In addition, many women offenders are primary caretakers of young children, with distinctive practical and emotional needs in this respect. It was therefore viewed as crucial that staff, in designing and implementing sentence plans, were mindful of these responsibilities and constraints, not least to ensure that contact times and targets were both realistic and achievable.[8] In terms of organisational culture this can be seen as running counter to the 'punitive turn' (Robinson and Ugwudike, 2012) and the bureaucratic demands of new managerialism that have had an impact in recent years on the Probation Service in England and Wales (see Annison et al, 2014). However, such an approach responds constructively to Corston's recommendation that 'community sentences must be designed to take account of women's particular vulnerabilities and domestic and childcare commitments' (Corston, 2007: 9).

## Probation engagement with women offenders – practice at the micro level

Attention to the issues outlined earlier thus endeavoured to put in place a safe and supportive environment for probation interventions with women offenders in Wales. In this respect it is important to acknowledge that while most women offenders do not present a high risk of harm, their pattern of offending – although relatively low level – may be persistent and accompanied by high levels of need in terms of personal and social problems (Gelsthorpe, 2011). This can present challenges to staff: sessions need to proceed at a pace that is tailored to engage with the issues that arise, and staff also need to respond to individual women's way of learning (Gelsthorpe, 2013).

Experience by one of the authors of this chapter (Kate Asher) is that most women offenders want to 'tell their story': many *really* want to tell their story and be heard, but many just don't know where or how to start. Furthermore, it is likely that they have tried before, many times, and have failed to be heard. It is thus important that probation staff help the women with such 'blockages' and allow the words to keep flowing, even at difficult times.[9] Women offenders often need reassurance and recognition of the effort used in making such disclosures and in reappraising their sense of identity (see Geiger and Fischer, 2005). In this respect, groupwork interventions such as the Women's Specified Activity Requirement can provide peer support (see Roberts, 2010): again, personal involvement (by Kate Asher) in such situations found instances of good practice when staff validated and supported such disclosures while other group members positively reinforced each other's achievements. Change is a slow and sometimes uncertain process; recreating a new identity is never easy, and sustaining the change in the long term is even harder.

Such women-centred engagement and the range of interventions within a holistic framework have generated significant results in recent years, particularly in the context of developing the women's skills and improving their sense of empowerment. While other factors may also be relevant, it is interesting to note that in terms of diverting women offenders from custody, in 2012 there was a 33% reduction in females being sentenced to custody for under 12 months in the Gwent area.

## The challenges posed by Transforming Rehabilitation

The policy and practice developments outlined earlier took place in the period following the Corston Report (2007) and leading up to the organisational changes brought about by the Transforming Rehabilitation reforms in 2014. In Wales – as across probation in England – the roll-out of the Transforming Rehabilitation programme meant that the Probation Trust was disbanded and staff in the existing organisation were allocated either to the National Probation Service (England and Wales),[10] or to the Wales Community Rehabilitation Company (CRC).[11] At the time of writing (October 2014) there is therefore an interim period being experienced ahead of the share sale planned for autumn 2014, after which the CRC will move into private ownership in April 2015.[12]

In the evidence to the Justice Select Committee Inquiry into Women Offenders in July 2013 it was stated that:

> Wales Probation considers the improvement in services to support Women offenders as a significant priority to achieve one of our core strategic objectives – to deliver the best services possible for the public in Wales. (Justice Select Committee, 2013: 1)

Wales Probation also confirmed its opinion that 'Baroness Corston's considerations and recommendations in 2007 remain crucial and relevant' (Justice Select Committee, 2013: 1), and cited progress made in Wales linked to the Corston Report recommendations:

> 3.7 The Corston Report and Recommendations have provided a key set of standards for service delivery which Wales Probation has been able to benchmark again, these have included developing Women only reporting times, offering choice of gender for report author and supervising officer. It is our view that further work can be done to build on these recommendations to ensure they become part of core service delivery and create safe environments for service delivery for women ...
>
> 3.8 Wales Probation has welcomed the development of One Stop Shops to enhance the level of service delivery to Women offenders and support the delivery of IAC [Intensive Alternatives to Custody] Orders. However there needs to be further work done to ensure that out reach service delivery in rural parts of the Country provide an equal level of access to services. (Justice Select Committee, 2013: 4)

The review within this chapter therefore indicates the strong sense of engagement from probation in Wales with the ethos and specific recommendations of the Corston Report (2007) and the impact this had had at macro, mezzo and micro levels in terms of policy and practice with women offenders in the community in Wales. This can be seen in tangible developments, such as the Women's Specified Activity Requirement and the establishment of the Women's Reporting Centre in the Neath, Port Talbot and Bridgend area at which 'women offenders can attend their appointments in a women-only environment while following a programme which tackles problem identification and solving and skills development' (Wales Community Rehabilitation Company, 2014a: 20).

The message conveyed by the new Wales Community Rehabilitation Company is of building on the legacy of the work of the Wales Probation Trust (see Wales Community Rehabilitation Company website, 2014b). As far as work with women offenders is concerned, it can be seen that innovative approaches have been developed, which are aligned to the recommendations for good practice in the Corston Report. Nevertheless, it remains to be seen how embedded these practices are, particularly in a time of considerable organisational change, disruption of staffing roles and resource constraints; without a constant focus on the underpinning value base and commitment to these aspects of policy and practice, it is possible that this pioneering approach may lose momentum and fade away in the face of other, more 'mainstream' demands.

These concerns are highlighted in the academic literature, with Gelsthorpe and Hedderman (2012) emphasising difficulties in relation to work with women offenders. These are:

> defining, estimating and measuring impact; achieving a level of change which is sufficient to attract suppliers; and an inability to value outcomes and to identify and allocate benefits. (Gelsthorpe and Hedderman 2012: 374)

Following an incisive review and critique of the situation in relation to Transforming Rehabilitation and the impact that this is likely to have on work with women offenders, Gelsthorpe and Hedderman state:

> Even if we could estimate and measure the reconviction benefits of community-based support services for women in the community with some accuracy, it is highly doubtful that new suppliers would be attracted into the marketplace. The level of demand in terms of sheer numbers is too small, and the complexity of women's needs is too great, to make this an area for easy or quick profits. Existing suppliers are operating from a sense of moral purpose, not financial reward. Perhaps they could be more efficient and more effective in the way they work with women, but until we know more about what works with which women in what circumstances, this approach is likely to stifle innovation. (Gelsthorpe and Hedderman, 2012: 387)

The situation thus remains uncertain, particularly in relation to the existing partnership arrangements between probation and third sector organisations. Indeed, the written evidence from Wales Probation to the Justice Select Committee Inquiry into Women Offenders stated that:

> 6.1 Wales Probation feel there is currently insufficient provision to meet the needs of Women offenders in the community fully and consistently. In our view closer

involvement of local voluntary and community sector bodies in the planning and delivery of these services would help address this deficiency ...

6.4 Women's community services are dependent upon a secure and robust third sector. However, the Wales Council for Voluntary Action State of the Sector Survey, May 2011, reported significant loss of funding, an increased demand for services and more complex funding and monitoring requirements. This raises considerable concerns regarding the volume range, quality and sustainability of community provision within such a vital sector for Women's provision. (Justice Select Committee, 2013: 6)

## Conclusion

In summary, innovative developments have been instigated and embedded into everyday practice with women offenders in Wales over the past few years, initiatives which have embodied the moral imperatives advocated in the Corston Report (2007). However, the imposition of external change from the ideologically driven Transforming Rehabilitation agenda leave much uncertainty about the immediate future for work in the community in Wales with women offenders. Evidence from Wales Probation to the Justice Select Committee conveyed such issues:

2.5 One of the difficulties that is fedback from operational staff is that it can take time for a new project to "bed in". Once the project is up and running, the funding often changes so the focus of the programme changes, this means that it can be difficult to keep referrals for some projects. There is concern that within the current financial climate projects may contract and this could have a detrimental impact on service delivery to Women. (Justice Select Committee, 2013: 3)

Sustaining change within organisations often poses challenges (see, for instance, Senge et al, 1999), but the current turbulence in this part of the criminal justice system presents particular uncertainty, which undoubtedly threatens the consolidation of progress that has been made so far. Senior's cautionary words summarise the problems that may emerge:

This wholesale organisational upheaval will spawn inexperienced organisations and individuals. This can of course stimulate innovative solutions but it also can lead to dangerous and costly mistakes which in a people business like probation puts communities and individuals at risk. The new partnerships created will be ones of convenience, not choice, driven by the commercial framework within which new relationships are being established. Of course many currently working in community justice will not become partners at all, as there is a real danger that smaller local VCS organisations will simply lose out. (Senior, 2013: 2)

This chapter thus charts the emergence of good practice that aligned closely with the spirit and the explicit recommendations of the Corston Report in relation to work with women offenders in the community in Wales. What remains unclear is how – and whether – these innovative developments can be sustained in the face of the changes that will be imposed by the Transforming Rehabilitation agenda.

**Notes**

[1]  This aligns with good practice which draws on motivational interviewing. For instance, Miller and Rollnick emphasise that 'good listening helps a person keep going, to continue considering and exploring what may be uncomfortable material' (Miller and Rollnick, 2013: 49).

[2]  The background to this change is summarised in the NOMS document as follows: 'There is extensive experience in Probation Areas/Trusts in Wales in relation to transition, merger and organisational change. In 2001 five of the seven Probation Services in Wales were subject to amalgamation and in 2008 two Probation Areas became First Wave Trusts and played their part in the NOMS "learning year" to assist in developing the Probation Trusts Programme' (NOMS, 2009: 25).

[3]  Plans under the Transforming Rehabilitation agenda anticipate that prisoners who receive prison sentences of under a year will also be subject to 12 months' supervision on release in the future (see Grayling, 2013).

[4]  These two additional pathways have generally been adopted – see, for instance the Women in Prison overview of the Corston Report 5 Years On, available at www.no-offence.org/pdfs/7.pdf.

[5]  Women offenders had reported that they felt claustrophobic and panicked by confined spaces, not least because they wanted to be able to access the exit at all times. Probation offices, in line with many public spaces, have

become increasingly risk averse, with the adoption of CCTV, panic alarms and escape doors for staff (Phillips, 2014: 123).

6  Such arrangements ensured that a woman was not forced to wait in the same room as her abuser or his family, friends or acquaintances, but also avoided more subtle reminders such as a man wearing similar clothes or the same aftershave as an abuser.

7  Many probation offices held one- or two-hour sessions, which were women-only reporting times. However, there were a few areas in Wales where the session involved staff visiting women offenders off-site in community provision.

8  Corston had drawn attention to the high level of receptions into custody following breach proceedings. She recommended that 'the restrictions placed on sentencers around breaches of community orders must be made more flexible as a matter of urgency' (Corston, 2007: 9). This was in fact addressed in a different way: revised National Standards were issued in 2011, which allowed 'frontline probation staff to manage their work with offenders as the risks of each case demands, using their knowledge and drawing on their professional training and experience' (Ministry of Justice announcement, 5 April 2011, www.gov.uk/government/news/new-probation-standards-to-slash-red-tape). These revised instructions allowed for more professional discretion in initiating breach proceedings by probation staff.

9  Women offenders' life experiences often include high rates of self-inflicted injuries and suicide attempts (Corston, 2007). Working with individuals who self-harm can be very difficult and challenging for probation staff. These difficulties need to be recognised and acknowledged in practice situations with women offenders: a huge amount of resilience and skill is required by staff members to cope with such challenges, and staff training and supervisory support is important in such circumstances.

10  Information on the Gov.UK website states: 'Sarah Payne is Director, National Offender Management Service (NOMS) in Wales. From 1 June 2014, Sarah will have responsibility for the new National Probation Service in Wales, as well as responsibility for all Welsh prisons in the public and contracted sectors' (www.gov.uk/government/people/sarah-payne).

11  This was an interim arrangement pending the government's decisions about the award of contracts to the Tier 1 'prime' companies as part of the privatisation of this part of the criminal justice system (see, for instance, the Clinks live resource webpage: www.clinks.org/criminal-justice/transforming-rehabilitation). An announcement on the Wales Probation website conveyed the information that 'Heading the Wales CRC will be Chief Executive Liz Rijnenberg, a former probation officer with 35 years experience of working in public, voluntary and private sectors' (www.

walesprobationtrust.gov.uk/news/2014/06/01/probation-changes-tackle-wales-reoffending-rates/).

[12] Wales CRC is now owned by Working Links, a public, private, voluntary company. Working Links is in partnership with Innovation Wessex, a mutual community interest company made up of former probation trust workers.

## References

Annison J., Burke L. and Senior P. (2014) Transforming Rehabilitation: Another example of English 'exceptionalism' or a blueprint for the rest of Europe?, *European Journal of Probation*, 6 (1): 6–23.

Amstrong, S. C. and McAra, L. (2006) Audience, borders and architecture: The contours of control, in L. McAra and S. C. Armstrong (eds) *Perspectives on punishment: The contours of control*, Oxford: Oxford University Press, 1-30.

Asher, K. (2013) *Work with women offenders recognised at Howard League Awards*, News Item, Wales Probation Trust.

Bauwens, A. (2013) *The 'architecture' of a probation office: Reflection of current probation policies? A comparative analysis between England and Wales and Belgium*, presentation at the Community Sanctions and Measures Working Group, European Society of Criminology, held at Liverpool Hope University on 25 April 2013, http://communitysanctionsblog.wordpress.com/conferences/

Bloom, B., Owen, B. and Covington, S. (2004) Women offenders and the gendered effects of public policy, *Review of Policy Research*, 21 (1): 31-48.

Byrne, C. F. and Trew, K. J. (2008) Pathways through crime: The development of crime and desistance in the accounts of men and women offenders, *The Howard Journal of Criminal Justice*, 47 (3): 238–58.

Chesney-Lind, M. and Pasko, L. (2013) *The female offender: Girls, women, and crime* (3rd edn), London: Sage.

Corston, J. (2007) *The Corston Report: A report by Baroness Jean Corston of a review of women with particular vulnerabilities in the criminal justice system*, London: Home Office.

Deering, J. (2011) *Probation practice and the new penology: Practitioner reflections*, Aldershot: Ashgate.

Geiger, B. and Fischer, M. (2005) Naming oneself criminal: Gender difference in offenders' identity negotiation, *International Journal of Offender Therapy and Comparative Criminology*, 49 (2): 194-209.

Gelsthorpe, L. (2011) Working with women offenders in the community: A view from England and Wales, in R. Sheehan, G. McIvor and C. Trotter (eds) *Working with women offenders in the community*, Abingdon: Willan, 127-50.

Gelsthorpe, L. (2013) *What works with women offenders?*, Presentation at the World Congress of Probation, October 2013.

Gelsthorpe, L. and Hedderman, C. (2012) Providing for women offenders: The risks of

adopting a payment by results approach, *Probation Journal*, 59 (4): 374–90.

Grayling, C. (2013) *12 months supervision for all prisoners on release*, Press release, 9 May 2013, www.gov.uk/government/news/12-months-supervision-for-all-prisoners-on-release

Houghton, J. (2013) *Work with women offenders recognised at Howard League Awards*, News item, Wales Probation Trust.

Howard League for Penal Reform (2009) *Women in the penal system: Second report on women with particular vulnerabilities in the criminal justice system*. Report from the All Party Parliamentary Group, under the chairmanship of Baroness Corston, www.howardleague.org/fileadmin/howard_league/user/pdf/Publications/Women_in_the_penal_system.pdf

Jewkes, Y. and Johnston, H. (2007) The evolution of prison architecture, in Y. Jewkes (ed.) *Handbook on prisons*, Cullompton: Willan.

Justice Select Committee (2013) *Inquiry into women offenders, Written evidence from Wales Probation*, www.publications.parliament.uk/pa/cm201314/cmselect/cmjust/92/92vw21.htm

Laub, J. H. and Sampson, R. J. (2001) Understanding desistance from crime, *Crime and Justice*, 28: 1-69.

May, T. (1991) *Probation: Politics, policy and practice*, Buckingham: Open University Press.

McIvor, G. (ed.) (2004) *Women who offend*, London: Jessica Kingsley.

McIvor, G., Murray, C. and Jamieson, J. (2004) Desistance from crime: Is it different for women and girls?, in S. Maruna and R. Immarigeon (eds) *After crime and punishment: Pathways to offender reintegration*, Cullompton: Willan.

Miller, W. R. and Rollnick, S. (2013) *Motivational interviewing: Helping people change* (3rd edn), NY: The Guilford Press.

Ministry of Justice (2007) *The Government's response to the report by Baroness Corston of a review of women with particular vulnerabilities in the criminal justice system*, http://webarchive.nationalarchives.gov.uk/20110110161733/http:/www.justice.gov.uk/publications/docs/corston-review.pdf

Ministry of Justice (2014) *Transforming rehabilitation*, www.justice.gov.uk/transforming-rehabilitation

NOMS (2009) *Wales Probation Trust: Business plan and organisational development plan 2010/11 – 2012/13.*

Phillips, J. (2014) The architecture of a probation office: A reflection of policy and an impact on practice, *Probation Journal*, 61 (2): 117-31.

Rex, S. (1999) Desistance from offending: Experiences of probation, *The Howard Journal of Criminal Justice*, 38 (4): 366–83.

Roberts, J. (2010) Women offenders: More troubled than troublesome?, in J. Brayford, F. Cowe and J. Deering (eds) *What else works? Creative work with offenders*, Cullompton: Willan.

Robinson, G. and Ugwudike, P. (2012) Investing in 'toughness': Probation,

enforcement and legitimacy, *The Howard Journal of Criminal Justice*, 51 (3): 300-16.

Senge, P., Ross, R., Kleiner, A., Roberts, C. and Roth, G. (1999) *The dance of change: The challenges of sustaining momentum in a learning organization*, NY: Doubleday.

Senior, P. (2013) Editorial: Probation: Peering through the uncertainty, *British Journal of Community Justice*, 11 (2-3): 1-8.

Wales Community Rehabilitation Company (2014a) *Reducing reoffending: Building a better future for Wales*, http://probation-institute.org/wp-content/uploads/2014/06/WALES_CRC_INTERVENTIONS_EDITION_21.pdf

Wales Community Rehabilitation Company (2014b) *Website*, http://walescrc.co.uk/

Wales Probation Trust (2012) *Wales Probation equalities annual report 2011/2012.*

Wales Probation Trust (2013) *Wales Probation equality information report 2012/2013.*

Wales Probation Trust (2014) *About us: The organisation.*

Worrall, A. and Gelsthorpe, L. (2009) 'What works' with women offenders: The past 30 years, *Probation Journal*, 56 (4): 329–45.

# SIX

# Youth justice practice with girls

*Becky Shepherd*

## Introduction

This chapter engages with the recommendations from the Corston Report (Corston, 2007) to explore key issues in relation to youth justice practice with girls. It engages with the academic literature and research findings and also draws on the author's professional knowledge and experience in this field. This review finds many parallels between policy and practice in relation to girls and women in terms of their experiences of being dealt with in the criminal justice system. However, there are some differences: from a positive viewpoint these can point to examples of good practice, which could be adopted more generally in relation to women as well as girls. Nonetheless, there are some areas of concern, particularly in relation to planned future developments that are highlighted here, not least to flag up the need for careful consideration from a gendered perspective before the implementation of major new approaches.

In the criminal justice system, girls are a minority within a minority in two senses. First, girls under 18 make up only a small proportion of the female offending population. Over the past few years, the number of girls in custody in England and Wales has remained constant at around 50, with exactly 50 girls in custody in June 2014. This contrasts with 3,932 adult women in custody in June 2014 (Howard League for Penal Reform, 2014a). Second, among juvenile offenders, themselves a small percentage of the overall offending population, there are far fewer girls than boys. Within the wider context of falling numbers of juveniles within the criminal justice system, the overall proportion of girls to boys has remained broadly consistent at approximately 20%/80%. In 2012/13, some 95% of young people in custody were male (Youth Justice Board, 2014). This indicates that the vast majority of offences seen by the courts as requiring custody continue to be committed by males.

It is clear, therefore, that within the wider offending population, girls are a very small proportion indeed. Their comparatively low number is relevant to their treatment within the criminal justice system, as this chapter will explore. Corston's criticism of the treatment by the criminal justice system of women who offend is highly relevant to the juvenile estate, although her report addresses adults only (Corston, 2007). Parallels can be drawn between how young females are treated within the microcosm of youth justice and how women are treated within the adult criminal justice system.

## Context – falling youth crime figures

The number of young people entering the criminal justice system each year has declined recently:

> The overall number of young people in the YJS [Youth Justice System] continued to reduce in 2012/13. Reductions have been seen in the number entering the system for the first time, as well as reductions in those receiving disposals in and out of court, including those receiving custodial sentences ... Since 2009/10, there have been 55 per cent fewer young people coming into the Youth Justice System and 36 per cent fewer young people (under 18) in custody. (Youth Justice Board for England and Wales, 2014a: 8)

More specifically, in terms of the decline in the numbers of first-time entrants (FTEs) into the youth justice system, the proportion of girls has declined the most:

> Females accounted for 24 per cent of all FTEs in 2012/13, compared to 32 per cent in 2009/10. Since 2009/10 the number of young females entering the Youth Justice System has fallen by 67 per cent, compared with 50 per cent for young males. (Youth Justice Board for England and Wales, 2014a: 24)

Although this is a positive development, given the fluctuations over past years it seems unwise to speculate whether this trend will continue, stabilise or reverse, or indeed how government policy makers may respond.

## Bail for girls

The Corston Report (2007) stated that bail support placements for women were inadequate. In this respect, juveniles are in a significantly better position: all youth offending teams (YOTs) are required to offer bail support packages to increase the prospect of bail being granted whenever feasible. Bail support packages can include a variety of requirements, including YOT supervision appointments, attendance at school if of statutory school age, residence, electronic monitoring (a tag) and appointments such as drug support (Thomas, 2005).

For those most at risk of being remanded into custody, an Intensive Supervision and Surveillance (ISS) requirement can be attached to bail, comprising 25 hours of monitored support per week (see Robinson, 2011). This always includes electronic monitoring. The timetable is based on a full educational week with additional activities including individual supervision, participation in groupwork programmes and constructive activities. Those not in education, training or employment would be required to attend for careers and education support sessions. However, bail support packages rarely provide gender-specific provision. From the author's professional experience of working within a YOT, the groupwork sessions often comprised all the young people on ISS bail, with boys being the majority of participants. Individualised and gender-responsive sessions, such as counselling or mental health work, were rarely included in ISS timetables, as there were ethical and legal difficulties in making these enforceable due to the need for consent.

The bail situation is thus significantly better for girls than for women, and the YOTs' statutory role in providing flexible and rigorous bail support packages is a considerable advantage. Nevertheless, it would be appropriate for YOTs to improve gender-specific bail support, including linking girls into appropriate community resources. However, as the number of girls on bail in many areas would be low, this would require individualised bail packages (for example, individual support to attend sexual health or domestic abuse support services, or gender-specific drug and alcohol treatment), which would have a cost implication in terms of staffing. However, even an intensive ISS bail placement is considerably cheaper than paying for a custody remand placement: custody costs £160,000 in a secure training centre (STC) and £215,000 in a secure children's home (SCH) per annum (Nacro, 2011).

## Remand for girls

Under the Legal Aid, Sentencing and Punishment of Offenders (LASPO) Act 2012, the responsibility for funding juvenile custodial remand places was devolved to local authoritiesa. Under LASPO, all children (aged between 10 and 17 years) remanded into custody become Looked After Children for the duration of the remand. A custody remand can be to a young offender institute (YOI), an STC or an SCH. The Act abolished the requirement for 17-year-olds to be remanded to a YOI. Following the abolition of female juvenile YOIs in 2013, girls can only be remanded to an STC or SCH, as with girls sentenced to custody. (For a full discussion of secure accommodation, see the 'Girls in custody' section of this chapter.)

Due to the cost of remand beds there followed an increased focus within local authorities on avoiding remands into custody. The alternatives for young people can thus also include a remand into the care of the local authority, which can mean placing in a non-secure children's home, a semi-independent unit, a foster placement or even with an appropriate relative (Lipscombe and Russell, 2008; Thomas, 2008).

In common with adult women, however, it would seem that girls are also being remanded into custody unnecessarily. Figures obtained from the Youth Justice Board show that 145 girls were remanded into custody in 2012/13 (Youth Justice Board, 2014). Of those, only 46 went on to be given a custodial sentence. These numbers are very small in comparison to boys and to adult women, but they are nevertheless illuminating and concerning. Approximately three times as many girls were remanded into custody in 2012/13 than were either sentenced to custody or given bail with ISS. It appears, therefore, that at least some of these remands into custody could reasonably have been avoided. It seems that being subjected to overzealous use of custodial remands is another burden that girls share with their adult counterparts.

## Sentencing bias and welfare concerns

It has long been argued that systematic bias is evident in sentencing decisions regarding women. Women and girls risk being subjected to 'double jeopardy', in which they are not only judged for their offence but also – particularly if the offence is violent – for their transgression of traditional gender roles (Heidensohn, 1985).

This is particularly so for black and minority ethnic (BME) women and girls, who suffer additional racial bias. The BME community – male and female – is disproportionately overrepresented in the criminal justice system at all levels: more likely to be arrested, more likely to be charged, less likely to get bail and more likely to receive a custodial sentence (see Kennedy, 1992; Bowling and Phillips, 2002; Phillips and Bowling, 2012).

In 2011-12, the All Party Parliamentary Group on Women in the Penal System's inquiry on girls produced a briefing paper: *From courts to custody: Keeping girls out of the penal system* (Howard League for Penal Reform, 2012). This report highlighted the unresolved tension between legitimate concern about up-tariffing of girls due to sentencers' welfare concerns (a key theme of the report), and recognition that problems in girls' lives outside their offending behaviour must also be addressed. Similar concerns have been raised by Nacro, namely that the 25 hours per week ISS requirement, which can be added to a community disposal, is being applied when it is not necessary in order to avoid custody, but to enable YOT staff to address welfare concerns (Nacro, 2011).

Practitioners often take the seemingly pragmatic view that while a girl is compelled by a community sentence to engage intensively, it is the ideal opportunity to get as much done as possible, motivated by attending to welfare needs as much as interventions in relation to offending behaviour. In fact, with many of those girls who are particularly vulnerable, it is not unheard of to get through an entire order without having been able to undertake structured offending behaviour work, as the young person lurches from one crisis to another, often without sufficient other statutory support (see Sharpe, 2011).

This lack of other avenues of support is noted in the Howard League inquiry *From courts to custody:*

> YOT workers felt that magistrates often expected the YOT to solve a girl's social problems and lacked a clear understanding of the obligations of the Local Authority to meet the needs of children under the Children Act 1989. YOT workers reported they faced difficulties in obtaining Local Authority support for girls with welfare needs ... One YOT worker had resorted to visiting children's services in person with a girl to demand that they reopen her social services file, which had been closed after she was placed under the supervision of the YOT. (Howard League for Penal Reform, 2012: 3)

This well-meaning but disproportionate tendency on the part of sentencers to 'beef up' a sentence as a means of providing support to which children are entitled under civil law means girls risk being sentenced more punitively than their offences may merit. Moreover, the interface between YOTs and social care staff can be extremely poor, with YOT practitioners often feeling that once a young person is under YOT statutory supervision, then social care departments 'pass the buck' for undertaking welfare tasks.

### Example from practice

A YOT worker supported a mother of a girl under YOT supervision to attend the local authority social care service to request accommodation for the child: the girl had robbed the mother repeatedly and the relationship had broken down. The YOT worker relayed concerns for the safety of both parties if the girl was not taken into care. The mother, in desperation, stated she would slit the girl's throat if she was not removed from home, in an attempt to get this request to be taken seriously. Even then, the request was initially refused. This experience highlights the problems arising from the fragmentation of services and lack of integration between the different agencies. It also illustrates concerns about the potential for escalation of problems in such situations rather than proactive interventions in a timely way.

## Community sentences [STARt]

The Corston Report (Corston, 2007) recommended that community solutions for non-violent women offenders should be the norm, and that community sentences must be designed to take account of women's particular vulnerabilities and commitments. This section now compares this standpoint in relation to girls.

The Criminal Justice and Immigration Act 2008 introduced the Youth Rehabilitation Order (YRO), a generic community sentence for young people under the age of 18. This replaced the variety of sentences previously available. The other main community sentence for juveniles is the Referral Order, a less onerous order imposed usually for first offences. This is not covered in further detail in this chapter, as the focus here is on girls who are subjected to more significant levels of intervention and, in particular, who are at risk of receiving custodial sentences.

YRO requirements are broadly similar to those available for an adult Community Order.[1] Four additional requirements of the YRO comprise: local authority residence; education (for those of statutory school age); intensive supervision and surveillance (ISS); and intensive fostering. The latter two are both a direct alternative to custody for those at risk of a prison term (see Moore et al, 2006), although ISS is more commonly used than intensive fostering.

Gender-specific provision for girls varies considerably between YOTs across England and Wales and sustainability of interventions is problematic, as Corston identified in relation to women. In 2009, the Youth Justice Board commissioned an extensive study of girls' offending in England and Wales – *Girls and offending: Patterns, perceptions and interventions*. This found that in 2004, a total of 45 YOTs out of 154 offered gender-specific interventions. It is of concern that by 2007 only 11 were still providing this (Youth Justice Board, 2009).

Due to the lack of a national approach to provision (see the 'Legislation, oversight and strategy' section of this chapter), gender-specific interventions for girls vary widely between YOTs, with some providing this by training existing staff, as in the Nottinghamshire projects (Matthews and Smith, 2009), or by buying in groupwork programmes from external third sector providers such as Barnardo's.[2]

The 2009 Youth Justice Board study found that for girls, developing a good relationship with staff was key to effective interventions. This finding is replicated across the research base (see, for example, Hubbard and Matthews, 2007) and is reinforced in practice by YOT workers: only when trust and mutual respect have been established do girls – particularly the many who have experienced abuse – feel able to engage fully with interventions. This has implications for sustainability. Many YOTs, particularly in London, rely on high numbers of locum staff, and the turnover of supervising officers can be high (see Barnett, 2014). This pattern risks reinforcing clients' difficulties with trust; just as girls start to build a relationship, they may have an abrupt change of supervising officer. The author's personal experience of this has been that this can lead to hostility and resentment, and cynicism about the YOT's commitment to help them, which is highly counterproductive.

Staff training is also central to the delivery of gender-specific interventions. Again, this varies enormously between YOTs and between individual YOT workers, who come from a variety of professional backgrounds, with differing levels of qualification and experience.[3] The challenging behaviour that girls can exhibit is a recurring theme in staff feedback (Pearce, 1995, in Worrall, 2001), leading to wider questions about practitioner bias and sociocultural expectations of female behaviour. Expecting girls to be difficult to engage can become a self-fulfilling prophecy, which is why gender awareness training for staff is so important. There is a requirement under the statutory Equality Duty for public bodies to provide a gender-responsive service[4] and equipping staff to do this properly is necessary to fulfil this obligation.

It is evident that there is much good gender-responsive practice within YOTs, but provision is patchy, and still too often dependent on the dynamism and commitment of local staff. The relevant recommendation in the Corston Report states:

> There must also be an investment in more rigorous training and ongoing support and supervision for those charged with meeting the complex needs of women. This training, which should include gender awareness and how community sentences can meet the needs of female offenders, should be extended to include all staff within the criminal justice system in contact with women, particularly those who make sentencing and bail decisions. (Corston, 2007: 13)

This is clearly directly relevant in terms of good practice in relation to girls, as well as women offenders, within the criminal justice system.

## Girls in custody

The Corston Report's key recommendations for custody can be broadly summarised thus:

- the prison estate to be replaced with geographically dispersed, small, multifunctional custodial centres;
- strip-searching minimised;
- custody reserved for protection of the public only;
- lessened use of unnecessary remand;
- abolition of prison for welfare reasons;
- increased use of bail support schemes;
- proper consideration of the impact on children of mothers being imprisoned;
- embedded strategic planning to reduce the need for custody. (Corston, 2007)

Again, these aspects are directly applicable to girls, and this section will apply a comparative critique in this respect.

The situation for girls in custody remains unsatisfactory: the problem of being imprisoned far from home and family is very acute for girls, despite the well-documented fact that maintaining such ties has a positive impact on rehabilitation (Ministry of Justice (MoJ), 2013). Families visiting prisoners in secure children's homes are not eligible for financial support from the Assisted Prison Visits Scheme, although while children are on remand, funding can be obtained through the relevant local authority.

In a situation directly comparable to women prisoners, girls who offend are disproportionately likely to have experienced trauma or abuse (Batchelor, 2005; Chesney-Lind and Pasko, 2013). Non-white children are overrepresented in custody and a significant number of children are Looked After Children (Nacro, 2011).

Until 2004, girls were held alongside adult women in prison. Often women found the girls' chaotic behaviour destabilising, and girls risked being inducted into the toxic culture of 'cutting up' (self-harming) endemic in women's prisons (Worrall, 2004: 55). In 2003, HM Inspector of Prisons described conditions for girls at Holloway Prison as 'grossly inadequate' with little awareness of child protection procedures (Gould and Payne, 2004). The notion of mixing children with adult prisoners now seems an unthinkable anachronism, although the change is in fact so very recent. After 2004, girls sent to custody were placed in mixed-gender SCHs, STCs or juvenile YOIs. SCHs are used for younger prisoners, while STCs usually hold 14- and 15-year-olds. Juveniles aged 16 and over would usually be held in YOIs, although they could be sent to SCHs or STCs if they would be particularly vulnerable in a YOI.

The LASPO Act 2012 removed the legislative requirement to remand 17-year-olds into YOI custody. In light of this, and also the recent decline in juvenile custodial numbers, the Coalition government decided to close all three female under-18-year-old YOIs. Girls in custody are now held solely in one of ten SCHs and four STCs. This is in some respects a positive development, as these establishments aim to have a more child-centred, education-focused ethos, in which the duty to promote the welfare of the child is (or should be) paramount. SCHs in particular, which hold the youngest children sentenced to custody, have much less of a 'prison' environment and more effort is made by staff to make them as homely as possible. The privately run STCs are more problematic, and concerns are raised regularly regarding the treatment of young people, including the use of restraint, which directly caused the death of 15-year-old Gareth Myatt in G4S-run Rainsbrook STC in 2004 (see Howard League for Penal Reform, 2014b).

At the time of writing (November 2014), no girls have died in custody; 16 boys have died in custody since 2000, all of them in either

STCs or YOIs (Youth Justice Board for England and Wales, 2014b). New restraint management techniques are being rolled out within the secure estate currently, although the then Justice Minister Chris Grayling's Secure College plans were attracting attention for a restraint policy which appeared to breach European human rights legislation (Joint Committee on Human Rights, 2014).

All girls are now held up to age 18 with boys who are usually under 16. Given that maturation tends to happen earlier in girls, this means that their male peer group, with whom they share education, leisure time and offending behaviour work, may not always be suitable. Boys held in SCHs and STCs are young, yet have offended seriously enough to have been given a custodial sentence. This includes sex offenders and those convicted of serious violence including murder. In practice this can risk re-traumatising girls who have been the victims or survivors of abuse.

**Example from practice**

One girl discovered that a friend of hers held in the same STC was serving a sentence for rape. She had herself been a victim of severe sexual abuse. She was sufficiently distressed by this to request transfer to another establishment, with the concomitant disruption to her education and therapeutic interventions.

Unlike the adult estate, where programmes are available specifically for women, offending behaviour work in SCHs and STCs is almost always delivered in mixed-gender groups, even though male and female routes into offending are often very different (Gelsthorpe and Sharpe, 2006).[5]

Information on gender-specific, offence-focused work available in SCHs and STCs was requested for this chapter. Responses were received from eight establishments: this showed that provision was varied, but that the majority provided girls with gender-specific intervention when it was identified as necessary. However, there was no evidence of a presumption of the necessity for gender-specific offending behaviour work, and the gender-specific work offered usually dealt with needs, although it was not directly related to offending. Apparently only one establishment provided gender-specific, offending-behaviour work (Clayfields House SCH in Nottingham).

Gender-specific interventions largely related to health awareness including sexual health, while recreational activities, such as segregated exercise and hair and beauty activities, demonstrated that traditional gendered expectations of girls' interests are reflected in the secure estate. Nevertheless, on a positive note, the flexibility that establishments have to respond to identified needs is encouraging, as it provides a refreshing contrast to the 'one-size-fits-all' approach within the adult prison estate, where interventions are often much less responsive to individual need.

## Strip-searching girls

The Corston Report (2007) was highly critical of automatic strip-searching in prisons, noting that the humiliation and violation of privacy of already highly vulnerable prisoners is inhumane and counterproductive to rehabilitation. This has been accepted by government: routine strip-searching of women in prison is being replaced with risk assessment and intelligence-led searches. Regrettably, the strip-searching position regarding juveniles is less clear-cut.

The issue of strip-searching of children in the secure estate was addressed by the Youth Justice Board in its *Review of full searches in the secure estate for children and young people* (Youth Justice Board, 2011). This stated that although some STCs and YOIs might need to undertake routine full searches on entry to the establishment, this was not desirable, and that strip-searching should be -risk assessment and intelligence-led whenever possible. The review stated that strip-searching in SCHs should not be required, due to the high levels of monitoring.

STC Rule 33 states that all inmates must be searched on reception into the establishment, and in practice this is routinely a strip-search. However, according to legal advice obtained from the MoJ, noted in the Youth Justice Board Review (2011), the requirement to search on reception is not a requirement for a strip-search. Therefore, if it is interpreted as such, strip-searching may be being overused in STCs.

SCHs are governed by the Care Standards Act 2000. Searching and strip-searching in SCHs is not covered in primary or secondary legislation, which means that practice and policy vary between establishments. The Youth Justice Board review (2011) found that the practice of strip-searching risked re-traumatising girls (and boys) who had previously experienced abuse. Practitioners noted discomfort in carrying out searches, as well as voicing concern about the impact of searches on vulnerable young people, particularly girls. Indeed, the review stated:

> There appeared to be distinct gendered reactions to how young people experienced full searches. While male young people expressed feelings of anger and frustration, young females often expressed feelings of anxiety and vulnerability:

"It makes me feel upset, embarrassed and really violating because I have been raped and it's awful being strip-searched." Young female.  (Youth Justice Board, 2011: 31)

The Youth Justice Board review (2011) noted that since 2009 the women's prison estate had adopted risk assessment and intelligence-led full searches, but this had not yet been adopted in SCHs and STCs, with some of both types of establishment using routine strip-searching on entry. In the absence of a national policy on full searching in STCs and SCHs, the situation seems to lack clear direction: this would appear to be one area in which more progress may have been made for women than for girls.

Overall, however, the situation for girls in custody appears to be somewhat better than that for women: facilities are better, provision of welfare services and non-offending behaviour interventions is better and more flexible, and the number of girls in custody remains quite low. However, mixing girls aged up to 18 with a younger cohort of boys, some of whom are serious offenders, is problematic. The long distance from home where girls are held is a serious disadvantage. The lack of gender-specific offending behaviour work highlights a deficit in provision. Moreover, the use of strip-searching has the potential to cause or reinforce trauma. In this respect there appears to be a postcode lottery in place, with variable quality of care and interventions dependant on which STC or SCH girls are placed in. Therefore, as with women, there needs to be a sharper focus on restricting the use of custody further and ensuring consistency in treatment for those in custodial settings.

## Legislation, oversight and strategy

Corston recommended interdepartmental ministerial scrutiny of the treatment of women who offend or are at risk of offending, embedded within both the criminal justice and local government agendas. She recommended the immediate establishment of a commission for women who offend or are at risk of offending, led at director level, with a remit of care and support for women who offend or are at risk of offending. She also recommended that systematic safeguards should be put in place so that good practice approaches are not lost. She did not recommend a separate sentencing framework for women, but stated that this should be reconsidered in the light of early experience of the statutory gender discrimination duty (Corston, 2007). Yet again there is direct relevance of these issues in relation to policy and practice for how girls are dealt with in the criminal justice system.

## Legislation

The criminal justice systems for adults and juveniles in England and Wales are notionally separate, but in fact intertwine and overlap. Adult and youth co-defendants can be tried together in adult court if deemed necessary; breaches of Youth Rehabilitation Orders imposed in the Youth Court must be heard in the Magistrate's' Court if the young person has turned 18 since sentence was passed, and young people charged with the most serious offences are tried in the Crown Court. The Sentencing Council has produced a Ddefinitive Gguideline, *Overarching principles – Sentencing youths* (Sentencing Council, 2009), which is the main reference point for courts. Advice on sentencing juveniles is also to be found in offence-specific sentencing guidelines to assist the judiciary.

As with women, girls have no separate sentencing arrangements from their male peers and there are no moves afoot to change this. If gender issues render a girl more vulnerable than a male peer, this should be addressed in detail in the pre-sentence report (PSR) prepared by the YOT. A well-written PSR represents the best opportunity to highlight particular vulnerabilities in a girl's circumstances to sentencers. This provides another example of how crucial gender-awareness training for YOT staff is. Youth PSRs are significantly longer and more detailed than those commonly prepared for adults: the author has found it of concern that magistrates have sometimes complained that the reports go into too much detail about the child's life circumstances – as if this information is somehow irrelevant.

The Definitive Guideline states:

> When sentencing an offender aged under 18, a court must have regard to:
>
> a) the principal aim of the youth justice system (to prevent offending by children and young persons); and
> b) the welfare of the offender. (Sentencing Council, 2009: 3)

The welfare principle is laid down in the Children and Young Persons Act 1933.[6] This is noteworthy: this principle results in significantly different sentencing for youths and adults. For example, young offenders convicted of robbery may receive community sentences, including for repeat offences of robbery. This is almost unheard of for adult offenders, who can expect a significant custodial sentence for the same offence (see Sentencing Guidelines Council, 2006).

## Oversight

Youth justice policy is set by the MoJ, and operational guidance on implementation and dissemination is provided by the Youth Justice Board. The Youth Justice Board is a non-departmental public body created by the Crime and Disorder Act 1998 to oversee the youth justice system for England and Wales and to support the strategic aims of the government. Welcome steps forward have been taken in relation to strategic focus on girls within youth justice, including the 2009 report mentioned earlier (Sentencing Council, 2009). In addition there has also been the development of an online Effective Practice library containing examples of good practice from around the country and groupwork guidance. Also in development is a checklist for YOTs to assess their progress against the statutory Gender Equality Duty. This will be made available on the Youth Justice Board website as a tool for YOTs to assess their own progress against the duty (YJB, 2009). However, strategic focus on girls could be more proactive, not least in terms of developing good practice in relation to work in this area.

Unfortunately, there is no centralised mechanism for assessing the standard of gender-responsive service provision: although the juvenile custodial estate and YOTs have a duty to provide gender-specific services for girls, the responsibility for assessing this falls to YOT management boards, within the remit of local authorities. Although all YOTs provide regular statistical returns to the Youth Justice Board, this in itself is not sufficient to assess how well services are being provided. Unless a statistical anomaly occurred (and was noticed), the statistical data would not flag up inadequate progress against the Gender Equality Duty.

This devolution of oversight to local authorities was part of the Coalition government's decentralisation agenda, one rationale being the wide variation in demographics: some areas will supervise almost no girls, and certainly none in custody. Others, notably inner-city areas, will have significantly more, with varying needs. Therefore the freedom to develop services specific to the local area makes sense. The flaw lies in the lack of centralised oversight of the provision. Without standardised scrutiny, some YOTs may be failing in their duty to provide gender-specific services, and if their YOT management board does not pick this up, there is no back-up mechanism.

## Strategy

The National Offender Management Service (NOMS) recognises seven rehabilitation pathways: housing, work, health, addiction, money, family, and behaviour (Social Exclusion Unit, 2002). The Corston Report (Corston, 2007) stated that these should be much better coordinated strategically for women, and recommended the addition of gender-specific pathways 8 and 9: support for women who have experienced abuse, and support for those who have been involved in prostitution. This has been accepted by government and incorporated into policy and practice for women offenders (see Worrall and Gelsthorpe, 2009). Meanwhile youth justice works to the same original seven pathways; pathways 8 and 9 have not been implemented for girls. This is a missed opportunity, given the high levels of abuse suffered by this group and it is to be hoped that this decision will be reviewed in the future.

Although the rehabilitation pathways apply to girls and women alike, in two areas there are key differences due to age: housing, and work – which for juveniles more commonly means education. The problem of homelessness is less acute for girls than women, as they are most likely to live with parents or carers, or in the care of the local authority, and are protected to an extent from homelessness by the local authority duty to accommodate children in need.[7]

However, girls accommodated by local authorities can be placed in inadequate 'semi-independent' accommodation (with access to staff, sometimes live-in, sometimes providing a set number of keywork sessions per week). This can be problematic, as semi-independent accommodation, provided by a multitude of private companies, is of highly variable quality. Although local authorities will have a list of preferred providers, when it is not possible to find a preferred placement, the author's experiences have shown that children can end up being placed in substandard accommodation with poorly trained, low-paid staff. Alternately, some supported accommodation is of very good quality, with dedicated staff providing a lifeline to vulnerable young people. The problem (again) is lack of consistency.

**Example from practice**

In one placement, although the local authority was paying for a 24-hour staffed placement, staff would go out and lock up. Meanwhile the girls would climb onto the roof to get in through a window as they were not allowed to have keys. This placement was subsequently closed after an arson threat was made to the property; it was suspected by YOT staff that this threat had been arranged by a resident, as she was so desperate to leave.

Each YOT provides education, training and employment guidance, which is a main focus within YOTs and within the secure estate, and should always be a target within every young person's intervention plan. Because many girls are still of school age, the focus on education, training and employment guidance is more consistent (and easier to access) than is currently the case for adult women. However, for those who are past statutory school age, the support for those who are functionally illiterate can be very poor. Often the available provision is limited to remedial basic skills classes in further education colleges. For those who have had a negative experience of statutory education, due to (for example) behavioural problems or a specific learning need such as dyslexia or ADHD, a classroom environment risks replicating previous humiliations. Yet individual teaching for those past statutory school age in the community is often poor or non-existent, and lack of functional basic skills is a severe barrier to engagement.

**Example from practice**

A girl under statutory YOT supervision was at risk of breach for persistently failing to attend reparation or education appointments as part of her ISS requirement. It transpired that she could not read street names or bus destinations but had been too embarrassed to disclose this.

## Concluding comments

Although there is no separate sentencing provision for girls, youth courts, alongside other public services, have a statutory duty to promote gender equality. This cannot realistically be achieved unless the specific difficulties that girls face are taken into account. With regard to sentencing, the best opportunity to ensure that this happens is via the PSR prepared by YOT staff. However, as identified earlier, pre-sentence issues such as bail and remand, and the conflation of risk and welfare issues, also need to be addressed.

Strategically, rehabilitation pathways largely mirror the position for women. However, failure to adopt Corston's recommended gender-specific rehabilitation pathways for girls with a history of abuse or sexual exploitation is a significant deficiency in view of the background and circumstances of this vulnerable group within the criminal justice system.

Although youth justice policy and practice is generally characterised as more progressive than its adult equivalent and the welfare principle is embedded in law, there is still insufficient focus on girls by the MoJ and a lack of centrally funded research on the needs of girls who offend. Despite the recently sharpened focus on girls at the Youth Justice Board, the lack of centralised oversight of how YOTs and the juvenile custodial estate fulfil their obligations under the Gender Equality Duty is a significant cause for concern. Without the incentive of centralised, high-level scrutiny – and without a greater commitment to the non-custodial, humanitarian, holistic direction of travel laid out by Corston – justice for girls risks remaining inconsistent, incomplete and unfair.

## Notes

[1] The various elements are: unpaid work; specified activity; programme; prohibited activity; curfew; exclusion; residence; mental health treatment; drug rehabilitation; alcohol treatment; supervision; attendance centre.

[2] See the relevant webpage 'Children in trouble with the law' at www.barnardos.org.uk/what_we_do/our_work/youth_justice.htm

[3] YOTs are multidisciplinary teams and will contain staff from a variety of professional backgrounds. A typical YOT contains youth offending officers, a seconded probation officer, a social worker, a seconded education worker, a drugs worker, and may also contain an in-house mental health team and other specialist interventions teams, for example providing groupwork or intensive ISS one-to-one support. Levels and type of professional qualifications can vary. Some YOTs require youth offending officers to be qualified at degree level in a relevant discipline, others do not.

[4] The 2011 public sector Equality Duty is a duty on public bodies and others carrying out public functions. It ensures that public bodies consider the needs of all individuals in their day-to-day work – in shaping policy, in delivering services, and in relation to their own employees. The new Equality Duty replaces the three previous public sector equality duties – for race, disability and gender. The new Equality Duty covers the following protected characteristics: age, disability, gender reassignment, pregnancy and maternity, race (this includes ethnic or national origins, colour or

nationality), religion or belief (this includes lack of belief), sex and sexual orientation.

5   The former Coalition government's plans to develop a network of Secure Colleges to replace the existent custodial estate engendered considerable anxiety among practitioners and campaigners. Former Justice Minister Chris Grayling had stated that Secure Colleges would be mixed-gender. In the view of many, placing girls in the Secure College estate would have been a disastrous move: the very small numbers of girls in custody would be sharing educational and other facilities with large numbers of boys, and the potential for intimidation, harassment and abuse would have been considerable. The House of Lords rejected the Coalition plans on Secure Colleges in December 2014, in part citing similar concerns.

6   Section 44, Children and Young Persons Act 1933 states: 'Every court in dealing with a child or young person who is brought before it, either as an offender or otherwise, shall have regard to the welfare of the child or young person, and shall in a proper case take steps for removing him from undesirable surroundings, and for securing that proper provision is made for his education and training.'

7   Local authorities can be loath to accommodate older teenagers – perhaps because if a young person has Looked After Child status for 13 weeks or more they become entitled to full care leaver's support, including eligibility for a council tenancy.

## References

Barnett, A. (2014) Some people make out like you're a crook trying to rip them off: A day in the lift of a locum YOT worker, Locum Today, 17 September 2014, www.locumtoday.co.uk/article.php?s=2014-09-17-some-people-make-out-like-youre-a-crook-trying-to-rip-them-off#.VH2zLiOsWMo

Batchelor, S. A. (2005) 'Prove me the bam!': Victimization and agency in the lives of young women who commit violent offences, *Probation Journal*, 52 (4): 358-75.

Bowling, B. and Phillips, C. (2002) *Racism, crime and justice*, Harlow: Pearson Education.

Chesney-Lind, M. and Pasko, L. (2013) *The female offender: Girls, women, and crime* (3rd edn), London: Sage.

Corston, J. (2007) *The Corston Report: A review of women with particular vulnerabilities in the criminal justice system*, London: Home Office.

Gelsthorpe, L. and Sharpe, G. (2006) Gender, youth crime and justice, in B. Goldson and J. Muncie (eds) *Youth crime and justice*, London: Sage, 47-62.

Gould, J. and Payne, H. (2004) Health needs of children in prison, *Archives of Disease in Childhood*, 2004; 89: 549-50, http://adc.bmj.com/content/89/6/549.full.pdf

Heidensohn, F. (1985) *Women and crime*, London: Macmillan.

Howard League for Penal Reform (2012) All Party Parliamentary Group on women in the penal system inquiry on girls: From courts to custody; Keeping girls out of the penal system, www.howardleague.org/appg-inquiry/

Howard League for Penal Reform (2014a) *Weekly prison watch bulletin*, www.howardleague.org/weekly-prison-watch/

Howard League for Penal Reform (2014b) *Custody for children*, www.howardleague.org/children0/

Hubbard, D. J. and Matthews, B. (2007) Reconciling the differences between the 'gender-responsive' and the 'what works' literatures to improve services for girls, *Crime & Delinquency*, 54 (2): 225-58.

Joint Committee on Human Rights (2014) *Legislative scrutiny: (1) Criminal Justice and Courts Bill and (2) Deregulation Bill, Fourteenth report of session 2013-14, HL Paper 189, HC 1293*, London: The Stationery Office.

Kennedy, H. (1992) *Eve was framed*, London: Vintage.

Lipscombe, J. and Russell, B. (2008) Remand fostering, in B. Goldson (ed) *Dictionary of youth justice*, Cullompton: Willan.

Matthews, S. and Smith, C. (2009) The sustainability of gender specific provision in the youth justice system, *Griffins Society paper 2009/04*, www.thegriffinssociety.org/Research_paper_2009_4.pdf

Ministry of Justice (MoJ) (2013) *Reforms for female offenders will improve family ties and employment links*, Press release, 25 October 2013, www.gov.uk/government/news/reforms-for-female-offenders-will-improve-family-ties-and-employment-links

Moore, R., Gray, E., Roberts, C., Taylor, E. and Merrington, S. (2006) *Managing persistent and serious offenders in the community: Intensive community programmes in theory and practice*, Cullompton: Willan.

Nacro (2011) Reducing the number of children and young people in custody, *Briefing paper*, www.nacro.org.uk/data/files/reducing-number-of-children-in-custody-953.pdf

Pearce, J. (1995) The woman in the worker: Youth social work with young women, *Youth and Policy*, 50: 23-34, in Worrall, A. (2001) Girls at risk? Reflections on changing attitudes to young women's offending, *Probation Journal*, 48 (2): 86-92.

Phillips, C. and Bowling, B. (2012) Ethnicities, racism, crime, and criminal justice, in M. Maguire, R. Morgan and R. Reiner (eds) *The Oxford Handbook of Criminology* (5th edn), Oxford: Oxford University Press.

Robinson, A. (2011) *Foundations for offender management: Theory, law and policy for contemporary practice*, Bristol: Policy Press.

Sentencing Council (2009) *Definitive guideline: Overarching principles – sentencing youths*, http://sentencingcouncil.judiciary.gov.uk/docs/web_overarching_principles_sentencing_youths.pdf

Sentencing Guidelines Council (2006) *Robbery: Definitive guideline*, http://sentencingcouncil.judiciary.gov.uk/docs/web_robbery-guidelines.pdf

Sharpe, G. (2011) Beyond youth justice: Working with girls and young women who offend, in R. Sheehan, G. McIvor and C. Trotter (eds) *Working with women offenders in the community*, Abingdon: Willan.

Social Exclusion Unit (2002) *Reducing re-offending by ex-prisoners*, London: HMSO.

Thomas, S. (2005) Remand management, in T. Bateman and J. Pitts (eds) *The RHP companion to youth justice*, Lyme Regis: Russell House Publishing.

Thomas, S. (2008) Remand, in B. Goldson (ed.) *Dictionary of youth justice*, Willan: Cullompton.

Worrall, A. (2004) Twisted sisters, ladettes, and the new penology: The social construction of 'violent girls', in C. Alder and A. Worrall (eds) *Girls' violence: Myths and realities*, NY: State University of New York Press.

Worrall, A. and Gelsthorpe, L. (2009) 'What works' with women offenders: The past 30 years, *Probation Journal*, 56 (4): 329-45.

Youth Justice Board (2009) *Girls and offending – patterns, perceptions and interventions* (Full Report), London: HMSO.

Youth Justice Board (2011) *Review of full searches in the secure estate for children and young people*, London: HMSO.

Youth Justice Board (2014) *Freedom of information response*, received 14 July 2014.

Youth Justice Board for England and Wales (2014a) *Youth justice annual statistics: 2012 to 2013*, www.gov.uk/government/publications/youth-justice-statistics

Youth Justice Board for England and Wales (2014b) *Deaths of children in custody, action taken, lessons learnt*, London: Youth Justice Board, www.gov.uk/government/uploads/system/uploads/attachment_data/file/362715/deaths-children-in-custody.pdf

SEVEN

# Women's centres

*Leeanne Plechowicz*

## Introduction

The Corston Report (Corston, 2007) made several recommendations to improve services for female offenders, a key proposal being the funding of the development of a large network of holistic, community-based 'one stop shops' for women in accordance with a centrally coordinated national strategic plan. Baroness Corston envisaged that women's centres should be used for women who offend or, crucially, are 'at risk of offending', as a diversion from police stations and court, as part of a package of intervention via community sentences, and to provide a 'real alternative to prison' (Corston, 2007: 10).

This chapter describes the concept of women's centres as encouraged by Baroness Corston in 2007, and considers why they were viewed to be such an important step in supporting female offenders and reducing risk of offending in England and Wales. It goes on to explore their progress (or lack thereof) over the intervening years and considers the implications for their future in light of the Transforming Rehabilitation agenda.

## The Corston Report

Momentum for providing interventions specifically designed to address female offending gathered pace through the early part of the new millennium and gained considerable attention in 2007 with the publication of three influential reports: The Corston Report (Corston, 2007); the *Women offenders accommodation pathfinders report for Wales* (National Probation Directorate, 2007); and a Fawcett Society commissioned report (Gelsthorpe et al, 2007). These brought together research findings on female offending related needs, what works with women, and the different models of good practice being utilised at the time (NOMS, 2007). The reports recommended women-only provision and a holistic approach, whereby women are treated as individuals with their own set of personal support needs and are empowered to take responsibility and desist from offending.

Among other commendable recommendations (many discussed elsewhere in this book), Baroness Corston proposed the funding of the development of a large network of holistic, community-based 'one stop shops' for women in accordance with a national strategic plan to be coordinated centrally. Her recommendation was inspired by visiting three 'one stop shops': Calderdale Women's Centre in Halifax, the Asha Centre in Worcester and the 218 Centre in Glasgow which, in different ways, all managed to provide this holistic approach to supporting women.

## Background and funding history

Prior to the Corston Report there were a handful of women's centres in England and Wales; these projects had been created independently to meet local need, some of which were in partnership with probation trusts. They included the well-funded Together Women pilots from 2005 in Yorkshire and Humberside and in the North-West of England.[1] However, it was Baroness Corston's recommendation of expansion that placed the concept of women's centres at the core of provision. In response, 20 philanthropic foundations formed the Corston Independent Funders' Coalition (CIFC), to create a funding stream to support the development of women's centres. Additionally, the Ministry of Justice (MoJ) set up the Criminal Justice Women's Strategy Unit in 2008 to encourage existing women's centres to develop working relationships with local commissioners. Finally, after much lobbying from the voluntary sector and the CIFC, in the financial year 2009/10, the MoJ provided £15.6 million for a two-year period within the 'New Opportunities Fund' for female offenders. While some criticised this funding for not going far enough (for example Fawcett Society, 2009), it was a welcome start.

Of the £15.6 million: £11.95 million was provided as voluntary sector grants for community-based alternatives to custody for women; £1.2 million was provided for enhanced bail support; £250,000 was provided for family intervention projects; £1.2 million remained unallocated; and £1 million was provided to the Women's Diversionary Fund, to expand women's centre provision, on the understanding that this £1 million was matched by the CIFC (National Audit Office, 2013). This Women's Diversionary Fund was a grant committee made up of representatives from the CIFC and the MoJ, and it awarded 24 grants in 2010 (14 to fund new women's centres and 10 to existing women's centres), with the expectation that any organisation awarded a grant would work towards sustainability in the post-grant period (Nichol, 2009 quoted in Radcliffe et al, 2013).

In 2011/12, the National Offender Management Service (NOMS) assumed responsibility for funding women's centres alongside the CIFC, and £3.2 million was provided to 31 women's centres, most of which had already received funding in 2009/10. Additionally, Women's Breakout was established in 2011 through CIFC funding, as an umbrella organisation to support existing women's centres in building relationships between each other, to make them more sustainable and to represent the network of centres at a national level. In 2012/13, a total of £3.78 million was ring-fenced by NOMS for community provision for female offenders in addition to £185,000 from Probation Trust cluster budgets.

In 2013/14, commissioning arrangements were made at a local level by probation trusts, although the funding went primarily to support the continuation of existing women's centres rather than any further expansion of provision. Around the same time, the House of Commons Justice Select Committee, 'appointed by the House of Commons to examine the expenditure, administration and policy of the Ministry of Justice and its associated public bodies' (House of Commons Justice Select Committee, 2013: 1), explored the development of policy and practice in relation to female offenders within the criminal justice system post-Corston, including funding arrangements. It welcomed written and oral evidence from key individuals and public, private and voluntary organisations as part of its examination. The CIFC in its written evidence to the House of Commons Justice Select Committee was critical of the government's commitment to local (as opposed to national) commissioning, describing it as 'a confused jigsaw of what is being planned, without any clarity of vision or on what outcomes are sought' (CIFC, 2013: 1).

In 2013/14, a total of £4.3 million was provided by NOMS to commission additional services in five regional probation clusters on a local need basis. Not all previously NOMS-funded women's centres received continuing funding on this occasion; instead 11 additional probation trusts received funding that had not previously received any, enabling an expansion of women's centre provision to new areas (NOMS, 2013). However, concerns were highlighted by the House of Commons Justice Select Committee that these funds might be spread too thinly over the probation areas, instead of providing appropriate funding to specific women's centres so that they could maintain their previous levels of service provision (House of Commons Justice Select

Committee, 2013). Furthermore the House of Commons Justice Select Committee also highlighted concerns that sustainability of women's centres would now rely on the capacity (or willingness) of the local probation trust to engage with voluntary sector providers. It highlighted the increased importance of local health and wellbeing boards, police and crime commissioners and criminal justice boards in this context, suggesting they act as 'brokers' between relevant agencies (House of Commons Justice Select Committee, 2013). Women in Prison (2012), a charitable organisation that campaigns and supports women involved in the criminal justice system, also highlighted that there was no guarantee that the money would be spent on women's centres run by the voluntary sector, as the funds were available for any community-based service for women and not ring-fenced for women's centres.

In October 2013, NOMS commissioned a stocktake of women's community services to assess the impact of the £3.78 million provided. It highlighted that in addition to this £3.78 million, a total of £5.8 million was already being spent on specific services for female offenders by probation trusts, well above the expected amount of £4.3 million (NOMS, 2013). This was, of course, encouraging. The NOMS stocktake recorded 53 women's centres in England and Wales, with various models and services offered. An additional 22 were predicted to be in existence by April 2014 once procurement processes were completed (NOMS, 2013).

This chapter now reviews the development and operation of women's centres over this period, before moving on to apply a more in-depth critique of the challenges posed within the context of the Transforming Rehabilitation agenda.

## Characteristics of women's centres

The Fawcett Society report (Gelsthorpe et al, 2007: 8) outlined nine characteristics of good practice for women's centres in the community. They should:

- be reserved for women only and provide a safe space for them to attend;
- integrate offenders and non-offenders;
- foster empowerment;
- take into account learning styles;
- be holistic and provide practical support;
- link with mainstream agencies;
- have capacity for women to return for support in the future;

- provide mentors or caseworkers;
- assist women to attend by providing practical support (such as childcare and travel reimbursement).

These recommendations have generally been followed by women's centres as they have subsequently developed. The majority, if not all, of the women's centres begin their contact with the female offender by allocating a caseworker to her, who then completes an assessment of support need. The referring agency, the woman herself, and the caseworker contribute to the assessment and thus develop a holistic understanding of the needs of the client; usually framed within the nine pathways to offending as outlined in the Corston report, : accommodation; skills/employment; health; drugs and alcohol; finance; children; attitudes; abuse; and prostitution (Corston, 2007: 41-6).

Data provided to NOMS in 2012 by 30 existing women's centres suggest that 41% of women were assessed as having four or more needs on referral, with 61% involved with the criminal justice system at the time (Women's Breakout, 2012). Women's centre clients' situations tend to be complex, with multiple areas of need that one agency alone cannot address. Services are therefore provided either directly by the caseworker or her colleagues, or by partner organisations, or by referral on to more appropriate agencies to address the areas highlighted in the support plan. Involving the client herself in the development of the support plan is considered to be empowering (Hedderman et al, 2008).

Plechowicz (2009) argued that the role of the caseworker is essential in empowering female offenders to desist from offending and drew on Attachment Theory to support this assertion. Having interviewed staff and clients of The Women's Turnaround Project (TWTP) Cardiff, Plechowicz purported that in engaging voluntarily with women's centres, women are subconsciously seeking a *secure base* through their relationship with their caseworker. A safe environment is developed by caseworkers, in which self-esteem and the ability to trust can be nurtured and independence and self-reliance achieved (Plechowicz, 2012). For example, women are at first escorted to partnership appointments by a caseworker, who then gradually withdraws her presence over time, enabling the client to increase her independence so that in the future the caseworker's support will not be needed; this is akin to the developmental model of a parent raising a child (see Ansbro, 2008).

Evaluations of women's centres generally support the view that the role of the non-judgemental caseworker is crucial in engaging the female offender (for example, Radcliffe et al, 2013). Easton et al (2010), in their evaluation of Together Women's Centres in Leeds, Bradford and Liverpool, found that several of the clients interviewed 'identified their turning point as the realisation that someone they did not know believed they could change and make better choices in the future' (Easton et al, 2010: 31). A process and impact evaluation on TWTP Cardiff in 2008 echoes this quality; this stated that the caseworkers' ability to be non-judgemental and to 'uplift and empower' their clients was particularly important to the 17 clients that they interviewed (Holloway and Brookman, 2008: 3). Finally, the Women's Breakout report *Experts by experience* (designed to be the 'collective voice' of the clients of 51 women's centre projects) highlighted the importance of caseworkers being non-judgemental and trusting in their clients' motivation and ability to desist from crime as being important in engaging women (Women's Breakout, 2014).

Most women's centres are exclusively for women and staffed by women, in an attempt to provide a safe environment for those vulnerable individuals, often the victim of violence at the hands of men. This is considered to encourage engagement and has often been valued highly by women when their views have been sought (see, for example, Radcliffe et al, 2013). In this respect:

> Safety, both physical and emotional, is a key benefit of women-only services. As a result, women feel supported and comfortable. They become empowered and develop confidence, greater independence and higher self-esteem. They are less marginalised and isolated and feel more able to express themselves. Women using these services feel that their voices are heard and listened to. Through sharing their experiences with other women to make sense of the world together, they develop a sense of solidarity. (Women's Resource Centre, 2007: 8)

Centres have close working relationships with key partner organisations that can contribute to the support plan, many of which are co-located within the women's centre. This ability to access multiple services under one roof may reduce the likelihood of disengagement by reducing barriers to attendance (Radcliffe et al, 2013).

In particular, strong relationships with probation have been cited as important and necessary by numerous evaluations, including the *Thematic inspection report: Equal but different?* in October 2011 (Criminal Justice Joint Inspection, 2011). Women's centres with underdeveloped relationships with probation were underused and thus, arguably, unsustainable in the long term. Important information was not always shared between these women's centres and probation, potentially causing increased risk to staff or the public, and communication channels were not appropriately 'systematic nor robust' (Criminal Justice Joint Inspection, 2011). Hedderman and Gunby (2013) also emphasised the importance of effective working relationships between women's centres and probation, highlighting probation's integral role in developing sentence awareness and confidence in women's centres.

## Conditional cautions and specified activity requirements

Engagement with women's centres is often voluntary, but in some areas is now enforced via 'specified activity requirements' within the community, or suspended sentence orders and conditional cautions. An element of coercion is inherent in such schemes. Plechowicz (2009) raised concerns about the enforcement or coercion of engagement with women's centres; voluntary attendance being considered to be crucial in empowering female clients and building strong attachment relationships to caseworkers. This concern was shared by the vast majority of staff and stakeholders interviewed by Hedderman et al who considered enforcement of attendance as 'unlikely to inspire genuine compliance as it robbed service users of choice' (Hedderman et al, 2008: iii).

However, McDermott (2012) highlighted the positives of enforcing engagement via specified activity requirements. For example, she pointed out that the female clients she interviewed were not aware of Jagonari Women's Education and Resource Centre in London until they were sentenced to a community order or a suspended sentence order with a specified activity requirement, and thus would not have engaged with it otherwise. The evaluation by Easton et al of conditional cautioning pilots in Leeds, Bradford and Liverpool (Easton et al, 2010) was also generally positive of the Together Women centre attendance being used as an enforceable diversion from court. They found that the women's conditional cautions had a positive effect on reoffending and other key areas (according to the clients themselves), with 20 out of 21 women reporting that they have not reoffended since attending the centres:

> The women's conditional caution can be seen as a catalyst to the creation of a different mindset among women offenders that allowed them to see that they had other, positive contributions to make and skills to draw on and

therefore encourage more meaningful engagement. (Easton et al, 2010: 32)

Unfortunately, analysis of reoffending rates against the Police National Computer was limited due to the short timeframe of the evaluation, and previous conviction data were not routinely held by the women's centres; hence firm conclusions on reducing reoffending could not be made. However, accepting the conditional caution allowed the women to engage with the centre to address their support needs and also to avoid the stigma of a court appearance and criminal conviction, which can only be considered a positive outcome. Conditional cautions were not considered to be resource-heavy for police compared with the alternative of court action, and the women's conditional cautions were welcomed by all stakeholders, especially the police, as it humanised female offenders.

However, a few concerns were raised in the pilot evaluation: first, there was evidence that some women's conditional cautions were made when a standard caution and voluntary self-referral would have been more in keeping with offence seriousness, thereby up-tariffing the offender on the basis of need. Additionally the differing interpretations of *Conditional cautioning for women offenders – A guide for practitioners* (Office for Criminal Justice Reform, 2008) by police pilot areas resulted in an inconsistency of application. In Liverpool and Bradford, the Women Specific Condition (WSC) was used in conjunction with existing conditions tailored to the individual; however, Leeds police interpreted the guidance to mean that the WSC superseded any other conditions and should be used on its own (Easton et al, 2010). Women in Liverpool and Bradford therefore may have received more onerous cautions than their Leeds counterparts, or paradoxically the Crown Prosecution Service in Leeds may have declined more conditional cautions because of their lack of onerousness. Furthermore, areas' interpretations of WSC completion was also an issue leading to inconsistency: women in West Yorkshire only had to attend the initial appointment to complete the condition, however in Liverpool women had to attend subsequent appointments as outlined in their support plan, totalling up to eight hours. Inconsistencies in interpretation of the guidance 'directly affect the fairness of the WSC' (Easton et al, 2010: 23) and the evaluation called for more clarity in future guidance.

Corston adamantly believed that women's centres should be utilised as a direct alternative to a custodial sentence in order to reduce the number of women serving custodial sentences and the impact this has on these vulnerable women, their families and the public purse

(Corston, 2007). The New Economics Foundation (Lawlor et al, 2008) completed a Social Return On Investment analysis on two women's centres in 2008 and concluded that £14 of social value is generated for every pound spent on supporting women in the community (as opposed to custodial sentences.) This estimation took into account the impact on the women and their children, their victims and society in general over a 10-year period. The value in the long term is therefore in excess of £100 million over 10 years (Lawlor et al, 2008). This presumes that women's centres are being utilised as a direct alternative to a custodial sentence by sentencers, as Corston encouraged.

Engagement with local women's centres has therefore been developed into specified activity requirements of community orders in numerous probation areas. In the financial year 2013/14, some 2,010 women were expected to complete such a requirement (NOMS, 2013). However, Radcliffe et al's evaluation of women's centre provision across a number of areas in 2013 raises concerns that magistrates' awareness of the availability of specified activity requirements to engage with a women's centre is inconsistent, even in areas where efforts have been made to promote the resource (Radcliffe et al, 2013).

Hedderman and Gunby (2013) also raised concerns with regard to the actual use of women's centres within sentencing practice. Their exploration of sentencers' perspectives in the north of England suggested that while sentencers welcomed women's centres, magistrates in particular did not consider them to be a direct alternative to a custodial sentence. Those magistrates interviewed felt that sentencing a woman to custody was an active decision as a response to the individual offender and offence seriousness when all other options were ruled out, not an action taken due to lack of alternatives (Hedderman and Gunby, 2013). Some sentencers interviewed also questioned whether women's centre intervention could be as worthwhile if engagement was made a mandatory part of an order, echoing Worrall's (2002) findings that some sentencers had ethical concerns with sentencing someone for help or support, as opposed to punishment, as this could lead to up-tariffing. Indeed, Radcliffe et al's (2013) evaluation suggested that women's centres were not being used as alternatives to custodial sentences, but were enhancing post-release licences and community orders instead. This raised the question, were women being up-tariffed compared to their male counterparts in a bid to help and support them? The Fawcett Society (2009) has argued that probation staff, when writing pre-sentence reports, have a crucial role to play in convincing sentencers that the use of women's centres can be an alternative to a custodial sentence in its own right.

## Criticism of government funding arrangements

One significant criticism of the government in relation to women's centres is insistence on annual funding arrangements, which has created sustainability concerns and thereby uncertainty for centres, their staff and their clients. Radcliffe et al (2013) found that this had had an impact on staff morale, with a high turnover of staff in some centres. Service provision was also affected, with staff and other resources being let go due to the uncertainty of funding, with a knock-on effect on the confidence of partners and sentencers and consequently referral numbers. Women's Breakout highlighted the value that women offenders place in the relationships they have with their caseworkers in its report *Experts by experience* (2014). Having interviewed and conducted focus groups with service users of multiple women's centres, it concluded: 'Services and key workers need to be consistent and not change at regular intervals. The development of a trusting and open relationship with a single professional can be key to a woman's journey of progress' (Women's Breakout, 2014: 8).

Losing these relationships due to funding issues is deeply regrettable in this context. Plechowicz (2009) argued that given the vulnerable nature of many women offenders and the strong bonds created between caseworkers and clients, the sudden loss of a centre or staff member could result in those clients' attachments to their caseworker replicating poor attachments experienced as a child and could greatly affect the women's self-esteem, willingness to trust and ability to manage emotions.

Additionally, the government has come under criticism from many sources for not vigorously pursuing Corston's recommendation to coordinate women's centres at a national level via an interdepartmental ministerial group and commission (see House of Commons Justice Select Committee, 2013). Seemingly reluctant to put this into practice, the creation of the Criminal Justice Women Strategy Unit was delayed until 2008 by the MoJ and was later disbanded in 2010 following a change in government. The new coalition government was in turn heavily criticised:

> It is regrettable that the Coalition Government appears not to have learnt from the experience of its predecessor that strong ministerial leadership across departmental boundaries is essential to continue to make progress, with the result that in its first two years there was a hiatus in efforts to make headway on implementing the important

recommendations made by Baroness Corston in 2007 ... We welcome the fact that, after we announced our inquiry, the Secretary of State for Justice assigned particular Ministerial responsibility for women offenders. Clear leadership and a high level of support from other Ministers will be essential in restoring lost momentum. (House of Commons Justice Select Committee, 2013: 40)[2]

It is perhaps not surprising in this context that Women in Prison highlighted that only four of Corston's 43 recommendation of 2007 were considered to be fully achieved by 2012, with 16 having had no progress made at all (Women in Prison, 2012). As Baroness Corston herself put it in her oral evidence to the House of Commons Justice Select Committee on 18 December 2012: 'if you don't have any kind of national guidance as to the fact that this is an important priority, it either doesn't happen or it can't be sustained' (House of Commons Justice Select Committee, 2012).

This lack of national oversight of women's centres has also resulted in an array of data collection and monitoring systems with limited consistency:

Despite consistent recommendations from evaluators on the need for women's community services to collect a common set of variables the Ministry of Justice short-sightedly allowed women's community services to develop their own monitoring systems, perhaps under the guide of 'localism'. (Radcliffe et al, 2013: 75)

Of those women's centres evaluated by Radcliffe et al (2013), no common support needs assessment tool existed – nor any agreed indicators of progress. Even the experienced centres within the Together Women demonstration project initiatives were criticised in 2008 by Hedderman et al, and subsequently in 2011 by Jolliffe et al, for failing to develop a standardised assessment measure and data-monitoring system across their own centres, from which firm evidence could be obtained and success measured. Furthermore, Jolliffe et al (2011) recommended that standardised data collection should include demographic data, to assist with statutory dataset matching (such as Police National Computer data) to measure reduction in reoffending – basic information that simply was not being collected. Failure to gather appropriate data from the outset of a project potentially hampers a women's centre's ability to obtain funding, since it cannot demonstrate its own effectiveness.

Strangely, while the MoJ would not subscribe to standardising the data parameters itself, it did start collecting quarterly reports from 2009 from women's centres, continued by NOMS until March 2012. This was intended to inform future funding, however it was fundamentally flawed by the inconsistencies of data collection and interpretation by women's centres (National Audit Office, 2013). In 2012, responsibility for managing women's centre data was moved to probation trusts but, perhaps unsurprisingly, this still did not allow for reoffending rates to be properly analysed due to a lack of data provided to them from women's centres.

## Transforming Rehabilitation

While NOMS asserts that the Transforming Rehabilitation agenda provides a great deal of opportunity for innovation in the provision of services for offenders (NOMS, 2013), many concerns have been raised with regard to the impact that the Transforming Rehabilitation agenda will have on women's centres.

### Payment by Results

The first concern raised is that Payment By Results, by its nature, does not fit well with female offenders or women's centres. While the Coalition government amended the Offender Rehabilitation Bill to ensure that 'contracts with future providers under the Transforming Rehabilitation agenda identify any specific provisions which are intended to meet the particular needs of female offenders' (MoJ, 2014: 3-4), there is nevertheless 'a very real possibility that many women's community centres will not survive in their present form' (Radcliffe et al, 2013: 13). With female offenders representing a minority of the total caseload of any community rehabilitation company (CRC), there is a potential risk of a privately owned company 'taking the hit' with regard to its reoffending rates against its Payment by Results payment, and concentrating its attention and funds on reducing the reoffending of its male service users (Maguire, 2012). Offenders with complex needs may find themselves written off as too troublesome and costly, and offered little support. As Gelsthorpe and Hedderman argue: 'The level of demand in terms of sheer numbers is too small, and the complexity of women's needs is too great, to make this an area for easy or quick profits' (Gelsthorpe and Hedderman, 2012: 387).

Additionally, if women's centres are going to compete in a Payment by Results environment, centres will need to improve their measuring systems to ensure that they are able to evidence their ability to reduce reoffending. Women's Breakout and NOMS are trying to address the data collection and monitoring issue, but this may well be too little too late:

> If these organisations are to compete in Payment by Results contracts and not be swallowed up by large private sector providers such as G4S – urgent consideration must now be given to investment in monitoring systems and training in monitoring and evaluation. (Radcliffe et al, 2013: 75)

Not surprisingly, there is now a growing impetus to develop common assessment tools (Radcliffe et al, 2013), but time will tell if these materialise.

### Those 'at risk of offending'

Second, the 2013/14 funding of £3.78 million was expressly provided to initiatives working with women who have offended, with an aim of reducing reoffending. This marks a shift away from supporting those at risk of offending, alongside those who have already done so. For many existing women's centres this represents a substantial challenge; while some centres may be able to redistribute other funding streams to support those clients engaging who are at risk of offending but who have not yet offended, others will have to turn away this client group (National Audit Office, 2013). Turning any vulnerable woman away from a service of support she is benefiting from is morally and practically difficult, and sends out a concerning message to the individual: we will only continue to support you if you commit a crime. Additionally, given the importance placed by the Fawcett Society (Gelsthorpe et al, 2007) on integrating offenders and non-offenders, it is disappointing that the Coalition government's dogged focus on reducing reoffending will negatively affect this. It is also potentially a waste of the work undertaken over the last few years by many women's centres to establish strong relationships with partners which, moving forward, may be become obsolete (Radcliffe et al, 2013).

### *Binary measure of reoffending*

Third, it will be especially frustrating for women's centres that commissioning decisions will, at the time of writing as at November 2014, revolve around a binary measure of reoffending rates. A binary measure of this nature does not take into account the holistic approach advocated by Corston (2007) and is unlikely to capture the more nuanced (and not always quantifiable) progress made in the pathways to offending areas that women's centres have been praised for achieving in the past. Until the government's Payment by Results designs 'recognise women as people involved in complex pathways to desistance' (McDermott, 2012: 49), and value the 'soft outcomes and incremental improvements' (Radcliffe et al, 2013: 16) made by their clients, women's centres will struggle to compete in the post Transforming Rehabilitation environment.

## Conclusion

Effective working links with partnership agencies, probation and, in some cases, sentencers will potentially be wasted – or at least disrupted – by the changes made to probation area boundaries and to commissioning arrangements for probation services post Transforming Rehabilitation. While it is hoped that bidders for CRC contracts will engage positively with existing women's centres, there is no guarantee that they will do so. Without CRC referrals and support, women's centres will struggle to survive.

However, if women's centres are able to demonstrate their effectiveness robustly, or if CRCs engage constructively in addressing the data collection concerns, there is a distinct possibility that the supervision of female offenders could be entirely carried out by women's centres in the future. It may be attractive to a private agency to effectively subcontract out the management of female offenders to a local women's centre, whose resources could be focused entirely on this minority – yet complex – group. Doing so would allow a CRC to direct its own resources to the bulk of its business – male offenders – and thus provide services tailored for the majority, with maximum impact on reoffending rates. If women's centres are canny and align themselves with those lead agencies bidding for CRC contracts at the earliest possible stage, they may find themselves in a stronger position than ever before. Time will tell.

## Notes

[1]  The Together Women provision was funded by the Labour government as demonstration projects for women offenders and those at risk of offending. There was an allocation of £9.15 million and the projects started to operate at five centres in the North-West and in Yorkshire and Humberside (Gelsthorpe, 2011: 139).

[2]  The Advisory Board on Female Offenders was chaired by Helen Grant from September 2012 to October 2013, at which point Simon Hughes, Minister of State for Justice, was appointed. The Advisory Board on Female Offenders sits four times a year (see www.gov.uk/government/groups/advisory-board-for-female-offenders).

## References

Ansbro, M. (2008) Using attachment theory with offenders, *Probation Journal*, 55 (3): 231-44.

Corston, J. (2007) *The Corston report: A report by Baroness Jean Corston of a review of women with particular vulnerabilities in the criminal justice system*, London: Home Office.

Corston Independent Funders' Coalition (CIFC) (2013) Written evidence from the Corston Independent Funders' Coalition (CIFC), in the Justice Committee (2013) *Second Report. Women Offenders: After the Corston Report*, London: The Stationery Office.

Criminal Justice Joint Inspection (2011) *Thematic inspection report: Equal but different? An inspection of the use of alternatives to custody for women offenders*, London: Criminal Justice Joint Inspection.

Easton, H, Silvestri, M., Evans, K., Matthews, R. and Walklate, S. (2010) *Conditional cautions: Evaluation of the women specific condition pilot*, MoJ Research Series 14/10, London: MoJ.

Fawcett Society (2009) *Engendering justice – from policy to practice. Final report of the commission on women and the criminal justice system*, London: Fawcett Society.

Gelsthorpe, L. (2011) *Working with women offenders in the community: A view from England and Wales*, in R. Sheehan, G. McIvor and C. Trotter (eds) *Working with women offenders in the community*, Abingdon: Willan.

Gelsthorpe, L. and Hedderman, C. (2012) Providing for women offenders: The risks of adopting a payment by results approach, *Probation Journal*, 59 (4): 374-90.

Gelsthorpe, L., Sharpe, G. and Roberts, J. (2007) *Provisions for women offenders in the community*, London: Fawcett Society.

Hedderman, C. and Gunby, C. (2013) Diverting women from custody: The importance of understanding sentencers' perspectives, *Probation Journal*, 60 (4): 425-39.

Hedderman, C., Palmer, E. and Hollin, C. (2008) *Implementing services for women offenders and those 'at risk' of offending: Action research with Together Women.* MoJ Research Series 12/08, London: MoJ.

Holloway, K. and Brookman, F. (2008) *The Women's Turnaround Project,* Cardiff: NOMS Cymru.

House of Commons Justice Select Committee (2012) *Minutes of evidence HC 92,* www.publications.parliament.uk/pa/cm201314/cmselect/cmjust/92/121218.htm

House of Commons Justice Select Committee (2013) *Second report. Women offenders: After the Corston Report,* London: The Stationery Office.

Jolliffe, D., Hedderman, C., Palmer, E. and Hollin, C. (2011) *Re-offending analysis of women offenders referred to Together Women (TW) and the scope to divert from custody,* MoJ Research Series 11/11, London: MoJ.

Lawlor, E., Nicholls, J. and Sanfilippo, L. (2008) *Unlocking value: How we all benefit from investing in alternatives to prison for women offenders. Measuring what matters,* London: New Economics Foundation.

Maguire, M. (2012) Response 1: Big Society, the voluntary sector and the marketization of criminal justice, *Criminology and Criminal Justice,* 12 (5): 483-505.

McDermott, S. (2012) *Moving forward. Empowering women to desist from offending. Exploring how women experience empowerment, compliance and desistance during enforced contact with a women's centre and probation,* London: The Griffins Society.

Ministry of Justice (MoJ) (2014) *Update on delivery of the government's strategic objectives for female offenders,* London: MoJ.

National Audit Office (2013) *Funding of women's centres in the community,* London: MoJ.

National Probation Directorate (2007) *Women offenders accommodation pathfinders report for Wales (From Homeless to Home),* Cardiff: NOMS.

NOMS (2007) *NOMS Wales: Commissioning and business plan 2008-9 Consultation Paper,* Cardiff: NOMS.

NOMS (2013) *Stocktake of women's services for offenders in the community,* London: NOMS.

Office for Criminal Justice Reform (2008) *Conditional cautioning for women offenders – A guide for practitioners,* London: Office for Criminal Justice Reform.

Plechowicz, L. (2009) *Is attachment theory and the concept of a 'secure base' relevant to supporting women during the process of resettlement? Observations from the Women's Turnaround Project, Cardiff*, London: The Griffins Society.

Plechowicz, L. (2012) Is attachment theory and the concept of a 'secure base' relevant to supporting women during the process of resettlement? Observations from the Women's Turnaround Project, Cardiff, Research and Reports article, *Probation Journal*, 59 (1): 71-3.

Radcliffe, P. and Hunter, G. with Vass, R. (2013) *The development and impact of community service for women offenders: An evaluation*, London: The Institute for Criminal Policy Research, School of Law, Birkbeck College.

Women's Breakout (2012) *Women's Breakout monitoring report 2011/2012.*

Women's Breakout (2014) *Experts by experience. The collective voice of women in the criminal justice system*, London: Women's Breakout.

Women in Prison (2012) *Corston Report 5 Years on*, London: Women in Prison.

Women's Resource Centre (2007) *Why women-only? The value and benefits of by women, for women service*, London: Women's Resource Centre.

Worrall A. (2002) Rendering women punishable: The making of a penal crisis, in P. Carlen (ed.) *Women and punishment*, Cullompton: Willan Publishing, 47-66.

EIGHT

# Older women prisoners and The Rubies project

*Jill Annison and Alma Hageman*

## Older women in prison

The Corston Report (Corston, 2007: 79) outlined 'the need for a distinct, radically different, visibly-led, strategic, proportionate, holistic, woman-centred, integrated approach' for female offenders. These recommendations related to all women within the criminal justice system but have particular resonance with respect to older women prisoners because of their relative invisibility (Wahidin, 2004). This chapter explores the situation with regard to older women prisoners and, in particular, turns the spotlight onto The Rubies, a project which runs for older women within Eastwood Park, a closed women's prison in south-west England.

## A descriptive overview of older women in the prison system in England and Wales

In terms of statistics, women represent a small proportion – around 5% – of the overall prison population in the UK (Women in Prison, 2014). The 2013 figures show that out of the 3,807 women in custody in the prison estate in England and Wales, 360 were aged between 50 and 59 years, while 99 were aged 60 and older (Ministry of Justice (MoJ), 2014).

As far as the types of offences are concerned, Wahidin and Aday (2013: 66) commented that the crimes committed by older women 'mirror those of young women', with a more detailed summary indicating that:

> The majority of the over 50 female prison population are serving sentences between four years and less than an indeterminate sentence; and the second highest category

is 12 months, and less than 4 years. The most common offences for this age group are: violence against a person, drug offences, and theft.[1] (Wahidin and Aday, 2013: 67)

Given this overall profile and the relatively small numbers, it is perhaps not surprising to find that there is little public awareness of older women prisoners.

In 2013, there were 13 women's prisons in the whole of England – there are no women's prisons in the NOMS South Central region or in Wales (Robinson, 2013).[2] Following an announcement in October 2013 by Justice Minister Lord McNally, this number was reduced to 12, with plans for two further women's prisons (Askham Grange and East Sutton Park) to close, as part of plans to develop resettlement prisons (NOMS, 2013; MoJ, 2013a; MoJ, 2013b). These developments are part of reforms that are intended to bring about improved family ties and employment links, although the geographical spread of these institutions means that many women will still be serving their sentences far away from their homes (Shaw, 2013).

Looking back at information from the HM Inspectorate of Prisons (2004) thematic review *'No problems – Old and quiet': Older prisoners in England and Wales* indicates that this is a long-standing issue, as it also noted the geographical distances for women prisoners from their homes (HM Inspectorate of Prisons, 2004). Such physical separation is problematic insofar as it:

> can result in women losing contacts and roles in the outside world, or in returning to families in which they have become an outsider, a misfit, literally a stranger to its younger members; at best, perhaps uneasily accommodated and 'at worst' meeting outright rejection. (Wahidin, 2004: 177)

In this respect, it should be noted that while there are some units within prisons specifically for older male offenders (for instance, Norwich Prison has an older prisoners unit and also an elderly lifer unit for male prisoners[3]), older women serve their sentences alongside all other women prisoners in penal establishments in England.

Having outlined the wider context, this chapter now investigates the particular needs and experiences of older women prisoners within prisons in England, before focusing more directly on The Rubies group at Eastwood Park Prison.

## Issues relating to older women prisoners

When considering the relatively small numbers of older female offenders within the prison estate, it is important to recognise their different routes into these custodial settings. For some, this will entail a period on remand in custody while awaiting sentence, but after receiving a custodial sentence there are typically five routes:

- The older first-time offender currently serving a term of imprisonment;
- The older offender who has had previous convictions but has not served a prison sentence before;
- The recidivist who may have spent a significant amount of her life in and out of prison;
- Prisoners fulfilling a life sentence who have grown old in prison;
- Long-term inmates. (Wahidin, 2011: 110)

It is important to acknowledge the heterogeneity of older women offenders, with such differences stemming from biological, social and cultural factors (see McCall, 2005). Indeed, Howse notes that 'there is enough diversity among older prisoners to undermine the theory that there is any such thing as a "typical" older prisoner with a fairly predictable set of needs' (Howse, 2003: 35).

While taking on board such issues and especially the need to acknowledge diversity, in terms of age there is general consensus that people in prison are 'older' from the age of 50. The 2013 *Bromley briefings* (fact files which are updated and published twice a year by the Prison Reform Trust), stated that: 'research to date suggests that older prisoners possess a physiological age approximately ten years in excess of their chronological age' (Prison Reform Trust, 2013: 48).

Although there is relatively little detailed research focusing on older women prisoners in England and Wales (Wahidin, 2011 aside), key concerns and issues have been the focus of campaigns in the penal field in relation to women prisoners in general in recent years (see, for instance, Soroptimist International, 2013; Prison Reform Trust, 2014; Howard League, 2014; Centre for Crime and Justice, 2014). In terms of recent developments, the House of Commons Justice Select Committee has drawn attention to the need to make available appropriate provision for all women prisoners – older women included – and advocated a strategy which adopts an intersectional approach 'in recognition of the multiple and overlapping ways that different identity characteristics interact' (Justice Committee, 2013: Evidence 94, Section 7.5).

It is within this wider context of issues that this chapter now turns its attention to The Rubies group for older women prisoners operating within Eastwood Park, a closed local prison in England.

## The context: Eastwood Park Prison

The Rubies group takes place at HMP/YOI Eastwood Park, a female closed local prison, which is situated at Falfield, South Gloucestershire. At the time of writing, as at October 2014, about 9% of the prison population at Eastwood Park is aged over 50, with the oldest prisoner up to this point being 83 years old.[4]

While Eastwood Park is described as a 'local' prison, it 'covers a wide catchment area extending over South Wales, the South, the Southwest, and the Midlands. It is the "local" prison to 72 courts' (HMP/YOI Eastwood Park Independent Monitoring Board, 2013: 3). Eastwood Park was not a purpose-built women's prison but opened as a female establishment in March 1996, having previously operated as a male juvenile detention centre and then a young offenders' institution.

The prison is spread across a range of residential wings: it has an operational capacity of 363 prisoner places, with the certified normal allocation of 315 places, which includes a mother and baby unit. It has a complex and vulnerable population of women of different ages: the 2012-13 report by the Independent Monitoring Board reported that 'a high percentage of women have continued to be admitted with mild to severe mental health problems' (HMP/YOI Eastwood Park Independent Monitoring Board, 2013: 3). Of particular note is the turnover of prisoners:

> The average prison population in the last year at any one time has been approximately between 300>310 with the average stay being approximately 39 days ... 50% of prisoners were at Eastwood Park for less than 2 months and 25% were at the prison between 1 and 14 days. The churn of prisoners is very high with the Prison effectively changing its population approximately 5.5>6 times a year. (HMP/YOI Eastwood Park Independent Monitoring Board, 2013: 3)

The executive summary from the Independent Monitoring Board's report stated that it was 'pleased to report on a number of positive changes at Eastwood Park during the reporting year' (HMP/YOI Eastwood Park Independent Monitoring Board, 2013: 5). It drew attention to the more than 25 partnership organisations working with the prisoners and highlighted that 'many of them, such as RECOOP who work with the over 50s, do an incredible job' (HMP/YOI Eastwood Park Independent Monitoring Board, 2013: 13).

Alongside the annual reports from the Independent Monitoring Board,[5] the prison has also been subject to inspections by HM Chief Inspector of Prisons. The unannounced inspection in November 2013 commended many aspects of the prison, awarding high scores against the healthy prison tests[6]: 4 for safety, 4 for respect, 3 for purposeful activity and 3 for resettlement. In his introduction to the report, Nick Hardwick, HM Chief Inspector of Prisons, wrote:

> Staff, managers and partner agencies at Eastwood Park, from top to bottom, should be proud of what they have achieved and the impressive mixture of compassion and professionalism we found on this inspection. The problems and needs they deal with go far beyond issues of crime and punishment. A large, closed institution, far from home, cannot be the best place to meet the needs we found among the women at Eastwood Park – and it is in view of those challenges that the outcomes achieved are all the more impressive. There are still areas where improvement is required but they should be seen in the context of these very positive findings overall. (Hardwick, 2014: 6)

## The Rubies

The Rubies project runs within Eastwood Park prison under the aegis of the independent charity RECOOP (Resettlement and Care of Older Ex-Offenders and Prisoners). RECOOP delivers support services and resettlement programmes, as well as being engaged in developing practice initiatives in relation to older offenders.[7] The Rubies project is funded from charitable sources and also by the prison.

The Rubies started running in 2011 and is now located in a quiet room within the prison, led by the RECOOP worker (one of the authors of this chapter) and a volunteer. In the early meetings, The Rubies was chosen by the women participants as the group name. The term has the advantage of being used to describe both the group itself and its participants. It thus avoids labelling of this group by age (as some of the other original name suggestions had done) and has gained positive connotations within the institution.

A well-being agreement was jointly put together when the group first commenced, to underpin the ethos of The Rubies. The themes of this agreement are revisited from time to time and the current version emphasises:

- respect – to respect every person as a unique individual;
- breaking of isolation and the fulfilment of the need for peer group companionship;
- creating a supportive, relaxed and quieter atmosphere;
- nourishing the need for creativity, new skills and interests;
- not talking about individual trials and cases.

The two-hourly group meetings take place twice a week and are available to both sentenced prisoners and women who have been remanded in custody. This approach means that the sessions are available to all prisoners aged over 50 at Eastwood Park. Nevertheless, the high turnover of this prison population means that there is a constant change in the composition of the group members, as The Rubies operates as an open group at all times. This situation poses complex challenges, not least because of the unpredictable dynamics and diversity of membership of such groups (Turner, 2011). However, the creative, varied and well-planned input (examples of recent sessions include: creative writing; mosaic making; a musical afternoon; sewing sessions; discussion sessions), together with the group leader's relevant professional experience, enables The Rubies to provide 'a space in a quieter environment' within the prison. The importance to the group members of their engagement and participation in these sessions is indicated by the overwhelmingly positive feedback that is given by the participants, with 100% satisfaction rates often returned on feedback forms. While on one occasion there was a score of 95%, the associated comment indicated that the 5% that was taken off was because the participant felt that "we should have more of this!"

The group composition varies from session to session, with anywhere between 5 and 15 women attending on a particular day. The focus of the meetings is to offer a creative space, with purposeful and restorative activities (for instance, craft activities produce garments and other products for outside charities, as well as cards and similar items for family and friends), while also providing a context where discussion and mutual support can take place. The importance of this opportunity for the older women to come together as The Rubies cannot be overstated, and is illustrated in the following poem which was written at the end of a series of sessions during which they had made mosaics:

> Days like splinters of broken glass –
> Pass by
> How to glue together my life
> Consisting of
> Shards of old broken crockery,
> Pretence
> And smashed-up experiences
> Will this prison sentence heal me / beautify me?
> Like a put-together mosaic
> Leaving cracks and scars –
> And a pretty picture…
>
> Poem by a Ruby

On some occasions, the input is more focused on specific aspects of information-giving, with particular engagement with problems or needs associated with the nine pathways out of crime. These pathways, which were identified as relevant within the Corston Report (Corston, 2007), are: Attitudes, Thinking and Behaviour; Accommodation; Drugs and Alcohol; Children and Families; Health; Education, Training and Employment; Finance, Benefit and Debt; Abuse; Prostitution. They are incorporated into the RECOOP project worker's planning for The Rubies sessions, albeit within a wider empowering approach, rather than focusing exclusively on a list of 'criminogenic needs' (Gelsthorpe and Sharpe, 2007). Indeed, it is clear that for many of the participants in The Rubies, they find a space where they can begin to reconnect with their inner resources: practical tasks (such as writing, drawing and sewing) can facilitate a general improvement in terms of well-being and enable some of the women to start to reflect on a pathway which could lead them to desistance from crime (see, for instance, Weaver and McNeill, 2010):

> DREAMS
>
> Getting out,
> Reuniting with my family,
> To feel the love we've lost out on,
> To hold my grandchildren again
> And never let go,
> To let my partner know

How much I care,
And to make decent friends,
Learning to trust,
And helping others
To trust us.

[...]

To hold no bitterness
And no revenge,
But also to forgive myself,
And treat myself with respect.

My dream is for freedom,
To get out
And stay out.

Extracts from a poem by a Ruby

Importantly within Eastwood Park, The Rubies provides a 'place to be', away from the noise and bustle of the main prison environment. As one participant commented: "I just love the quiet, the coffee and the kind listening ear when I am in the Rubies,"[8] while another group member wrote a poem which muses on what this experience had given her:

I am so glad
To leave HMP EWP
And listen to the silence
No more clanging of gates
Grating metal on metal, scratching my Soul

[...]

BUT...
I am so sad
To leave the Rubies
Those glorious Rubies
Now my friends, my sisters, the chats, the respect...

I am glad, but I am sad too.

Extracts from a poem by a Ruby

The heterogeneous nature of the older women within prison has been noted earlier, and this becomes of particular relevance within The Rubies group meetings: for those group members for whom this is their first experience of prison there may be feelings of bewilderment, shock, shame or anxiety, while for many participants physical and mental health problems become more acute and difficult to deal with in the institutional setting. In addition, the problems inherent in the nine pathways impinge on their lives inside and often weigh heavily. For instance, one woman said: "Coming to the Rubies helped me through the limbo of uncertainty, despair, apathy and denial. I feel calmer now." Another member of The Rubies summarised her feelings in the final lines of the poem she wrote about spring:

> Does spring still come?
> On the 'outside'
> When inside my prison walls
> No one hears my silenced cry
> For understanding and hope.

Extract from a poem by a Ruby

The crucial importance of instilling hope as a therapeutic factor and its role in 'motivating energy that promotes goal development, reduction of negative emotions, and coping ability' has been noted in the academic literature (Nedderman et al, 2010: 117) and seems particularly pertinent within this setting.

The ethos and atmosphere of The Rubies group are thus vital elements, together with the professional skills and experience of the project worker (see Turner, 2011). Within this setting, the range of different creative approaches provides both a constructive activity and also a sense of cohesion and inclusion for the older women. A recent example of such a task was the collective making of a Rubies quilt, which was bordered with the words: 'Creativity works as all women have velvet in their hearts', and 'Safety'; 'Resettlement'; 'Respect'; 'Purposeful Activity'. As one of the women involved said: "When life gives you scraps, make quilts!" The quilt was submitted for the 2014 Koestler Awards,[9] where it received the highest accolade of a platinum award. In addition, the poems included in this chapter, together with others in a collection called 'Ruby Red', received a commendation.

While such activities clearly fall outside the structure of more focused interventions within the categories of psychology, education or training, they do provide 'more varied and diverse responses to offenders' needs', as advocated by Parkes and Bilby (2010). Such approaches are also supported by Nugent and Loucks (2011) in their evaluation of an arts programme within Cornton Vale, Scotland's main prison for women, with their concluding statement that:

> The evidence nationally and internationally, and the findings presented here ... have been able to show that the arts can have a significant positive impact on offenders, especially in building self-confidence, self-esteem and social capital. They can also be particularly useful in working with those who have mental health issues. (Nugent and Loucks, 2011: 367)

The potential for improving or stabilising psychological well-being within the context of undertaking creative activities is mirrored within The Rubies sessions, with its ethos of creating a mutually supportive atmosphere. For instance, knitting serves as a purposeful activity, while its rhythmic nature can reduce stress levels and increase levels of concentration and self-esteem. Moreover, crafts like this sometimes have additional spin-offs, such as the transfer of these skills to the wings and to younger prisoners, thus establishing a new and more positive dynamic between women of different ages and backgrounds. Similarly, other creative skills can promote diversity and bring together women from different cultural backgrounds: at one Chinese New Year there was a sharing of Chinese horoscopes, fortune cookies and traditional readings. Meanwhile the reading group concept was introduced, facilitating different perspectives being presented to group members, with an opportunity to relate their own stories and to 'allowing us to start finding the words to describe some difficult thoughts and feelings' (O'Connor, 2012).

These group sessions for The Rubies thus provide a calm space for older women within the prison, while the wider remit and connections of RECOOP mean that external speakers are sometimes invited to the sessions. In addition, signposting can be made to other staff members and different interventions to address issues while in prison and also looking ahead to resettlement. Most of all, the unity of these different approaches for The Rubies is significant: for example, issues relating to the pathway involving children and families are focused upon under the wider umbrella of 'keeping in contact', with discussions about relationships taking place alongside creative activities such as making cards, friendship bands or dream catchers. Nevertheless, such an approach should not be romanticised: for many there are ongoing concerns about the future, not least because of rejection by family members and shame and stigma arising from local publicity and reactions from friends, work colleagues or neighbours. A Ruby wrote poignantly about her feelings:

TASTE

Here
In this prison cell
I only know one taste:
The taste of sadness
Turning to bitterness:
Impossible to swallow
A sour, fermented, stale bile
Left on a plastic plate
Wasted
Like the hours, ticking away my life.

Poem by a Ruby

Finally, it is important to remember that all of the women who attend The Rubies have lost their liberty, with all of the attendant privations that such a situation brings about. This is poignantly captured by a Rubies group member in her seventies at the end of her poem 'Before I Die':

The one thing I want to do before I die
Is to be FREE,
To be ME again.

Extract from a poem by a Ruby

## Conclusion

This chapter has investigated the situation with regard to older women offenders in prison and has presented a review of issues and problems that arise in connection with this relatively small – and constantly changing – population within the prison system in England and Wales. Research emphasises the importance of age-appropriate, timely and holistic interventions, not least to provide an environment for such offenders that meets their needs 'in the areas of health, safety, protection, recreation, and socialization' (Aday and Krabill, 2013: 203).

Drawing on Corston's advocacy of the need for a distinct approach (Corston, 2007), her distinction of the differences between male and female offenders was further extended in this chapter to emphasise the diverse needs among older women in prison. As Codd has pointed out: 'older prisoners have different needs, problems and experiences of imprisonment compared with young prisoners, relating not only to the physical environment but also to prison regimes and recreation opportunities' (Codd, 1995: 152).

The example of The Rubies group for older women within Eastwood Park, a closed prison in England, has shown how provision by a charity, in collaboration with and with the support of the prison authorities, can provide an innovative, flexible and constructive response. While wider controversies about penal policy with regard to women offenders continue, particularly in the face of the challenges posed by the government's Transforming Rehabilitation agenda (Gelsthorpe and Hedderman, 2012), The Rubies provides a haven for the older women participants, where they can feel (according to one Rubies group participant) "that a new beginning, even at our age, is possible!"

## Notes

[1]  Precise information is not available on the women attending The Rubies group, but impressionistically there appear to be an increasing number who have been charged with finance-related offences including benefit fraud and embezzlement from their work situations.

[2]  The 13 women's prisons were: Askham Grange (North Yorkshire), Bronzefield (Surrey), Downview (Surrey), Drake Hall (West Midlands), East Sutton Park (Kent), Eastwood Park (Gloucestershire), Foston Hall (Derbyshire), Holloway (London), Low Newton (Durham), New Hall (West Yorkshire), Peterborough (Cambridgeshire), Send (Surrey), Styal (Cheshire).

[3]  See www.justice.gov.uk/contacts/prison-finder/norwich

[4]  At the time of the most recent inspection of the prison by HM Chief Inspector of Prisons (11-22 November 2013), there were 13 women prisoners aged 50-59 years old (4% of the overall prison population), there were 3 women prisoners aged 60-69 years old (0.9% of the overall prison population), and there was 1 woman prisoner aged over 70 years old (0.3%) (HM Chief Inspector of Prisons, 2013: 67).

[5]  The work of the HMP/YOI Eastwood Park Independent Monitoring Board is summarised within the Annual Reports.

[6]  The four criteria of a healthy prison are: Safety – Prisoners, particularly the most vulnerable, are held safely; Respect – Prisoners are treated with respect for their human dignity; Purposeful activity – Prisoners are able, and

expected, to engage in activity that is likely to benefit them; Resettlement – Prisoners are prepared for release into the community and helped to reduce the likelihood of reoffending (HM Chief Inspector of Prisons, 2012: 9). The rating scores are from 1-4, with 4 being the highest (HM Inspectorate of Prisons, 2009: 8-9).

[7] For further information on RECOOP, see www.recoop.org.uk/pages/home/index.php

[8] All quotes and extracts from writing by The Rubies group members are anonymous to respect their privacy. They are included with the permission of the Governor of Eastwood Park Prison and the RECOOP project worker, and with thanks to the individual authors.

[9] See www.koestlertrust.org.uk/pages/awards.html

## References

Aday, R. H. and Krabill, J. J. (2013) Older and geriatric offenders: Critical issues for the 21st century, in L. Gideon (ed.) *Special needs offenders in correctional institutions*, London: Sage, 203-32.

Centre for Crime and Justice (2014) *Justice matters for women*, www.crimeandjustice.org.uk/justice-matters-women

Codd, H. (1995) Older offenders and criminal justice, *Probation Journal*, 42 (3): 152-5.

Corston, J. (2007) *The Corston Report: A report by Baroness Jean Corston of a review of women with particular vulnerabilities in the criminal justice system*, London: Home Office.

Gelsthorpe, L. and Hedderman, C. (2012) Providing for women offenders: The risks of adopting a payment by results approach, *The Probation Journal*, 59 (4): 374-90.

Gelsthorpe, L. and Sharpe, G. (2007) Women and resettlement, in A. Hucklesby and L. Hagley-Dickinson (eds) *Prisoner resettlement: Policy and practice*, Cullompton: Willan, 199-223.

Hardwick, N. (2014) Introduction, in HM Chief Inspector of Prisons (2014) *Report of an unannounced inspection of HMP Eastwood Park, 11-22 November 2013*, www.justice.gov.uk/publications/inspectorate-reports/hmi-prisons/prison-and-yoi/eastwoodpark

HM Chief Inspector of Prisons (2012) *Report of an unannounced short follow-up inspection of HMP & YOI Eastwood Park, 21-23 February 2012*, www.justice.gov.uk/publications/inspectorate-reports/hmi-prisons/prison-and-yoi/eastwoodpark

HM Inspectorate of Prisons (2004) *'No problems – Old and quiet': Older prisoners in England and Wales. A thematic review by HM Chief Inspector of Prisons*, London: HM Inspectorate of Prisons.

HM Inspectorate of Prisons (2009) *The prison characteristics that predict prisons being assessed as performing 'well': A thematic review by HM Chief Inspector of Prisons*, http://socialwelfare.bl.uk/subject-areas/services-client-groups/adult-offenders/hminspectorateofprisons/prison09.aspx

HMP/YOI Eastwood Park Independent Monitoring Board (2013) *Annual Report, 1 November 2012-31 October 2013*, www.justice.gov.uk/downloads/publications/corporate-reports/imb/annual-reports-2013/eastwood-park-2012-13.pdf

Howard League (2014) *Women in prison*, www.howardleague.org/women1/

Howse, K. (2003) *Growing old in prison: A scoping study on older prisoners*, Centre for Policy on Ageing and Prison Reform Trust, www.prisonreformtrust.org.uk/uploads/documents/Growing.Old.Book_-_small.pdf

Justice Committee (2013) *Women offenders: After the Corston Report, Second Report of Session 2013–14, Volume I: Report, together with Formal Minutes, Oral and Written Evidence*, London: The Stationery Office.

McCall, L. (2005) The complexity of intersectionality, *Signs*, 30 (3) (Spring 2005): 1771-1800.

Ministry of Justice (MoJ) (2013a) Press Release citing Announcement by Lord McNally, published 25 October 2013, www.gov.uk/government/news/reforms-for-female-offenders-will-improve-family-ties-and-employment-links

MoJ (2013b) *Government response to the Justice Committee's Second Report of Session 2013-2014. Female offenders.* CM 8279, London: HM Stationery Office.

MoJ (2014) *Prison population statistics*, www.gov.uk/government/collections/prison-population-statistics

Nedderman, A. B., Underwood, L. A. and Hardy, V. L. (2010) Spirituality group with female prisoners: Impacting hope, *Journal of Correctional Health Care*, 16 (2): 117-32.

NOMS (2013) *Women's custodial estate review*, conducted by Cathy Robinson, London: NOMS.

Nugent, B. and Loucks, N. (2011) The arts and prisoners: Experience of creative rehabilitation, *The Howard Journal*, 50 (4): 356-70.

O'Connor, S. (2012) 'The Rubies', *Inside Time* newspaper, April 2012 http://insidetime.org/the-rubies/

Parkes, R. and Bilby, C. (2010) The courage to create: The role of artistic and spiritual activities in prisons, *The Howard Journal*, 49 (2): 97-110.

Prison Reform Trust (2013) *Bromley briefings prison factfile*, Autumn 2013, London: Prison Reform Trust.

Prison Reform Trust (2014) *Women*, www.prisonreformtrust.org.uk/ProjectsResearch/Women

Robinson, C. (2013) *Women's custodial estate review*, London: NOMS.

Shaw, D. (2013) *Askham Grange and East Sutton Park women's prisons to close*, news report, BBC News, www.bbc.co.uk/news/uk-24669657

Soroptimist International (2013) *Reducing women's imprisonment: Action pack*, London: Prison Reform Trust.

Turner, H. (2011) Concepts for effective facilitation of open groups, *Social Work with Groups*, 34: 246-56.

Wahidin, A. (2004) *Older women and the criminal justice system: Running out of time*, London: Jessica Kingsley.

Wahidin, A. (2011) Ageing behind bars, with particular reference to older women in prison, *Irish Probation Journal*, 8: 109-23.

Wahidin, A. and Aday, R. (2013) Older female prisoners in the UK and UK: Finding justice in the criminal justice system, in M. Malloch and G. McIvor (eds) *Women, punishment and social justice: Human rights and penal practices*, Abingdon: Routledge, 65-78.

Weaver, B. and McNeill, F. (2010) Travelling hopefully: Desistance theory and probation practice, in J. Brayford, F. Cowe and Deering, J. (eds) *What else works? Creative work with offenders,* Cullompton: Willan, 36-60.

Women in Prison (2014) *Statistics,* www.womeninprison.org.uk/statistics.php

# NINE

# Gendered dynamics
# of mentoring

*Gillian Buck, Mary Corcoran and Anne Worrall*

## Introduction

> There are some crimes for which custody is the only resort
> in the interests of justice and public protection, but I was
> dismayed to see so many women frequently sentenced for
> short periods of time for very minor offences, causing
> chaos and disruption to their lives and families, without any
> realistic chance of addressing the causes of their criminality
> … These are among the women whom society must
> support and help to establish themselves in the community.
> (Corston, 2007: i)

The term 'mentoring', rather surprisingly, does not appear in the
Corston Report but, as the quotation above indicates, it would
seem to be compatible with the aims and ethos of that report. In the
period since its publication, mentoring has had an increasingly high
profile in both statutory and voluntary sector work with women
in prison and those newly released in the community. Yet for all its
commonsensical 'feelgood' benefits, it has been subject to very little
evaluation. In this chapter we examine some of the positive and negative
features of mentoring programmes for women who have experienced
imprisonment.

Our original intention was to base this chapter on the results of our
current research, in which we are evaluating a mentoring programme
for young women released from prison. The programme is run by a
voluntary sector organisation and includes both peer mentors (recruited
in prison) and community-based volunteer mentors. In the event,
the programme has faced a number of challenges – many of which
reflect prevalent obstacles that have been identified in the literature on
mentoring, both generally and in criminal justice settings in particular.
Consequently, our data collection has proceeded at a slower pace than

we had anticipated. We decided, therefore, to change direction and to write what might be termed 'an illustrated literature review'. The core of the chapter is a literature review but, wherever appropriate, we have illustrated the review with data from our interviews with volunteer and peer mentors and a case study constructed from mentee files. We make no claims for this data, other than that they reinforce both the opportunities and the challenges of mentoring already highlighted in the research of others.

## What is mentoring in the criminal justice context?

> A voluntary, mutually beneficial and purposeful relationship in which an individual gives time to support another to enable them to make changes in their life. (Mentoring and Befriending Foundation, 2013)

Mentoring is an approach that is widely used in UK youth justice services and is increasingly being utilised in adult rehabilitation services. Given the definition of mentoring offered above, it is easy to see why such an approach may appeal to different, even conflicting expectations. These variously range from improving the quality of life for offenders, smoothing the route to resettlement or, most contentiously, having a demonstrable impact on reducing law-breaking behaviour. Despite its popularity, however, there is relatively little evidence of the impact of this approach. Not only is there a relative shortage of empirical studies in this field, but there is a huge diversity of mentoring practices (Bozeman and Feeney, 2007; Sprawson, 2011; South et al, 2012) that may have an impact on the possibility of making claims about value. There is a further challenge for mentoring services, given that 'the impact of their service can take years to manifest [and it is] difficult to broadcast the successes of mentoring effectively' (Clinks and Mentoring and Befriending Foundation, 2012: 13). There are, however, a number of points we can take from the research that has been done.

In summarising the state of the available evidence on mentoring, Jolliffe and Farrington concluded that mentoring 'reduced subsequent offending by 4 to 11 per cent' (2007: 3), although they added the caveat that 'this result was primarily driven by studies of lower methodological quality' and that the 'best studies, designed to provide the most accurate assessment of the impact of mentoring, did not suggest that mentoring caused a statistically significant reduction in re-offending' (2007: 3). They also found that mentoring was only successful in reducing reoffending when it was one of a number of interventions given, suggesting that mentoring on its own may not reduce reoffending and that the benefits of mentoring may not persist after the mentoring ended. While this assessment provides a good picture of the potential of mentoring for criminal justice, it is relevant to note that of the 18 studies assessed by Jolliffe and Farrington, only two were based in the UK, and both of those were focused on young people. In 2008, Tolan et al (2008) reviewed 39 studies. They concluded that 'mentoring for high-risk youth has a modest positive effect for delinquency, aggression, drug use, and achievement' (2008: 3) and noted that the effects were stronger when *emotional support* was a key feature of the intervention and when *professional development* was an explicit motive for participation of the mentors.

Turning to adult mentoring, an evaluation of seven projects in Great Britain concluded that 'the projects as a whole appeared to have no significant effect on one-year reconviction rates of their participants, even when controlling for risk' (Brown and Ross, 2010: 33). Yet their study did identify '*relational factors*' as some of the main benefits, including 'confidence and peace of mind' and 'someone to talk to/ mentor' (Brown and Ross, 2010: 34). This point about the additional benefits of mentoring appears to be important. While there is clearly only limited evidence that mentoring can help to reduce reoffending, there is substantiation of other benefits associated with the practice. These include: increasing young people's involvement in education, training and work (Newburn and Shiner, 2006); reducing high-risk behaviours and improving education and employment outcomes (de Anda, 2001; Dubois et al, 2002); and improved attitudes and behaviours towards substance abuse, violence and interpersonal relationships (Parkin and McKeganey, 2000; Clayton, 2009).

Some further, albeit contentious, benefits of mentoring are its affordability and capacity, particularly in times of austerity:

> Offender mentoring ... gives fiscally stretched non-government organisations the capacity to leverage the services of community volunteers as a way of providing a greater range of services ... [These services] involve relatively high levels of contact time between mentors and mentees. In contrast, the contacts between professional support workers and their clients are likely to be brief and episodic. (Barry, 2000, in Brown and Ross, 2010: 32)

These benefits are clearly relevant in the current context of reduced public and third sector budgets. In the health sector, however, putting volunteers 'at the heart of the health service' gave unions concern 'that volunteers might be used to replace lower grade paid staff, or to fill gaps in the event of industrial action' (Neuberger, 2008: 18). Freedman (1993, in Colley 2001: 180) has similarly warned of the danger that mentoring may operate as a form of social control in eras where governments are driven by economic considerations to reduce welfare spending, but fear the social unrest that this may create. Indeed, even without these ethical concerns, it has been noted that 'the anticipated chief advantage of mentoring programmes, low cost, was not proven; other interventions produced similar results at a lower cost' (Finnegan et al, 2010: 8).

## What is peer mentoring?

As with generic mentoring, the notion of people with convictions mentoring their 'peers' is growing in popularity in criminal justice practice and policy. One of the most consistent claims of peer mentoring is that people benefit from the knowledge of shared experience:

> Ex-offender mentors' personal insight into prison life makes it easier for the young people to bond with the volunteers and provides the all-important initial hook with which to engage them in the project. (Hunter and Kirby, 2011: 1)

Peers 'are more likely to have specific knowledge ... and an understanding of realistic strategies to reduce risk' (Devilly et al, 2005: 223). The combination of personal experience and an ability to inspire/give hope to newly released prisoners is regarded as the unique characteristic of peer mentoring (Boyce et al, 2009: 19-20). As one of the peer mentors in our own research said: "Because you've got that experience, do you get what I mean? And I think an ex-offender would feel better with another ex-offender because we've both got that experience" (Peer mentor 3). Peer mentors understand that mentoring is not a panacea, but that it works as part of a range of supports. The success of mentoring is also based on the motivations of the mentees:

> 'I don't think that mentoring alone would just help somebody. I think it's a combination of things. Because with mentoring, you are there for the person and everything, but it's about the person and it's about them getting control of their lives and everything. You're not doing it for them, they're doing it for themselves, I suppose.' (Peer mentor 1)

While there is much optimism for this approach, however, there is also a lack of evidence that peer mentoring 'works', not least because, like generic mentoring, there is such a variety of peer models in operation (South et al, 2012). Yet while the research into peer mentoring in criminal justice settings is too scarce and varied in focus to be generalisable, there are some promising messages emerging from studies undertaken to date. Evaluations of the UK-based St Giles Trust Peer Support Charity, for example, claim that its reoffending rate is 40% lower than the national reoffending rate (Frontier Economics, 2009: 15) and 'the reconviction rate for WIRE (female ex-offender led service) participants was 42%, against 51% for the national average for women offenders' (The Social Innovation Partnership, 2012: 5).

As with mentoring more generally then, there is some evidence of wider benefits from peer mentoring, in addition to the often prioritised impact upon recidivism. Sheehan and colleagues, for example, noted that following a peer mentoring intervention, children were less inclined to tolerate violence (1999: 50). Burns et al (2010: 218) found that 'peers and especially friendship networks within groups were influential in desisting bullying'. Summarising some of the American studies, Parsons et al (2008: 5) noted: 'classic model peer mentoring programmes have concluded that participating young people are less likely to use drugs and alcohol, less likely to be violent, have improved school attendance and performance and improved relationships with their parents and peers'.

In the UK context, peer education has been found to improve attitudes and behaviour relating to substance misuse (Parkin and McKeganey, 2000: 302). There are also some indications that peer mentoring can increase the 'agency', or self-direction of service users, by enabling young people to resolve their own problems without professional assistance (Walker and Avis, 1999: 576). This finding may be of particular significance, given that the success of people in maintaining desistance from crime is often linked to their sense of self-control or agency (Maruna, 2001; Zdun, 2011). Young people involved with the Prince's Trust ex-offender mentoring pilot have reported practical benefits, such as help with benefit claims, dealing with frustrations, housing or employment (Hunter and Kirkby, 2011: 4). Such personal connections and links into support networks represent an increase in 'social capital', described by McNeill and Weaver as 'relationships, networks and reciprocities within families and communities' (2010: 20), a key factor in desistance theory (Sampson and Laub; 1993; Farrall, 2004). Indeed the social capital benefit of peer mentoring may pertain to the mentor as much as the mentee, given that 'volunteering can enhance social capital, which is a precondition to "making good" on the part of offenders' (Corcoran, 2012: 20). On a very practical level then, the availability of peer mentoring opportunities offers a valuable opportunity to people who often find it difficult to obtain work otherwise, due to having a criminal record (Clinks and Mentoring and Befriending Foundation, 2012). This opportunity to prove oneself is once again central to rehabilitation, given that 'desistance requires the involvement and cooperation of the offender as well as access to opportunities' (Boyce et al, 2009: 27). Finally, volunteers have described their work as fulfilling to a point where 'their involvement in the project had increased their self-confidence' (Boyce et al, 2009: 13).

While there are some encouraging messages from research into peer mentoring to date, there are also several inconsistencies in the findings. Frankham (1998, in Pawson, 2004: 49) highlighted how disjuncture can occur between the *ideal* and the *reality* of peers as role models. She noted how most of the mentors in the project she studied were 'academic high fliers' and not 'to the taste of other members of the group', leading one participant to ask: "they're a bunch of wimps, why should I follow them?" Pawson goes on to warn that 'the internal dynamics of peer mentoring can build up resistance to the programme message' (2004: 49). Pawson contextualises such resistance in reference group theory and social identity:

> The success of mentoring turns minutely on the mentee's appetite for change. The basic concept is that mentees come to the relationship with different levels of identification with their present status and this 'reference group affiliation' is a key to determining whether, how and in what respects they might be persuaded or helped to change. (Pawson, 2004: 4-5)

Operating structures can provide further barriers to achieving desired aims. UK voluntary agencies working in prisons have experienced obstacles with obtaining security clearance for volunteers, especially if their volunteers have criminal records. Additionally, the transfer of prisoners to other establishments or other probation areas has led to loss of contact, and hence the breakdown of mentoring relationships (Clinks and Mentoring and Befriending Foundation, 2012: 8). Jaffe's (2012) doctoral study on the Listener programme traced the experiences of prisoners who were trained Samaritans working with their peers in four prisons. Jaffe observed the lack of private places where confidential discussions could take place. Moreover, burnout was a particular risk, given the closed environment of the prison and the fact that Listeners are known to their clients and under constant demand. There have also been warnings that volunteering, particularly in prison settings, can take a high personal toll, with harms including burnout, post-traumatic stress, injury or even death (Buck and Jaffe, 2011).

Although there is something redemptive about the process of being a peer mentor, there is great complexity to a process that assists both mentor and the mentee to take 'transformational' journeys. Careful distinction should be drawn between the separate and different needs of mentors and mentees/protégés, of which project staff and/or volunteer supervisors need to be mindful. Some volunteers may make significant personal strides through participation in programmes, but might not be ready or suitable for one-to-one mentoring. Similarly, mentors may experience relapses, which might adversely affect their self-image as 'role models'. One response has been to recognise that volunteers are often at different stages in their own 'recovery' and this should be carefully calibrated against the corresponding levels of responsibility they receive (Buck, 2013: 3).

## Women and mentoring

Many of the identified benefits of mentoring for women in the criminal justice system are intangible or indirect. Trotter (2011: 293), for example, contends that '[m]entoring programmes ... can be instrumental in providing support to women in prison, [by] promoting individual change, developing healthy relationships, and also encouraging successful reintegration after release' (2011: 293). Trotter also argues that having strong social ties to non-incarcerated individuals and having a 'seamless set of systems' beginning in prison and continuing on release can be essential to encouraging successful reintegration and reducing recidivism rates among women in prison (2011: 294). Rumgay similarly asserts that since women offenders complain of lack of opportunities for participation in rehabilitation programmes, mentoring programmes 'might provide one mechanism for facilitating this transition process, while also offering access to a prosocial source of support, independent from the insecure networks that may be available within the social environments of women offenders' (Rumgay, 2004: 415).

The importance of mentoring as a source of support was also a feature for Taylor (2008: 21), who highlighted, 'how important it was to have someone from inside the prison, to whom the women could turn for support'. Servan and Mittelmark, whose research focused on women in Norway, found that their respondents unanimously 'emphasized the importance to coping well of having some close relationships providing emotional and practical social support' (Servan and Mittelmark, 2012: 254). In their report on the provision of gender-specific resettlement services for women, Gelsthorpe et al (2007: 8) recommended 'that women have a supportive milieu or mentor to whom they can turn when they have completed any offending-related programmes, since personal support is likely to be as important as any direct input addressing offending behaviour'.

Brown and Ross's (2010) study focuses exclusively on women in a criminal justice setting and goes some way to explaining why this social and emotional support may be so important. They noted how one of their 'most striking findings' was the 'level of social isolation' of mentoring participants and 'the tenuousness of their links with other human beings' (Brown and Ross, 2010: 42). Not only did the social capital provided by mentors (in forms of links into the community and advocacy) have practical benefits, but it was also seen as 'evidence of trust and affirmation of their status as a person' (Brown and Ross, 2010: 43). While this study found little evidence of 'the transmission of a distinct body of knowledge or skills from mentor to mentee', it argued that a positive mentoring experience might offer 'new experience and practice in relationship building'. The authors also pointed to 'the enormous potential of the pool of residual social capital that lies largely untapped within our communities', such as mentors providing job or tenancy references or character references in court proceedings (Brown and Ross, 2010: 48). While Brown and Ross made sense of mentoring in terms of opening up new life avenues, Radcliffe and Hunter (2013) considered how these may be maintained. They highlighted the importance of women being encouraged to seek support in the future, should they need it when formal mentoring has ended. Equally, however, they noted that:

> staff are keen that women do not become overly reliant on individual case workers and described an ideal gradation of intervention from intensive one-to-one support at times of crisis, shifting to group activities within the centre, and then to volunteering, mentoring, work experience and educational activities with external agencies. (Radcliffe and Hunter, 2013: 37)

Pollack (2004) examined peer support services as an example of anti-oppressive practice for women in prison: 'the fact that the group was co-facilitated by prisoners, rather than by professional staff, greatly enhanced a sense of self-reliance and the autonomy of prisoner participants who have so few opportunities to author their own stories and define their own needs' (Pollack, 2004: 703).

Crucially, Pollack suggests that peer support 'helps counter the notion that women in prison have few skills, are unable to assume responsibilities, cannot be trusted and are emotionally unstable'. Consequently it could constitute a move 'away from a deficit model to one that emphasises women's strengths and acknowledges their varied and skilful modes of coping' (Pollack, 2004: 704; see also Burnett and Maruna, 2006).

In summary, there is a broad consensus that what appears to work best for women is the provision of support that helps women to 'cope' with prison but also with release and reintegration. Such social ties are also important post-release, as women often lack secure or safe social networks and thus experience high levels of social isolation. Mentoring can offer emotional and practical social support in this void, while also giving women experience of developing healthy relationships, thus affirming their status as a person. In other words, it can decrease isolation and increase self-worth and autonomy. Finally, mentoring appears to work by emphasising women's strengths and skills, which promotes positive individual change. Where there is greater uncertainty converges on whether mentoring might promote sustained self-sufficiency. Programmes may lack clear step-down or exit strategies which, coupled with the sudden termination of services or the unforeseen departure of service users, are serious and real contributors to 'failure'. This is discussed in the next section, but this risk can be anticipated by providers who may keep services open informally, while encouraging individuals to gradually progress towards constructive activity or work.

## Challenges and pitfalls

On a less positive note, Colley (2001) warns that programmes should be vigilant against the power dynamics inherent in mentoring. Drawing on feminist critiques, she argues that traditional notions of mentoring derive from hierarchical and directive pedagogical models developed in all-male social environments, and that these paternalistic principles may be unintentionally reproduced in all-female mentoring relationships:

Within such traditional frameworks, the mentor is construed as the powerful member of the dyad, the mentee as the powerless or disempowered, and the process as the transmission of a reified concept of knowledge from the experienced mentor to the novice mentee, reinforcing established practice and invalidating the new. (Colley, 2001: 180)

One aspect of the power dynamics of mentoring concerns the extent to which the mentoring relationship is perceived to be 'professional' or, alternatively, a 'friendship'. An exchange with a volunteer mentor in our own research nicely illustrates the dilemma:

Mentor 3:      I think that if you had a scale, professionals are at number 10, friends are at number, say, 1.

Interviewer:   Where would a mentor be on that scale?

M:             To a mentee, I think we'd be number 8.

I:             Much closer to the professionals?

M:             Yeah, than to friends.

I:             And are you happy with that, or would you like it to be at a different point?

M:             I'd like it to be a different point because I think it'd be easier to maintain that relationship. I'd rather be at number 5. I'd rather be in the middle, because if I was at the top, if I'm too far at the top, then the relationship's not like the same relationship as you need it to be to get a result. And if I'm too far at the bottom, then the boundaries are blurred.

Reflecting an intuitive, but critical, awareness of power disparities, then, this mentor reflects on the difficulties in balancing the demands of being a 'role model' and 'peer'. This sensitivity to new forms of being is especially relevant to women, given that: 'female prisoners not only lack the amount and quality of vocational programs normally available in men's prisons, but the existing programs tend to reflect historical stereotypes of "feminine" occupations such as housekeeping, food services, sewing and cosmetology' (Urbina, 2008: 82-3).

When considering why mentoring may not 'work' as expected, Spencer's (2007) approach provides some insight. She conducted interviews with male and female participants in a community-based, one-to-one mentoring programme whose mentoring relationships ended prematurely. She found 'six salient factors that contributed to the demise of these mentoring relationships'. These were: 'mentor or protégé [mentee] abandonment; perceived lack of protégé motivation; unfulfilled (or mismatched) expectations; deficiencies in mentor relational skills, including the inability to bridge cultural divides; family interference; and inadequate agency support' (Spencer, 2007: 331). Considering these factors in turn, we are able to illustrate the frustration experienced by two of the volunteer mentors in our project.

## Abandonment

'Mentor or protégé [mentee] abandonment' usually involved a partner simply disappearing. Some of Spencer's (2007: 339-340) respondents described having 'the most unfortunate experience of excitedly awaiting a mentor who simply never arrived for a scheduled outing'. In turn, mentors also reported being abandoned by their mentees. The ensuing disappointment led to diminished interest in the programme for both mentors and mentees. In our study, one mentor had experienced no fewer than three mentees failing to turn up for agreed meetings:

> 'I kind of feel like I'm not really doing anything or getting anywhere. Like, as much as I'm ringing them and chasing them around, I'm not actually doing what the project is there for, helping them get on the straight and narrow.' (Mentor 5)

## Perceived 'lack of protégé motivation'

The perceived 'lack of protégé motivation' referred to mentees who 'were not all that interested in having a mentor' (Spencer, 2007: 340). Spencer recorded at least one mentee who had enrolled on the programme without realising the commitment it involved. Another 'had just gone along with the idea' at the suggestion of his mother (Spencer, 2007: 340). Mentor 5 in our research was initially pleased that a mentee's mother "actually came along to the meeting and was, like, really pushing her to go forward with the project". But it soon became clear that the mentee herself was not motivated, "just didn't engage" and "didn't show" at meetings. Furthermore, the mother soon began to collude and make excuses for her daughter.

## Unfulfilled expectations

'Unfulfilled expectations' included a 'romanticized, characterization of a mentoring relationship' being countered by 'the reality of forging such a bond with an unrelated and, in most cases, a highly vulnerable young person' (Spencer, 2007: 340-1). Some mentors in Spencer's study, for example, had 'expectations about the needs of the protégé – that they would need both more and less from a mentor than they actually seemed to' or 'expectations about some of their own needs being met, such as feeling "good" about the time spent with the young person' (Spencer, 2007: 341). Mentor 5 in our study reflected on the naivety of some of her expectations:

> 'Ideally, when I started, I got in my head that I'd be meeting this offender, they'd tell me all their problems, tell me what they wanted from me, and I'd go and I'd help them do it. And then at the end of it, they'd be [in a position to say] "I've got myself a house, I've got myself a job or voluntary work, or education." Just turning their lives around really, that's what I *really wanted* to do [emphasis added].' (Mentor 5)

Equally, mentees also had unrealistic expectations as to what made a 'good match' with mentors, leading some to consider terminating the relationship if they found there was not a 'closer, more personal relationship', or where there was 'doubt about the fit between the mentor's interests and [mentee's] current needs' (Spencer, 2007: 344). Another of our volunteer mentors experienced a mentee requesting the mentoring to stop because the mentor did not drive and could only offer telephone support:

> 'I think it was because all we could offer her was phone support and I could see her once a month, if she wanted me to, but she didn't feel like the support was enough, so she [decided] she'd rather not have it.' (Mentor 6)

## Deficiencies in mentor relational skills

'Deficiencies in mentor relational skills' can entail: (a) lack of youth focus; (b) unrealistic, or developmentally inappropriate, expectations of the youth, and (c); low awareness of personal biases and how cultural differences shape relationships (Spencer, 2007: 344). We found no explicit evidence of this among our volunteer mentors, although it is perhaps worth noting that several were university students who had enlisted to fulfil the requirements of a course module. Although they were subject to the same recruitment and training processes as other mentors, their life experience was more limited and there was also a question mark over the length of time that they would be available for the work.

## Family interference

'Family interference' may materialise when family members put 'a halt to their mentoring relationship' either deliberately or tacitly, by failing to pass along telephone messages from the mentor to the mentee for example (Spencer, 2007: 347). Mentor 5 gave a graphic account of a mentee having a loud argument with her sister in the street outside the café where a meeting had been planned and then walking away from the appointment, without realising that the mentor had witnessed the incident: "Her sister didn't want her to take part in this project for some reason, she didn't think she needed the help." The same mentor also experienced problems with another mentee, who did not have her own mobile phone and could only be contacted through an unreliable partner.

## Inadequate agency support

Finally in terms of 'inadequate agency support', too much or too little involvement can lead to unforeseen consequences. Spencer (2007: 348) cited the example of breakdown in communication occurring because a mentor reported difficulties with scheduling a meeting with project staff to discuss an issue of personal safety. Another mentor complained of project staff becoming 'too involved in her relationship with her protégé, creating indirect communication patterns' (Spencer, 2007: 348). In contrast, all our mentors spoke well of the support they received from the project staff. Nevertheless, evidence that we obtained from other data sources suggested to us that project staff were struggling to sustain many of the mentoring relationships for a number of organisational reasons, including high staff turnover, failure to recruit sufficient numbers of mentors, problematic relationships with the referring prisons, absence of any systematic database and a general lack of experience in this area of work.

## Case study

Despite the challenges and pitfalls associated with mentoring women on release from prison, we have found some uplifting examples of relationships that have 'worked', and we present one of these here as we draw together the threads of this chapter.

Milly is 21 years old and had served three custodial sentences when she initially joined the mentoring programme. Milly had been assessed by the project while still in custody in preparation for her release into the community, where her mentoring took place. Milly was initially classified as a 'high risk' by both prison and probation, so that her mentor had to have accompanied visits for the first few months until her risk classification could be reduced. Her previous convictions were for arson, provocation of fear, possession of offensive weapons and criminal damage. Milly was also returned to custody during the mentoring period for nine weeks for breaching her curfew, theft and possession of a weapon, but she re-engaged with the programme after her most recent release. Milly has complex needs and a history of fractured family relationships, self-harming, homelessness and serial short-term relationships with different partners. She disclosed to her mentor historical sexual abuse by male relatives. She has lived alternately with different partners or with a family member in the mentoring period. On entering the programme, Milly's goals were: to work to reduce her high-risk status; address her self harming; find appropriate accommodation; find support for anger management; and engage in sporting activities.

Sophie was assigned to Milly as her mentor while the latter was still in custody and has been her mentor since then. Sophie has been involved in complex and numerous interventions to support Milly to access welfare and related services including: CAB; counselling; the Prince's Trust; Healthy Minds; probation and children's services. Sophie supported Milly during her court appearance for breach of sentence requirements during the first phase of the mentoring relationship, encouraging Milly to engage with probation and solicitors, and to gather supporting statements from family and agency staff. Sophie also organised a special birthday surprise for Milly's 21st birthday (indoor rock-climbing).

Once the essential trust and confidence was in place in the mentoring relationship, Sophie was able to successfully challenge Milly to address her behaviour and set realistic goals for herself. For example, on one occasion when Milly threatened to harm herself because she was not getting the response she wanted from an agency, Sophie met with her and: "went through anger management scales and techniques with her". Milly gradually gained confidence in dealing with difficult situations.

Sophie is aware that consistency of support is crucial to encouraging Milly to stay the course, especially at times when Milly is struggling or frustrated. On an occasion when Milly got drunk and injured herself, they came to an agreement that Milly should avoid alcohol, but crucially, this was a preface to Milly making a bigger decision to seek treatment for her substance misuse.

It is too early to conclude what the outcome of this mentoring relationship will be. Milly committed serious breaches of her sentence conditions during the early phase of mentoring, and is still at risk of reoffending. However, not only has the intervention of her mentor helped Milly to access services, but she has also gained some skills and begun to build emotional resources and resilience. More intangibly, but just as importantly, it has helped her to prepare for difficulties and potential conflicts, to anticipate 'triggers' to her own misbehaviour, and to manage some of her negative reactions. By the time of her first review, Milly had achieved her initial action points and was aspiring to further goals, including securing training and employment (voluntary or paid) in the sports and leisure industry and applying for access to her child. She successfully completed a Sport for Life course and a volunteering placement with the Prince's Trust.

## Conclusions

While there are some promising messages emerging from studies into mentoring and peer mentoring, it is relevant to note that most of this evidence is from an American context and the majority of studies focus on young people in a variety of settings other than those directly related to criminal justice or resettlement. There is a scarcity of evidence on the impact of peer mentoring in UK adult criminal justice settings, especially in prisons. There is a particular lack of focus on women's mentoring in either community or custodial settings. Much of the work that has been done to date has been small-scale, isolated evaluations of particular projects.

On a broader scale, 'there does not appear to be a development of significant theoretical concepts or models of mentoring comparable to those in the fields of guidance or counselling' (Colley, 2001: 178). Perhaps as a result, 'work continues to be both descriptive rather than analytical, and to be biased in its favourable view of mentoring'

(Colley, 2001: 178). There is, therefore, space for mentoring to be more rigorously theorised and critiqued.

In this chapter we have begun to address some of the theoretical, policy and practical issues relating to mentoring in general and to mentoring women in particular. We have concluded that mentoring has a place in the reintegration of women ex-prisoners, but is by no means a panacea and should not be burdened with unrealistic expectations of either directly reducing reoffending or saving money.

## References

Boyce, I., Hunter, G. and Hough, M. (2009) *The St Giles Trust peer advice project: Summary of an evaluation report*, London: The Institute for Criminal Policy Research, School of Law, King's College.

Bozeman, B. and Feeney, M. K. (2007) Toward a useful theory of mentoring: A conceptual analysis and critique, *Administration and Society*, 39 (6): 719-39.

Brown, M. and Ross, S. (2010) Mentoring, social capital and desistance: A study of women released from prison, *Australian & New Zealand Journal of Criminology*, 43 (1): 31-50.

Buck, G. (2013) *Peer mentoring briefing paper*,. www.academia.edu/3628751/Peer_Mentoring_Briefing_Paper

Buck, G. and Jaffe, M. (2011) 'Volunteering in criminal justice' Seminar Report, *ESRC Seminar Series: The third sector in criminal justice*, Keele: Keele University.

Burnett, R. and Maruna, S. (2006) The kindness of prisoners: strengths-based resettlement in theory and in action, *Criminology and Criminal Justice*, 6 (1): 83-106.

Burns, S., Cross, D. and Maycock, B. (2010) 'That could be me squishing chips on someone's car.' How friends can positively influence bullying behaviors, *Journal of Primary Prevention*, 31 (4): 209-22.

Clayton, A. N. (2009) *Mentoring for youth involved in juvenile justice programs: A review of the literature*, MA: University of Massachusetts.

Clinks and Mentoring and Befriending Foundation (2012) *Supporting offenders through mentoring and befriending: Clinks and MBF survey findings September 2012*, www.mandbf.org/wp-content/uploads/2012/10/Clinks-and-MBF-survey-report-findings-final-version-Sept-2012.pdf

Colley, H. (2001) Righting rewritings of the myth of mentor: A critical perspective on career guidance mentoring, *British Journal of Guidance and Counselling*, 29 (2): 177-97.

Corcoran, M. (2012) 'Be careful what you ask for': Findings from the seminar series on the 'Third sector in criminal justice', *Prison Service Journal*, No. 24.

Corston, J. (2007) *The Corston Report: A report by Baroness Jean Corston of a review of women with particular vulnerabilities in the criminal justice system*, London: Home Office.

de Anda, D. (2001) A qualitative evaluation of a mentor program for at-risk youth: The participants' perspective, *Child & Adolescent Social Work Journal*, 18 (2): 97-117.

Devilly, G. J., Sorbello, L., Eccleston, L. and Ward, T. (2005) Prison-based peer-education schemes, *Aggression and Violent Behavior*, 10: 219-40.

Dubois, D. L., Holloway, B. E., Valentine, J. C. and Cooper, H. (2002) Effectiveness of mentoring programs for youth: A meta-analytic review, *American Journal of Community Psychology*, 30 (2): 157-97.

Farrall, S. (2004) Social capital and offender reintegration: Making probation desistance focused, in S. Maruna and R. Immarigeon (eds) *After crime and punishment: Pathways to offender reintegration*, Devon: Willan.

Finnegan, L., Whitehurst, D. and Denton, S. (2010) *Models of mentoring for inclusion and employment: Thematic review of existing evidence on mentoring and peer mentoring*, London: Centre for Economic and Social Inclusion.

Frontier Economics (2009) *St Giles Trust's through the gates: An analysis of economic impact*, London: Pro Bono Economics.

Gelsthorpe, L., Sharpe, G. and Roberts, J. (2007) *Provision for women offenders in the community*, London: The Fawcett Society.

Hunter, G. and Kirby, A. (2011) *Evaluation of working one to one with young offenders*, London: Prince's Trust.

Jaffe, M. (2012) *Peer support and help-seeking in prison: A study of the listener scheme in four prisons in England.* PhD Thesis, Keele: Keele University.

Jolliffe, D. and Farrington, D. (2007) *A rapid evidence assessment of the impact of mentoring on re-offending: A summary*, 11/07, Cambridge: Cambridge University.

Maruna, S. (2001) *Making good; How ex-convicts reform and rebuild their lives.* Washington, DC: American Psychological Association.

McNeill, F. and Weaver, B. (2010) *Changing lives? Desistance research and offender management, Research report 255*, The Scottish Centre for Crime and Justice Research, www.sccjr.ac.uk/pubs/Changing-Lives-Desistance-Research-and-Offender-Management/255

Mentoring and Befriending Foundation (2013) *Definition of mentoring*, www.mandbf.org/guidance-and-support/what-is-mentoring-and-befriending

Neuberger, J. (2008) *Volunteering in the public services: Health and social care*, Baroness Neuberger's review as the Government's Volunteering Champion, March 2008, London: Cabinet Office.

Newburn, T. and Shiner, M. (2006) Young people, mentoring and social inclusion, *Youth Justice*, 6 (1): 23-41.

Parkin, S. and McKeganey, N. (2000) The rise and rise of peer education approaches, *Drugs: Education, prevention and policy*, 7 (3): 293-310.

Parsons, C., Maras, P., Knowles, C., Bradshaw, V., Hollingworth, K. and Monteiro, H. (2008) *Formalised peer mentoring pilot evaluation*, Canterbury: Canterbury Christ Church University.

Pawson, R. (2004) *Mentoring relationships: An explanatory review*, Working Paper 21. Leeds: University of Leeds.

Pollack, S. (2004) Anti-oppressive social work practice with women in prison: Discursive reconstructions and alternative practice, *British Journal of Social Work*, 34 (5): 693-707.

Radcliffe, P. and Hunter, G. (2013) *The development and impact of community services for women offenders: An evaluation*, London: The Institute for Criminal Policy Research, Birkbeck College.

Rumgay, J. (2004) Scripts for safer survival: Pathways out of female crime, *The Howard Journal of Criminal Justice*, 43 (4): 405-19.

Sampson, R. J. and Laub, J. H. (1993) *Crime in the making: Pathways and turning points through life*, Cambridge, MA; London: Harvard University Press.

Servan, A. K. and Mittelmark, M. B. (2012) Resources for coping among women ex-offenders, *International Journal of Mental Health Promotion*, 14 (5): 254-63.

Sheehan, K., Dicara, J. A., Lebailly, S. and Christoffel, K. K. (1999) Adapting the gang model: Peer mentoring for violence prevention, *Pediatrics*, 104 (1): 50.

South, J., Woodall, J., Kinsella, K., Dixey, R., Penson, B. and de Viggiani, N. (2012) *Peers in prison settings (PiPS)*, Expert Symposium, 23 May 2012 Conference Proceedings. Leeds: Leeds Metropolitan University.

Spencer, R. (2007) 'It's not what I expected': A qualitative study of youth mentoring relationship failures, *Journal of Adolescent Research*, 22 (4): 331-54.

Sprawson, A. (2011) *Mentoring in criminal Justice*, A one day conference organised by A. Hucklesby and E. Wincup, Leeds: University of Leeds.

Taylor, C. (2008) *Volunteering for all? A qualitative study of women ex-offenders' experiences of volunteering*, London: The Griffins Society.

The Social Innovation Partnership (2012) *The WIRE (Women's Information and Resettlement for Ex-offenders) Evaluation Report*, London: The Social Innovation Partnership, see http://site.stgilestrust.org.uk/media/22/6593/1sgt-report-final.pdf

Tolan, P., Henry, D., Schoeny, M. and Bass, A. (2008) *Mentoring interventions to affect juvenile delinquency and associated problems*, Campbell Systematic Reviews, 16, Oslo: The Campbell Collaboration.

Trotter, C. (2011) Mentoring, in R. Sheehan, G. McIvor and C. Trotter (eds) *Working with women offenders in the community*, Cullompton: Willan.

Urbina, M. G. (2008) *A comprehensive study of female offenders: Life before, during, and after incarceration*, Springfield, IL: Charles C. Thomas.

Walker, S. A. and Avis, M. (1999) Common reasons why peer education fails, *Journal of Adolescence*, 22 (4): 573-77.

Zdun, S. (2011) Immigration as a trigger to knife off from delinquency? Desistance and persistence among male adolescents from the Former Soviet Union in Germany, *Criminology and Criminal Justice*, 11 (4): 307-23.

# TEN

# 'Serious therapy' for serious female offenders: the democratic therapeutic community at HMP Send

*Alisa Stevens*

'I've never been anywhere before here that made me feel better about myself, or made me think that I could be a better person. That's a bit sad, isn't it?' (Sarah)

As Baroness Corston (Corston, 2007) was keenly aware, most women in prison are serving short sentences for non-violent offences. This remains the case: of all women offenders sent to prison in 2013, a total of 77% were given a determinate sentence of less than 12 months; while, as of June 2014, only 12% of women prisoners were serving an indeterminate term (Ministry of Justice, 2014a). Forty per cent of women received into prison in 2013 were sent there for the offences of theft and handling stolen goods, compared to 14% imprisoned for violence against the person (Ministry of Justice, 2014b). The long-serving female prisoner, whose serious offending represents a risk to the general public, is therefore a rarity.

For this statistically unusual and qualitatively different population, an unusual and different form of rehabilitative intervention exists: the democratic[1] therapeutic community (TC). It is unusual because only four men's prisons, and one women's prison, in England and Wales offer one or more TCs; collectively accommodating less than 1% of the total prison population. It is different because, in contrast to the cognitive-behavioural model of change that informs most programmes approved for use in custodial and community settings, the TC's accredited treatment modality rests upon a combination of psychodynamic psychotherapy and self-consciously pro-social communal living. The TC is also as equally concerned with 'hidden' causes and holistic cures as the minimisation and management of reoffending.

The focus of this chapter, then, is the rehabilitative work undertaken at the TC located within HMP Send, a closed women's prison in

Surrey, south-east England. Illustrated by verbatim excerpts from semi-structured interviews with staff and 'residents' – as prisoners are called in TCs – that the author conducted at Send[2] as part of a wider ethnographic and phenomenological study of three prison-based TCs (Stevens, 2013), this chapter highlights the gendered nature of serious female offenders' therapeutic needs. It further argues that immersion in "serious therapy" (Natalie) contributes to the kind of agentic renegotiation of one's image of self and redirection of one's life trajectory that has been observed in ex-offenders by scholars of desistance. First, however, there follows a necessarily brief explanation of what a TC is and does.

## Prison-based democratic therapeutic communities

The contemporary TC originates from innovations in the care of traumatised military veterans during World War Two. A handful of psychoanalytically informed psychiatrists, concerned with the psychodynamic significance and therapeutic climate of the hospital setting, essentially re-envisaged 'treatment' as a collaborative enterprise between patients as architects of their own rehabilitation, and staff as enablers of that rehabilitation. The central premise that has since evolved is that troubled people need a supportive, enabling environment within which to re-experience, and hence come to recognise and understand, the ways of thinking and behaving which have harmed them and, certainly among serious offenders, contributed to their infliction of harm upon others. A TC is thus simultaneously a psychosocial intervention and an all-encompassing 'living-learning experience' (Jones, 1968: 106), in which the community collectively shares responsibility for creating and sustaining an egalitarian, tolerant, yet constructively challenging 'culture of enquiry' (Main, 1946) and for ensuring that its 'total resources' are positively 'pooled in furthering treatment' (Jones, 1968: 85; and see also Rapoport, 1960; Haigh, 1999).

As unlikely as it admittedly sounds, TC principles and practices were imported into the English penal system with the opening of HMP Grendon in Buckinghamshire in 1962. Grendon remains the only prison to operate entirely as a collection of TCs; the other TCs are housed on one wing or unit within an otherwise 'mainstream' prison. While each TC creates its own written constitution and develops its own character, they must all meet the same accreditation standards, as an offending behaviour programme *and* as a therapeutic community. The prison-based TCs therefore share a common regime, the 'purposeful activity' of which revolves around group work: thrice-weekly small group psychodynamic psychotherapy and bi-weekly community meetings.

The small groups typically comprise around eight residents, facilitated by one or more psychotherapists, psychologists, or (uniformed) prison officers who have undertaken some additional therapeutic training. With its origins in Freudian psychoanalysis, a fundamental premise of the psychodynamic approach is that distress and dysfunction derive from unresolved, unconscious (that is, not in one's immediate awareness) internal conflicts and drives. This subjective, inner (psychic, emotional) world of experience must therefore be unearthed, reflected upon and spoken about, if the initial and continuing 'meanings' of – and reverberations from – those experiences are to be fully understood (Yalom, 1995; Bateman et al, 2010). The work of the small groups is therefore to encourage residents to relate their complete personal and offending history, but crucially over the course of which, they move beyond factual recitation of 'what happened' to interpretations of 'what this meant' for the resident's inner world, and just as importantly, continues to mean, for her ways of behaving, relating to others, and managing her emotions within the TC. After each small group, the community reconvenes to receive a summary of – or 'feedback' on – the material discussed, thereby ensuring that all community members are aware of each other's problems and invested in each other's therapeutic progress. Community meetings, by contrast, serve a number of functions, but chiefly exist to provide the whole community with a forum for deliberating upon, and ideally resolving through negotiation, any issues which affect the community's safe and effective functioning. These meetings are chaired by a resident, elected for a specified term on the basis of the therapeutic challenge that leadership will represent for her.

## The therapeutic community at HMP Send

Just as the 'Cinderella status' of women offenders has ensured that their custodial and rehabilitative needs have always been a distant afterthought to men's, so it took a further four decades after the opening of HMP Grendon for women to be given the opportunity to access TC treatment. The original plans for Grendon actually envisaged a mixed user site, of 50 women and girls in 'a smaller separate section', 250 men and 50 boys (Snell, 1962: 789); but while young offenders were accommodated until 1989, the prison never admitted women. It was not until the 1990s that provision for women was seriously reconsidered, when research suggested that 6–8% of women prisoners would be clinically suitable for, and could benefit from, TC treatment (Maden et al, 1994; Kennedy, 1998, cited in Stewart and Parker, 2007). These estimates of need provided the 'business case' for the opening of a women's TC; finally realised in 2003 with the opening of a TC with a capacity of 80 at West Hill, a lower-security annexe within the walls of the men's local prison, HMP Winchester in Hampshire. Within a year, however, the function of West Hill was changed to become a men's resettlement unit. This unhappily obliged the embryonic TC to transfer to HMP Send, and without any of the uniformed prison staff to whom the women had become attached. The entirely predictable result was some unsettled, anxious and angry residents, half of whom subsequently left the TC. 'A crisis of confidence' about the TC's ability to survive soon followed (Stewart and Parker, 2007: 76).

This early, insecurity-inducing concern about the TC's long-term viability periodically re-emerged because, notwithstanding the identified clinical need, the best marketing endeavours of TC staff, and the clarion call of HM Chief Inspector of Prisons (2006: 71: para 8.52) to take 'national action and responsibility' to promote its services, the TC never managed to recruit enough women to fill the 40-bed wing that HMP Send initially reserved for it.

Presently (as at December 2014), Send TC occupies 24 of the 32 beds on the upper residential landing of a two-storey wing and thus, except for sole use of therapy rooms on both floors, the TC still does not enjoy exclusive use of clearly demarcated space but shares its residential accommodation with 'lodgers' (non-TC women). In consequence, and in comparison with the men's TCs, its situated distinctiveness and social cohesiveness as a TC has been compromised. Moreover, even when a waiting list of prisoners seeking admittance has developed, the TC's ability to accept these women, and to run additional activities for the community, has been restricted by persistent staff shortages. Officers detailed to work in the TC have been redeployed to operational duties elsewhere in the prison, while mainstream officers have predominately overseen the residential area (HM Chief Inspector of Prisons, 2008, 2010).

While all TCs located within mainstream establishments are vulnerable to the multiple, internally determined and externally imposed priorities for, and pressures on, the 'host' establishment, as the inglorious history of 'terminated' TC units attests (see Stevens, 2013), the structural context within which Send TC operates is therefore especially challenging. Ideally, and as staff and residents interviewed for this research requested and HM Chief Inspector of Prisons (2010, 2014) has recommended, the TC would be housed in a discrete unit and supervised only by prison officers wholly involved in, and committed to, the TC regime and ethos.

Women who transfer to the TC are typically serving very long, if not indeterminate, sentences for offences of extreme interpersonal violence (including murder and manslaughter), arson or robbery. Certainly they must have at least two years still to serve, in order to complete the required minimum treatment duration of 18 months. They must also voluntarily apply (and be clinically assessed as suitable) for admission, which presupposes that they know about the TC's existence, what it does and whom it best suits. For this, the recommendation of an influential (and accurately informed) professional such as an offender manager can be crucial: such 'criminal justice system followers' are an important source of new recruits to the men's TCs (Stevens, 2013). An encouraging development for Send TC, then, is its inclusion (along with the men's TCs) as a recognised custodial 'pathway' in the emerging Offender Personality Disorder Programme (see NOMS/NHS England, 2014). With more referrals, and the benefit of the kind of strategic promotion that HM Chief Inspector of Prisons advocated, the TC's future would feel more assured. This chapter now turns to the rehabilitative experience that awaits women who do commit to "serious therapy".

## A gendered focus on 'serious therapy'

> 'Relationships are a *major* issue for our women; they're important for men as well, but I think relationships are even more pertinent for women. Women carry a huge amount of shame about the things that have been done to them, and somehow there's a magical process whereby talking about it in a group of other women, coming into contact with the feelings about it, and being reassured by other women that they're not alone with having those experiences and those feelings, is just so incredibly powerful.' (Elizabeth, therapist)

To explain convincingly how the many constituent parts of a treatment intervention as complex as the democratic therapeutic community combine to effect personal change among offenders is beyond the scope of this chapter (but for which see, among others, Genders and Player, 1995; Morris, 2004; Stevens, 2013; Brown et al, 2014). Instead, one aspect which has particular resonance for women is highlighted: the therapeutic work undertaken on interpersonal relationships and emotional bonds or 'attachments'. In TCs, attachment experiences are explored narratively in psychotherapy and re-experienced emotionally and psychologically in the relationships formed with residents and staff.

Attachment theory anticipates that a child whose basic needs were not met, because her primary 'attachment-figure' (care-giver) was indifferent, abusive and/or inconsistent, develops 'internal working models' (cognitive maps and affective schemas), which negatively shape how she perceives, and limits what she expects from, herself and others (Bowlby, 1988). As an adult, psychosocial and emotional impairment, including personality disorder, and a range of maladaptive (avoidant, ambivalent or disorganised) attachment styles, coping strategies and defence mechanisms, and repetition compulsions may then emerge. In conjunction with other simultaneously operating risk factors, this predisposes the individual to violent offending (de Zulueta, 1993; Fonagy, 2004). It is therefore neither surprising nor coincidental that TC residents, and 'heavy end' forensic populations more generally, have often experienced abandonment, loss, neglect, cruelty and/or abuse, usually within the context of familial relationships, during their formative years (Shine and Newton, 2000; Adshead, 2004). Indeed, Adshead (2004: 149, emphasis added) notes that it is 'highly unusual for offender patients ... to have had early childhood experience which *would* promote attachment security'.

The relevance of attachment deficits to serious female offending is underscored when one considers that women's violence is overwhelmingly relational and expressive and occurs within the private sphere of the home (Swan and Snow, 2002; Motz, 2008); and their involvement in serious violence and other gender atypical crimes (such as robbery, burglary and drug trafficking) increases when one or more male co-offenders is present (Becker and McCorkel, 2011; see also Jones, 2008). Women also appear to demonstrate greater criminogenic needs (risk factors associated with the probability of recidivism) than men in relation to familial and marital relationships and emotional and personal factors (Hollin and Palmer, 2006). Certainly among the author's research participants, essentially their offending was either 'about' or involved (and arguably would not have been committed without the instigation or participation of) 'significant others'. The women's need to talk about their attachments in general, and their partners in love, sex and/or criminal activity, and their children specifically, and at the more profound, painstaking level of depth and detail demanded by the psychodynamic approach, was therefore acute. As prison officer Heidi observed, "'I'd say relationships are the biggest thing that brings women to us; they often identify relationships straight off as their biggest problem" (Heidi, prison officer).

To be able to talk candidly, however, requires trust in one's group and the wider community. One of the immediate difficulties which must be overcome in a forensic TC, then, is an entirely understandable reluctance to trust among women whose lives have been episodes in rejection, betrayal and deceit; a learned reticence compounded by the inherently low trust environment of the prison. In 'normal' prisons, the women reported, it was "not sensible" to be too "open" with others, because to do so was to render oneself vulnerable to prisoners who might then "take advantage", emotionally or materially, or break confidences. Prison-based TCs, however, demand strict observance of confidentiality within the TC, so that when new arrivals saw that "nothing bad seemed to happen to the girls[3] who did speak about their stuff", they realised, "well, maybe I can trust [other residents]" (Theresa).

Once basic trust has been secured, residents are encouraged to 'open up' and share their own, and comment on each other's, life stories. These disclosed experiences typically included: recurrent episodes of multiple forms of trauma in childhood; extended periods in local authority care as an adolescent; adult relationships characterised by – often as the victim, but sometimes the perpetrator, of – sexual abuse and exploitation, physical violence, psychological manipulation and domination, emotional volatility, irrational jealousy and unhealthy co-dependency; involvement in sex work; and a history of self-harming behaviours, from 'cutting up' and eating disorders to suicide attempts. Unsurprisingly, to revisit discursively such experiences in psychotherapy was "very, very difficult and really painful" (Sarah), and thus to *persist* in psychotherapy, in the full knowledge that "when you go to the dark places of your life, your sadness, your upset, you're going to feel that pain" (Josephine), required, beyond courage and resilience, faith that the process was, or would eventually be, worthwhile. One of the cited advantages of group, as opposed to individual, therapy, however, is its 'strength in numbers' (Manor, 1994: 251); and accordingly, the encouragement and affirmation of the community, especially 'senior' (therapeutically advanced) residents, was pivotal to less experienced residents' motivation and ability to endure the "terrible turmoil and pain" (Jenny) of psychotherapy.

Sharing a "past that I didn't want to share, that I felt embarrassed about" (Josephine) was also made easier by discovering that such disclosures were routinely met not with the disloyalty or exposure one would risk in the mainstream, but with sensitivity, empathy and respect. This augmented the women's confidence in each other as responsible and responsive auxiliary therapists, who would neither judge nor reject them, not least because residents soon realised that their apparently unique problems were, in fact, familiar to and understood by others: "We all have the same sort of issues, so the shame is taken away" (Belinda). This resonance of experience and resulting reassuring confirmation of 'universality' (Yalom, 1995) powerfully lessened residents' embarrassment, social isolation and loneliness; increased their understanding and acceptance of themselves and their self-diagnosed 'abnormality'; and helped them to access their repressed, and often little understood, emotions which, psychodynamic theory argues, unconsciously motivate dysfunctional and anti-social behaviour:

> 'I hadn't felt no feelings about things that had happened to me before but here, hearing other people's stories, just to know you're not the only one that's gone there or done that, it does help … Just hearing the other girls talk about things what they've been through, and their feelings about it, makes it easier for me to feel my feelings and get support with them feelings … Here, because we do go deep with each other, it makes for a different relationship. There's a lot more support and care for everyone and you know they ain't going to go around and chat your business, so you can trust them.' (Caroline)

Notably, there was comfort to be found in acknowledging the culturally endorsed shame that some women felt *as* women offenders. The 'doubly deviant' female offender has already failed to conform to the stereotypical norms of her gender, as well as having failed as a law-abiding citizen. When that offending related to the intimate and maternal relationships at which women are 'supposed' to excel, feelings of embarrassment and self-disgust were only exacerbated. This was particularly evident among women who had experienced loss or separation from their mothers (or other primary care-giver) in childhood and now had to accept that their actions and resulting imprisonment have caused them to lose their own children: the magnified "guilt and shame" of one who has "failed as a mum" (Adele).

Having been through "the same sort of issues" also made it easier for residents to work together, and under the guidance of the therapeutic staff, to understand what they 'mean': to draw on their experiential knowledge and pool their acquired therapeutic perceptiveness to be able to make sense of behaviours and incidents which previously had "made no sense at all" (Jenny). Typically, this included analysis of the origins of behaviours that were self-defeating or harmful; and making connections between pain that a resident had experienced, personally or vicariously, and pain she had inflicted, on herself or her victim. Psychodynamically, for example, the woman who murders her lover is psychically redirecting and physically re-enacting her unprocessed, denied and sublimated feelings (rage, disgust, fear) about previous experiences of trauma and victimisation; or 'acting out' her unconscious, internal fantasy world, in which she gains revenge upon the (actual or symbolic representation of the) person who caused that trauma and victimisation. Essentially, she remembers the trauma of abuse by repeating the trauma of abuse (Cordess and Williams, 1996; Welldon, 1988; Motz, 2008). As Louise explained:

> 'You make links from when you was a kid and then you can see how you went wrong. The things that was done to me as a kid has made me do what I've done today; you link it all up. See, I'm in for murder and I always thought, I done what I done and it's not linked to nothing, but when you go into it really deep with your group, you see that it is. Especially [another resident], me and her have been through similar things ... [and] she's helped me to see how everything is connected and leads to other things.'

As practitioners of psychotherapy and self-help movements have long appreciated, then, there is a cathartic process of healing to be experienced in sharing one's adverse and abusive experiences and 'shameful' problems among people who truly understand those experiences and problems. As 'helpees' and helpers, recipients and donors of support and advice and, in time, as proficient auxiliary therapists and respected role models and mentors to one's appreciative peers, residents deepened their understanding of their own and other's "issues" and gained a sense of competency, self-efficacy and intrinsic worth (Riessman, 1965; Yalom, 1995). This enhanced their self-esteem and provided reassuring and tangible evidence of their personal development, compelling them to reassess positively what qualities they possessed and of what they were, and of what they might be, capable. Moreover, and in accordance with attachment theory, the safe frame provided by the therapeutic milieu, and their communal experience of "serious therapy", offered the women the opportunity to establish and enjoy perhaps the first trusting, reliable, secure, and hence palliative, attachments of their adulthood, which positively challenged their expectations of themselves and of others, both in the TC and prospectively for the future.

## Becoming 'a better person'

'I'm getting to the root of my problems and making sure
that I won't be coming back to prison ... TC can work,
if you want it to. You're allowed to change in here, they
want you to change. I always knew there was someone
else underneath, not just the person who used drugs and
violence and got into trouble, but she got lost a long time
ago. And here, I've found her again. I've been able to let
go the woman I was, and go right back to find me again,
the real me.' (Louise)

Women's accounts of progression towards personal change can be
usefully framed theoretically by drawing on desistance research. This
literature seeks to understand and elucidate the events and processes
associated with the cessation of criminal activity. One, relatively
recent, aspect of desistance research has noted that people who give up
crime make subjective, purposive (re-)evaluations or 'cognitive shifts'
(Giordano et al, 2002) in the ways in which they conceptualise their
identity and life story.

This is not as fanciful as may first appear: all human beings actively
create and continuously recreate a conception of self, or identity, based
on the knitting together of 'the stories we live by' (McAdams, 1993)
and (metaphorically and literally) tell ourselves and others about who
we are. Of course, this 'storied self' (McAdams, 1996) has to account
for all the key episodes common to any life and reflect the observable
reality of the individual's present situation. Furthermore, the storyline
must be able to accommodate incidents, decisions or omissions which
were ill-fated, ill-judged or just plain indefensible; and this is frequently
achieved by, consciously or otherwise, applying a revisionist gloss,
which makes those missteps more tolerable to the narrator and, when
required to be retold, acceptable to her audience. The construction of
a narrative identity, which credibly and sequentially accounts for the
past, logically develops the plotline to the present, and into which one's
new or continuing image of self neatly 'fits', is therefore a situated and
ongoing accomplishment of the symbolic project of the self (Giddens,
1991; Elliott, 2001).

Two seminal studies are now frequently cited as evidence of how
such 're-authoring' benefits the would-be and actual former offender.
Shadd Maruna (2001) found that successful desisters most frequently
told a 'prototypical reform story' or 'redemption script'. The narrator
was able to plot a coherent, subjectively *and* objectively convincing,

route map from 'going wrong' to 'making good', which enabled her to distance herself progressively from the offender she was, to the non-offender she 'really' is now (or always 'really' was). In Peggy Giordano and colleagues' (2002) theory of 'cognitive transformation', the potential desister was someone who latched onto a 'hook for change', by which she could begin to envision and fashion 'an appealing and conventional "replacement self"' (Giordano et al, 2002: 1001). When sustained over time, she developed a 'cognitive blueprint' about 'how one is to proceed as a changed individual' (Giordano et al, 2002: 1035), which no longer cohered, cognitively or emotionally, with offending. In other words, and almost by default or as a fortuitous by-product of this alteration in one's sense of self, a return to offending became inherently incompatible with the preferred 'new me'. Additionally, and of particular relevance for the gendered aspect of the TC's work emphasised in this chapter, is Mary Eaton's (1993) study of women who transformed their lives after a period of imprisonment. She argued that women need 'redirection' (motivation), 'recognition' and 'reciprocal relationships' or mutuality in order to successfully desist: they need to feel that they are people of worth, who can change and contribute to society, and to have these changes recognised and confirmed in pro-social relationships.

In a similar vein, then, the TC can represent for serious offenders the necessary 'hook for change', and provide them with the beneficial 'reciprocal relationships' to assist with changing. Many of the residents in this study had been drawn to the TC in search of self-understanding and, even if only acknowledged retrospectively, self-forgiveness; a tangible need "to find out [about myself and my crime] and to grow and become more self-confident" (Theresa). Telling one's story in therapy enabled the resident to "find out" and come to understand her life in its entirety, "like a jigsaw puzzle, with all of these pieces on the table, and I've got to put them in, one by one, to make the full picture of my life" (Jenny). Elements of the life story that had seemed wholly unconnected, or had been deliberately 'split off', denied and compartmentalised, were now understood to be interlinked, so that "everything is connected and leads to other things": the inner conflicts and painful memories which the resident had been unable to tolerate, and her self-defeating cognitive maps and maladaptive patterns of attachment, had contributed to her descent into offending. To "make links" in this way did not excuse the offending, but by enabling it to be situated within, and hence contextualised by, the resident's life story, it allowed for both her offending and her life story to be more fully, and hence, accurately understood. For as Maruna's desisters had discovered, beginning to understand, and hence to be able to explain to oneself and others, how one "went wrong" is the essential precursor to beginning to 'go right' in the future.

Moreover, by embedding a culture of reciprocal disclosure and advice, and emboldened by the sacrosanct promise of confidentiality within the TC, the community provided the setting within which to share one's problems, gain the social support to address them, and to explore and regulate one's emotional response to those problems. In so doing, it emerged that no matter how unique or 'embarrassing' one's problems seemed, they were in fact known to and understood by others. This lessened the sense of incorrigible, intractable 'deviancy' that some women had internalised; and helped to instil the therapeutically important experience of hope (Yalom, 1995), notably by the inspirational example of senior residents: "I say to the new girls, if *I* can change, so can they!" (Belinda). Positive changes were approvingly noticed and endorsed by other community members, further enhancing the resident's self-esteem and (self-)perceived capacity for personal agency and self-efficacy.

Combined with other contributory factors in 'the TC way' of offender rehabilitation (Stevens, 2013), the result was that the women came to discern in themselves the emergence of a 'replacement self' and to formulate for themselves a 'redemption script'. This could take the form of the creation of an entirely 'new me': someone "*completely* changed" (Belinda) from who they were, and for whom the past was no longer relevant to their present and future ideal self. Alternatively, it could take the form of a more subtle emergence of "the me that I always wanted to be, but was never allowed to be" (Natalie), or re-emergence of "the real me" who had "got lost a long time ago" (Louise). The women gained new insights, practised new ways of being and relating, and forged new expectations of themselves and of others – more positive, more expansive – which directly enhanced their self-esteem. These accounts of personal change, reflected in and reinforced by their changed ways of thinking about themselves, their experiences, and how they related to others, therefore revealed residents' agentic negotiation of a new image of self, and the scripting of a more adaptive self-narrative, in which both were more closely aligned to the achievement of pro-social goals and values including, ultimately, long-term desistance from crime.

## Concluding comments

> 'This is serious therapy. It does my head in! It really does, it's *such* hard work. But it's good … I really wish I had done this years ago; maybe I wouldn't be here now if I had. And, you know, there's lots of girls in the system who could do with this, who would benefit from it. Because here, you can change, you really can.' (Natalie)

As Baroness Corston (2007: 5) recognised, 'it is demanding a great deal of women to delve into issues they prefer to block out'. To misinformed outsiders, the prison-based TC, with its caring and compassionate ethos and 'residents' who seem primarily concerned with pursuing self-understanding and the possibilities of personal change, may appear to be a 'soft' option. Yet, "TC is the hardest way you can do prison" (Belinda) *because* it requires the pursuit of self-understanding and exposes the possibilities of personal change. The democratic therapeutic community at HMP Send represents precisely the kind of small, custodial unit that Corston envisaged, for the minority of women offenders from whom the public requires protection, and promotes precisely the kind of holistic 'woman-centred' approach to rehabilitation that Corston advocated. It allows women with similar "issues" and a similar desire "to grow", to come together and share, often for the first time and in confidence, the traumatic experiences which have burdened them for so long, and fundamentally warped their sense of worth. Within the 'secure base' (Bowlby, 1988) of the TC, the outcome can be a truly transformative, 'corrective emotional experience' (Yalom, 1995: 24), which enables the resident to "feel better about myself" and, not unconnectedly, to progress towards becoming "a better person". As appreciation of the work of Send TC grows, and if its potential for expansion is realised, it is therefore to be hoped that more serious female offenders will be able to profit from undertaking "serious therapy".

### Notes
[1] North American readers will be more familiar with TCs that are described as 'hierarchical', 'concept' or 'addictions', in which the primary focus of treatment is substance abuse. This chapter discusses only the 'democratic' model, for personality and attachment disordered offenders.

[2] Of 16 women residing in the TC at the time of the fieldwork (2007), 10 volunteered to be interviewed, together with one therapist and two prison officers. The average duration of residents' TC experience at the

time of interview was 12 months. With their consent, interviewees were tape-recorded to ensure accuracy of quotation; and pseudonyms have been applied to preserve participants' anonymity. The fieldnotes and interview transcripts were analysed using a grounded theory approach.

[3] The women habitually referred to each other as 'girls'. As Owen (1998: 38) notes, 'girl' may sound inappropriate to 'free world' or feminist ears but, in prisons, 'seems to carry little negative connotation'.

## References

Adshead, G. (2004) Three degrees of security: Attachment and forensic institutions, in F. Pfäfflin and G. Adshead (eds) *A matter of security: The application of attachment theory to forensic psychiatry and psychotherapy*, London: Jessica Kingsley, 147-66.

Bateman, A., Brown, D. and Pedder, J. (2010) *Introduction to psychotherapy: An outline of psychodynamic principles and practice* (4th edn), London: Routledge.

Becker, S. and McCorkel, J. (2011) The gender of criminal opportunity: The impact of male co-offenders on women's crime, *Feminist Criminology*, 6 (2): 79–110.

Bowlby, J. (1988) *A secure base: Clinical applications of attachment theory*, London: Routledge.

Brown, J., Miller, S., Northey, S. and O'Neill, D. (2014) *What works in therapeutic prisons: Evaluating psychological change in Dovegate Therapeutic Community*, Basingstoke: Palgrave Macmillan.

Cordess, C. and Williams, A. H. (1996) The criminal act and acting out, in C. Cordess and M. Cox (eds) *Forensic psychotherapy: Crime, psychodynamics and the offender patient*, London: Jessica Kingsley, 13-21.

Corston, J. (2007) *A Report by Baroness Jean Corston of a Review of Women with Particular Vulnerabilities in the Criminal Justice System*, London: Home Office.

de Zulueta, F. (1993) *From pain to violence: The traumatic roots of destructiveness*, London: Whurr Publishers.

Eaton, M. (1993) *Women after prison*, Buckingham: Open University Press.

Elliott, A. (2001) *Concepts of the self*, Cambridge: Polity Press.

Fonagy, P. (2004) The developmental roots of violence in the failure of mentalization, in F. Pfäfflin and G. Adshead (eds) *A matter of security: The application of attachment theory to forensic psychiatry and psychotherapy*, London: Jessica Kingsley, 13-56.

Genders, E. and Player, E. (1995) *Grendon: A study of a therapeutic prison*, Oxford: Clarendon Press.

Giddens, A. (1991) *Modernity and self-identity: Self and society in the Late Modern Age*, Stanford, CA: Stanford University Press.

Giordano, P., Cernkovich, S. and Rudolph, J. (2002) Gender, crime and desistance: Toward a theory of cognitive transformation, *American Journal of Sociology*, 107 (4): 990-1064.

Haigh, R. (1999) The quintessence of a therapeutic community: Five universal qualities, in P. Campling and R. Haigh (eds) *Therapeutic communities: Past, present, and future*, London: Jessica Kingsley, 246-57.

HM Chief Inspector of Prisons (2006) *Report on an announced inspection of HMP Send, 13-17 February 2006*, London: HM Inspectorate of Prisons.

HM Chief Inspector of Prisons (2008) *Report on an unannounced short follow-up inspection of HMP Send, 18-22 August 2008*, London: HM Inspectorate of Prisons.

HM Chief Inspector of Prisons (2010) *Report on an announced inspection of HMP Send, 6-10 December 2010*, London: HM Inspectorate of Prisons.

HM Chief Inspector of Prisons (2014) *Report on an unannounced inspection of HMP Send, 3-14 February 2014*, London: HM Inspectorate of Prisons.

Hollin, C. and Palmer, E. (2006) Criminogenic need and women offenders: A critique of the literature, *Legal and Criminological Psychology*, 11 (2): 179-95.

Jones, M. (1968) *Social psychiatry in practice: The idea of the therapeutic community*, Harmondsworth: Penguin.

Jones, S. (2008) Partners in crime: A study of the relationship between female offenders and their co-defendants, *Criminology and Criminal Justice*, 8 (2): 147-64.

Kennedy, H. (1998) *Women's therapeutic community feasibility study*, London: Prison Service's Women's Policy Group.

Maden, T., Swinton, M. and Gunn, J. (1994) Therapeutic community treatment: A survey of unmet need among sentenced prisoners, *Therapeutic Communities*, 15 (4): 229-36.

Main, T. (1946) The hospital as a therapeutic institution, *Bulletin of the Menninger Clinic*, 10: 66-8.

Manor, O. (1994) Group psychotherapy, in P. Clarkson and M. Pokorny (eds) *The Handbook of psychotherapy*, London and NY: Routledge, 249-64.

Maruna, S. (2001) *Making good: How ex-convicts reform and rebuild their lives*, Washington, DC: American Psychological Association.

McAdams, D. (1993) *The stories we live by: Personal myths and the making of the self*, NY and London: Guilford.

McAdams, D. (1996) Personality, modernity, and the storied self: A contemporary framework for studying persons, *Psychological Inquiry*, 7 (4): 295-321.

Ministry of Justice (2014a) *Statistics on women and the criminal justice system 2013,* London: MoJ.

Ministry of Justice (2014b) *Offender management annual tables 2013: Receptions 2013*, London: MoJ.

Morris, M. (2004) *Dangerous and severe – Process, programme and person: Grendon's work*, London: Jessica Kingsley.

Motz, A. (2008) *The psychology of female violence: Crimes against the body* (2nd edn), Hove: Routledge.

NOMS/NHS England (2014) *Brochure of women offender personality disorder services*, London: NOMS/NHS England.

Owen, B. (1998) *'In the mix': Struggle and survival in a women's prison,* Albany, NY: State University of New York Press.

Rapoport, R. (1960) *Community as doctor: New perspectives on a therapeutic community*, London: Tavistock Publications.

Riessman, F. (1965) The helper therapy principle, *Social Work*, 10 (2): 27-32.

Shine, J. and Newton, M. (2000) Damaged, disturbed and dangerous: A profile of receptions to Grendon therapeutic prison 1995-2000, in J. Shine (ed.) *A compilation of Grendon research*, Grendon Underwood: HMP Grendon, 23-35.

Snell, H. (1962) H. M. Prison, Grendon, *British Medical Journal*, 2 (5307): 789-92.

Stevens, A. (2013) *Offender rehabilitation and therapeutic communities: Enabling change the TC way*, Abingdon: Routledge.

Stewart, C. and Parker, M. (2007) Send: The women's democratic therapeutic community in prison, in M. Parker (ed.) *Dynamic security: The democratic therapeutic community in prison*, London: Jessica Kingsley, 69-82.

Swan, S. and Snow, D. (2002) A typology of women's use of violence in intimate relationships, *Violence Against Women*, 8 (3): 286-319.

Welldon, E. (1988) *Mother, madonna, whore: The idealization and denigration of motherhood*, London: Free Association Books.

Yalom, I. (1995) *The theory and practice of group psychotherapy* (4th edn), NY: Basic Books.

# Part Three
## Towards best practice

# ELEVEN

# Breaking the cycle for women through equality not difference

*Martina Feilzer and Kate Williams*

## Women first, offenders second?

There has been a growing reform movement to reduce the imprisonment of women in England and Wales. Concern over the treatment of women in prison goes back at least to the days of Elizabeth Fry's visits to Newgate in the early 19th century, but recently there has been a sustained and vocal reassessment of the punishment of women; and an increasing concern about the punitive way in which female offenders were being treated (Fawcett Society, 2004). As a result, the Women's Offending Reduction Programme was launched by the government in 2004 to tackle women's offending and to reduce the number of women in prison. Concerned about the rise in female incarceration, the government ordered a review of female offenders in the criminal justice system. Baroness Corston's resulting 2007 report concluded:

> ... it is timely to bring about a radical change in the way we treat women throughout the whole of the criminal justice system. ... This will require a radical new approach, treating women both holistically and individually – a woman-centred approach. (Corston, 2007)

The Corston Report, along with many others (such as Fawcett, 2004 and 2009) seemed to confirm what some researchers already claimed: that women were incarcerated for lesser offences than men and earlier in their offending careers and that, since 1990, the situation had been getting steadily worse. Thus, the most recent call for reform goes beyond adjusting how sentences are delivered, both in the community and in prison, to the use of a particular sentence and its abolition – imprisonment.

In 2012, the Prison Reform Trust published a three-year strategy to reduce the imprisonment of women in the UK (Prison Reform Trust, 2012a) and, in June 2014, again called for a reduction in women's imprisonment (Prison Reform Trust, 2014). In Scotland, similar calls were made (Burman, 2012; Scottish Commission, 2012), and Clinks published a similar message calling for a gender-responsive approach to sentencing (Clinks, 2012). The Howard League for Penal Reform has worked since the 1990s to reform penal policy for women, and in June 2014 its Chief Executive, Frances Crook, called for the abolition of imprisonment for female offenders (Crook, 2014). She summarised the main arguments for treating women differently from men when it comes to sentencing as: women's offending is different; women are more often primary carers of children or other family members, and thus their imprisonment is disruptive and damaging for family cohesion and child development; and women respond differently to imprisonment. Crook acknowledges that this selective abolitionism could be discriminatory, but sees it as a first step towards 'doing pretty much the same thing for men' (Crook, 2014).

The call for the reduction and eventual abolition of women's imprisonment is not restricted to reform groups alone. In the early years of the 21st century, the then Labour government was alerted to the problem of women in the penal system when the proportion of women in prisons peaked at 6% of the prison population in 2002 (Berman, 2011: 5; Fawcett Society, 2004). The Labour government invested in the Women's Offending Reduction Programme (Home Office, 2004; see also Government Action to Reduce Women's Offending, 2004) and ordered Baroness Corston's review of the treatment of female offenders in the criminal justice system (Gelsthorpe and Morris, 2002; Deakin and Spencer, 2003; Hedderman, 2004). In response, Corston concluded that, for women, prison should only be used when necessary to deal with serious and dangerous offenders (Corston, 2007).

From this discussion, it would appear as if all researchers agree that women are disadvantaged at the sentencing stage, but this is not the case. At least two views of the treatment of women dominate in relation to the criminal justice system. One, based on feminism, decries the treatment of women in the criminal justice system as harsher than that of men. It is suggested that female offenders are seen by the courts as doubly deviant, deviating from both social norms stipulated in criminal law and from their 'appropriate' gender roles (Heidensohn and Silvestri, 2012: 351). The other view, often based on classical positivist views of female crime, suggests that police and courts treat women more leniently than men due to male chivalry, and that lower rates of offending in official statistics reflect this differential treatment (Pollak, 1950). Evidence on whether women are treated more leniently or more harshly at the sentencing stage is contested and subject to significant debate (for a discussion and overview, see Heidensohn and Silvestri, 2012: 350-53; and Easton and Piper, 2012: 307-9). The purpose of this chapter is not to enter this debate, but rather to explore the merit of the argument that women should be treated differently from men.

In discussions of whether or not women should be treated differently within the criminal justice system, two issues seem to be conflated. First, whether gender should influence the decision of which sentence is imposed by magistrates' courts and Crown Courts; this discussion forms the core of the present chapter. Second, once a sentence has been imposed, the administration and delivery of that sentence needs to be sensitive to gender-specific as well as cultural and health-related needs, and this includes the administration of community programmes as well as imprisonment. This is where Corston (2007) placed most of her argument:

> I have concluded that there needs to be a fundamental re-thinking about the way in which services for this group of vulnerable women, particularly for mental health and substance misuse in the community are provided and accessed; there needs to be an extension of the network of women's community centres to support women who offend or are at risk of offending and to direct young women out of pathways that lead into crime. (Corston, 2007: 2)

The difference in administration and delivery of sentences may be acceptable depending on one's concept of equality. The legal duty to respect equality arises out of the Equality Act 2006, which requires all public authorities to respect gender equality. This legislation allows assessment on both equality of treatment and equality of outcomes, so equality does not necessarily mean identical treatment. Therefore, different treatment of women from men in the delivery of a sentence is acceptable; some even argue that it is required, if it delivers a more equal outcome.

It is this shift in official approaches to equality – linked to official, practitioner and academic expressions of concern about the paucity of criminal justice policy in relation to female offenders – that opened the door to permitting consideration of the distinct needs of female offenders, and to a radical rethink of the way in which women should be treated in the criminal justice system. Therefore, differences in the administration of sentences – and in the provision of services which respond to gender-specific needs – are now regarded as appropriate and have been introduced. Sentences are imposed following gender-neutral consideration, so the overall punishment is equal; it is merely delivered or administered differently, for example through the use of different interventions. We accept this difference as just and fair, but question which, if any, gender differences justify differential treatment taking the form of different sentences at the sentencing stage. Would equality of outcome permit a form of distributive justice to be applied that permits gender-specific levels of punishment? Before answering this, it is necessary to test some of the arguments in support of differential treatment.

## Why treat women differently: theoretical positions

The debate surrounding the treatment of female offenders is not new and a number of theories have been proposed to justify differential treatment, some of these theoretical positions are considered below.

### Classical views of female crime

Biological determinism influenced the earliest discussion of causes of crime. Even Lombroso, often termed the 'Father' of criminology, devoted significant research effort in trying to establish the atavistic features of female offenders as biologically, intellectually and morally inferior to men. Lombroso explained that, despite atavistic features, women's lower levels of female criminality were explained by their maternal and compassionate characteristics, which prevent them from following their more primitive instincts (extract from Lombroso and Ferrero, 1893 in Rafter, 2009: 174). Lombroso compared women with children, a comparison still relevant in today's debates, and called for the treatment of their 'sickness' rather than punishment (Burke, 2005: 126). Generally this has not been officially used in sentencing, although there is one gender-specific defence in England and Wales: infanticide (a partial defence to murder available only to mothers who kill their children within one year of birth as a result of post-natal depression, Infanticide Act 1922).

Although coming from a different perspective, some other early work on female crime highlighted the need to consider alternatives to traditional forms of punishment, and proposed a greater focus on the environmental conditions in women's lives. In 1889, Tarnowsky, a female anthropologist who focused on prostitution, called for an improvement in women's lives, in particular providing access to employment, which would allow them to escape their miserable conditions as well as the 'bad advisors who counsel debauchery and vice' (extract from Tarnowsky, 1889 in Rafter, 2009: 181). This argument is also used in contemporary debates on women's crime, namely that women are pushed into crime by men, often partners (for example Prison Reform Trust, 2012a; Jones, 2008).

Many early 20th-century theorists equated sexual deviance and prostitution with criminal behaviour, and while psychologists moved on from a purely biological and physiological view of criminal behaviour, their view of causes of female crime was no more flattering. Female offenders were regarded as poorly socialised into their appropriate gender roles, suffering from penis envy, or were neurotic or insane (Burke, 2005: 125-6).

Each of these positions invests women as less worthy and rational than men, and many wanted that to be addressed in sentencing. Happily, these positions were never officially incorporated into sentencing policy, although they may be used informally by sentencers (Heidensohn and Silvestri, 2012: 351).

## Feminist perspectives

Apart from these early accounts of women as fundamentally 'bad or mad', there was relative silence about female offenders in the early parts of the 20th century. Women made up a small proportion of offenders, and the focus of research and interest was on the causes and responses to male offending. The theories developed for understanding (male) criminal activity not only neglected to take account of women and women's offending but, importantly, the differences in patterns and frequency of offending between men and women (Heidensohn and Silvestri, 2012: 336-7). In the 1960s, this began to change, and criminologists explored female offending and offenders, building up knowledge of crime patterns, responses to female crime, and sentencing patterns. Theories centred on notions of female conformity to social norms, including criminal law, which emerged to explain the gender gap (Heidensohn and Silvestri, 2012: 344). Some suggested that once women were liberated from male and structural oppression, this gap would close (see Adler, 1975; Simon, 1975) but others disagreed (see Smart, 1979; Box and Hale, 1983).

Criminologists also began to look at how women were treated in the criminal justice system, and some of the work was based on assumptions that the criminal justice system served to further oppress women (for example Fawcett Society, 2004 and 2009; Corston, 2007; Women in Prison, 2011; James-Hanman, 2014). Research on the differential treatment in criminal justice experienced by women and by members of minority ethnic groups has greatly enhanced our understanding of criminal justice, sentencing processes and the effects of penal interventions. It is from this new understanding that many of the calls for different treatment of women arise.

## Equality

Different notions of equality were briefly discussed earlier. In some, differential treatment, or positive discrimination/action in relation to minority groups is argued to be acceptable, in order to compensate for existing structural inequalities that disadvantage particular groups disproportionately. Recently, this thinking has become more acceptable, and some argue that it should be applied to women in the criminal justice system.

The UK government has signed up to the United Nations Rules for the Treatment of Women Prisoners and Non-Custodial Measures for Women Offenders, which in the main deal with the administration of sentencing and the gender-sensitive provision of services in prison. However, the UN rules go further, in suggesting that member states should develop gender-specific diversionary measures and alternatives to custody, 'taking account of the history of victimisation of many women and their caretaking responsibilities' (UN, 2010, Rule 57). This approach suggests support for the idea that sentences should 'be calculated in an effort to counteract discriminatory forces that are known to operate more widely' leading to 'positive discrimination' (Ashworth, 2010: 240). In relation to its application to the sentencing of women, Player (2014: 280) refers to this as a form of distributive justice, which draws on Rawls' principle of allowing differential treatment of differently situated groups in order to improve 'the life prospects of the least advantaged' (Rawls was a moral philosopher who wrote one of the most famous tracts on the principles of justice, see Rawls, 1971). However, as Ashworth (2010: 248) argues, there remains a debate as to whether women should be sentenced on the 'same principles as men, or whether there should be special principles applicable to women'.

Arguing that women need to be sentenced differently runs the risk of pathologising their offending behaviour. So, while regarding male offenders as rational, rights-bearing citizens who should be treated as such by the criminal justice system, women might not be given the same status. It is unlikely that the modern, often feminist, proponents of changing the sentencing for women would want women's rationality questioned.

Currently, sentencing guidelines would not support different sentencing principles dependent on gender. These guidelines are designed to ensure equality and consistency in sentencing decisions. In England and Wales, sentencing is based on proportionality – since 1991 the core of decision making in sentencing is that the punishment should be proportionate to the seriousness of the crime (in terms of harm and culpability), and the punishment should be no more than required by the elements of the offence. Therefore, to argue for different punishment for women, one needs to claim that:

- the offences women commit are less serious – in most cases, this is true and therefore this position assumes that women are presently more harshly punished than are men (for similar crimes); equality principles require that sentencing be altered (a correction in the way sentences are imposed on women to bring them in line with men), so that men and women are treated equally according to the proportionality principle; or
- women are less culpable – this reaches back to the 19th- and early 20th-century theories suggesting that women are, by nature or intellect, less able to understand or control their actions and therefore possibly less culpable; it seems unlikely that the recent calls for different treatment are willing to accept this idea, although many seem to drift this way; or
- sentencing considerations and guidelines, especially those relating to personal mitigating factors, are either incorrect or incorrectly applied – either seriousness is being too harshly assessed or sentences are not being reduced when they should be (see the later discussion concerning, for example, primary carers).

None of these would assume a blanket differential treatment from men. Equality before the law is a fundamental principle of the criminal justice system in England and Wales. In some respects, this equality may clash with differential treatments of groups of citizens to remedy existing structural inequalities (Ashworth, 2010: 255; Easton and Piper, 2012: 300) although, as seen earlier, difference may be necessary to guarantee equality of outcome. How far deviation from the principle of equality before the law is justifiable is the crux.

## Are female offenders different?

One of the fundamental assumptions underpinning the argument for abolition of imprisonment for women is that female offenders are different from male offenders in important respects. The Prison Reform Trust's 2014 briefing sets out a compelling list of differences between male and female prisoners (see also Clinks, 2014; Crook, 2014; Prison Reform Trust, 2012a; Burman, 2012; and the Scottish Commission, 2012).

Our approach to the question of difference is to ask whether differences in offending patterns, previous experiences of victimisation, levels of coercion, and so on, would routinely be taken into account, for example, as mitigation when passing sentence in the courts. If this is the case, then gender should not be important, as sentencing would routinely respond to such factors and thus be sensitive to gender difference. However, if such factors are not routinely taken into account in sentencing, the question is whether they should be and on what theoretical basis, for both men and women or only for women, considering the evidence of gender differences.

To some extent, the answer to this depends on the penal theory employed, but in England and Wales sentencing is guided by the statutory sentencing rationales as listed in ss. 142 and 143 of the Criminal Justice Act 2003. In deciding on the appropriate sentence, s. 142 requires sentencers to '... start by considering the seriousness of the offence' and have regard to five purposes of sentencing: punishment; reduction of crime; reform and rehabilitation; protection of the public; and the making of reparation. In 2004, the Sentencing Guidelines Council stipulated that seriousness was a fundamental principle of sentencing: 'the seriousness of an individual offence should be judged on its own dimensions of harm and culpability' (Sentencing Guidelines Council, 2004: 9). The proportionality principle is mediated by consideration of aggravating and mitigating circumstances, which can relate to the harmfulness of the offence or the culpability of the offender (Ashworth, 2010: 168). Jacobson and Hough (2007: 15) list four broad factors of personal mitigation that they found were used by sentencers: the wider circumstances of the offender at the time of the offence; the response of the offender to the offence; the offender's past; issues in the offender's present and future life. Generally, personal factors are considered for each individual rather than for a group or category such as 'all women'. Consideration for personal mitigation is also given to factors that fall 'just outside criminal law defences such as insanity, duress, necessity or mistake of law' (Ashworth, 2010:

169). With these general sentencing principles in mind, we turn to the arguments made for treating women differently.

## Gender differences in offending

There is no doubt that official crime statistics, as well as statistics based on self-reported offending, provide evidence of significant differences in patterns of offending between men and women. Women make up only a small proportion of known offenders (about 20%) and an even smaller proportion of serious offenders (between 5% and 12%) (Home Office, 2006 and 2009). Female offenders start offending at an early age but also desist from offending earlier than male offenders (Fawcett Society, 2004 and 2009). As a result, on average, they accumulate fewer convictions than men (Carlen and Worrall, 2004).

The 2012 statistics on adult females in the criminal justice system, suggest that in 2010/11, about a third of arrests of women were for violence against the person (34%), the same proportion as males arrested (33%). The main difference was in the proportion of thefts: 30% of all arrests of women were for theft, whereas this accounted for only 20% of male arrests (Ministry of Justice (MoJ), 2012a: 42). In terms of sentencing, out of all the sentences imposed in both magistrates' courts and Crown Courts in 2011, a higher proportion of women (77%) than men (61%) received a fine; a lower proportion of women (10%) than men (15%) received a community sentence; and a significantly lower proportion of women (3%) than men (10%) were sentenced to immediate custody (MoJ, 2012a: 57). The differences in disposals are largely a result of:

- differences in the types of offences coming before the court – women tended to face less serious charges (MoJ, 2012a: 13);
- differences in the extent of previous criminal record – more women (15%) than men (9%) sentenced for indictable offences had no previous cautions or convictions; more men (32%) than women (25%) had 15 or more previous convictions (MoJ, 2012a: 69).

A clean slate used to be a mitigating factor in sentencing. Now a criminal record is a factor that increases culpability and so seriousness of the crime (this has the effect of an aggravating factor, but it is hidden in the decision-making in that it is not specifically referred to as an aggravating factor). This change may well have negatively affected women as their prior 'good' behaviour no longer reduces their sentence (see Sentencing Guidelines Council, 2004: 6). The change in sentencing guidelines might be seen as indirect discrimination, as it has a greater negative impact on women than on men.

Ashworth (2010: 246) notes that courts respond differently to female offending, regarding female offenders as 'troubled' rather than 'troublesome' because their offending is less serious or their criminal record less troubling. However, there may be cases where women are differently sentenced because of their sex, but it is unclear whether this results in harsher sentencing (because they breach both legal and societal norms) or more lenient sentencing (because, by nature, women are thought to be less threatening).

Conversely, what reformers call for is different sentencing for women, regardless of the offence. However, the same outcome, fewer women in prison, could be achieved if the sentencing guidelines or concepts of seriousness were altered for everyone – men and women – for example, if property offences were non-custodial (Ashworth, 2013: 10). In 2012, this would have affected sentences for 21% of female prisoners and 8% of male prisoners. Furthermore, reinstating no previous convictions as a mitigating factor would serve to lower both men's and women's sentences, although the impact would be greater on women as more have a 'clean slate' (in 2011, some 26% of female prisoners had no previous convictions compared to 12% of male prisoners (Prison Reform Trust, 2012b: 1)). Each of these measures would be non-discriminatory, improving sentencing decisions for both men and women, but would have a greater impact on women.

## Women offenders as victims of crime

Reference is often made to research establishing significant levels of victimisation among female offenders, including sexual, physical and psychological abuse. Official statistics on the extent of victimisation of the general population paints a complex picture in relation to gender.

While a higher proportion of men (4% of adult males) than women (2% of adult females) report being victims of violence, more women (7% of women responding to a self-completion module on intimate violence in the Crime Survey for England and Wales 2011/12) than men (5%) report being victims of intimate violence. Gender differences become more marked when including all experiences since age 16 (31% of women report intimate violence compared to 18% of men). Sexual assaults are reported more frequently by women (3%) than men (0.3%) in the self-completion module (MoJ, 2012a: 18-22). However, when it comes to the most serious violence in the form or manslaughter and murder, there are fewer female victims (32% in 2010/11) than male victims (68%). Women are more likely to be killed by someone they know (78% of women killed were killed by a partner or acquaintance, compared to 57% of males), and among those who knew their 'killer' most commonly by a partner or ex-partner (60% of women compared to 8% of males).

It is more difficult to estimate victimisation levels among offenders, but there is established evidence of a significant overlap between offender and victim populations (Roe and Ashe, 2008: 29). As far as direct comparisons of levels of victimisation among female and male offenders are concerned, Williams et al (2012) shed some light on previous experiences of prisoners participating in the Surveying Prisoner Crime Reduction cohort study. They found extensive levels of previous victimisation among prisoners, especially female prisoners: 53% of women in prison suffered abuse as children (including emotional, physical and sexual abuse) compared to 27% of men. Two thirds (67%) of women who reported experiencing such abuse had suffered sexual abuse compared to 24% of men (Williams et al, 2012: 9).

If victimisation were recognised as a mitigating circumstance, it would reduce sentences for more women than men and so not taking account of victimisation may be seen as discriminatory in its outcome. It might, therefore, be argued that rules should be designed so that previous victimisation can be taken into account in decisions about the amount of punishment an individual should receive. However, at the moment, previous victimisation is not regarded as a mitigating factor unless it is immediate and leading up to the crime, for example issues of self-defence. This is probably the correct approach, as any consideration of victimisation would raise questions about how far back to look, which types of victimisation would be relevant, and why this should be considered in sentencing an offender for an offence. Until these concerns are resolved, victimisation might be more relevant in decisions as to types of intervention than to type of disposal or severity of punishment (for both men and women).

## Women offenders as primary carers

The effect of the sentence on the offender and on others, including the offender's dependants, is considered a factor that can be used as personal mitigation (Ashworth, 2010: 183; Easton and Piper, 2012: 205). In 2011, in its guidelines on common assault, the Sentencing Council recognised that being a sole or primary carer for dependent relatives should be a gender-neutral factor reducing seriousness or affecting personal mitigation. However, judges have been reluctant to make allowances for caring responsibilities, as it deviates from the principle of proportionality and so, although it is sometimes used, this is not common (Jacobson and Hough, 2007: 13). Ashworth (2010: 187) calls for this issue to be resolved by policy makers. Adherence to the guidelines would improve sentencing decisions for both sexes, although as many more women are primary carers, the impact on their sentencing would be greater: in 2003, for example, some 33% of female prisoners (and only 5% of male prisoners) were primary carers (Prison Reform Trust, 2014: fn 34). Imprisoning primary carers has a detrimental impact on: the carers themselves – being separated from their children (dependants), their chances of rehabilitation, their psychological wellbeing and their mental health; and the dependants – when a carer is imprisoned.

Stewart (2008: 9) found that similar proportions of male and female prisoners had children under the age of 18 (just over half) and had lived with at least one child (just over a third), and lone parents made up 6% of prisoners surveyed (Stewart, 2008: 9). The Prison Reform Trust's briefing (2014: 5) suggests that a third of mothers were lone parents before imprisonment. Easton and Piper (2012: 302) confirm the distinct effect that maternal imprisonment has on the welfare of dependent children: a significant proportion end up in care (in 2010, some 17,000 children were separated from their mothers due to imprisonment (Prison Reform Trust, 2014: fn 34)).

Clearly, the imprisonment of either parent – mother or father – has a significant detrimental impact on dependent children, and imprisonment of the primary carer has the most severe impact. All children have a right to the best care and life chances possible (United Nations Convention on the Rights of the Child, 1989), so imprisonment of primary carers should only be used where absolutely necessary. Therefore, sentencers should be required to mitigate the sentence for primary carers – male or female. If this were done, it is likely that female imprisonment would be substantially reduced.

### Women suffer from addictions and health problems

Light et al (2013: 3) discovered both that rates of illegal drug use are far higher among prisoners (male and female) than either the general population or offenders sentenced to community sentences, and that levels of alcohol consumption (even hazardous drinking levels) among prisoners did not differ by gender. However, women are more likely than men (50% versus 29%) to report needing help with a drug (or alcohol) problem, and to associate substance misuse with their offending

(Light et al, 2013). The Corston Report found that 70% of women but only 50% of men needed clinical detoxification on arrival in prison (Corston, 2007).

Female prisoners were far more likely to be suffering from anxiety or depression (female 61% and 65% respectively; male 33% and 37%), although again the largest difference was between prisoners and those in the general population. Physical health problems seem to afflict both sexes equally (Light et al, 2013: 4 and 29).

Clearly, both male and female offenders misuse substances, although the effects may be more acute for women who are imprisoned. They also both suffer greater health problems (including mental health problems) than the general population. Both substance misuse and mental health problems are also associated with reoffending, so they need to be addressed. Sentencers should ensure proper treatment through required interventions for both men and women. This might take precedence over punishment, certainly in offences that do not involve violence. Interventions should be focused, depending on the needs of the offender (this might require gender differences to be taken into account in delivery of the intervention), but the overarching way in which it would impact on the sentence would be similar for men and women.

## Women respond differently to punishment

Another key argument in the campaigns to reduce or abolish women's imprisonment is that women seem to respond differently and more adversely to imprisonment than men, or they are more severely affected by punishment (Fawcett Society, 2004 and 2009; Corston, 2007; Burman, 2012; Clinks, 2014; Prison Reform Trust, 2012a and 2014; Scottish Commission, 2012). As there are fewer women's prisons, women are more likely to be held far away from home and, as a result, are more likely than men to lose contact with their families (Prison Reform Trust, 2014: 5-6).

There are important differences in terms of sentences served as well as some demographics. In 2011 a greater proportion of women (21%) than men (10%) in prison were serving short-term sentences of 12 months or less; a greater proportion of women (13%) than men (6%) were serving a prison sentence for theft and handling; and a greater proportion of women (21%) than men (15%) were serving a short prison sentence for drug offences; and women in prison are, on average, older than men (MoJ, 2012a: 84-90). Rates of reoffending one year after a criminal justice disposal also differed for women and men, with men having a greater rate of reoffending in the one-year follow-up of 29%, compared to 19% proven reoffending among women (MoJ, 2012a: 92). Compliance with community sentences and suspended prison sentences was higher for women (70% completed a community sentence and 74% a suspended sentence order) than for men (65% completed a community sentence and 66% a suspended sentence order) (MoJ, 2012a: 94).

In the sentencing process, there are a number of points at which sentencers can consider the impact of the sentence imposed. The potential impact of the sentence on the offender can be regarded as grounds for personal mitigation (Jacobson and Hough, 2007: x, 11, 34), although it is not often used. Additionally, whether the purpose of sentencing (as set out in s.142 Criminal Justice Act 2003) can be achieved should be considered in light of the impact on the offender. In terms of the chances of rehabilitation, for example, the courts should weigh up the adverse impact of a prison sentence, such as the loss of employment, housing, and so on, with the potential of access to rehabilitation schemes. Again, whether the purpose of a sentence such as rehabilitation can be achieved is not often considered. What many  proponents of different sentencing for women assume, though do not rigorously debate, is that the greater impact suffered by women should necessarily reduce the use of prison, otherwise there is inequality of impact of punishment. To implement this, there are possible reasons to intervene. Women are different in nature, such that punishment necessarily affects them more severely; this would require different treatment in order to deliver an equal outcome. Many women's social standing and place in society means that they are likely to be more severely affected by punishment, particularly imprisonment. If women are more severely affected by punishment then, to guarantee equality of outcome (equal suffering therefore equal punishment), there needs to be disparity in sentencing (probably not justified) or there need to be different rules to ensure that the correct outcome is achieved (equal punishment for both men and women for similar crimes). This last would not be discriminatory and might be achieved by application of the possible ways in which impact of punishment can be taken into consideration in present rules and/or clearer guidelines for men and women.

### Imprisonment: self-harm and mental health problems

Concerns have been raised about women's ability to cope with imprisonment in relation to compliance with prison discipline and rates of self-harm and suicide. A limited indication of problematic behaviour in prisons is the rate at which inmates are punished for offences against prison discipline, which includes disobedience as well as assault against other inmates or staff. In 2011 rates of offences punished within prisons were higher for women (130 offences punished per 100 female prisoners) than men (106 offences punished per 100 male prisoners), but assault rates were slightly lower for women (167 per 1,000 prisoners) than men (180 per 1,000 prisoners) (MoJ, 2012a: 94-100). Rates of self-harm have fallen for female prisoners, but they are still almost 10 times higher than for male offenders – the rate of self-harm incidents was 1,750 per 1,000 female prisoners and 194 per 1,000 male prisoners in 2012 (MoJ, 2012b: 6); and in 2011, the equivalent of 29% of female prisoners self-harmed compared to 7% of male prisoners (MoJ, 2012a: 96). Acts of self-harm appear to be more severe, that is ending in hospital attendance, for males (9%) than females (2%), however. The risk of self-harm is highest in the early days of a prison sentence and thus the higher proportion of female offenders serving short-term sentences has an impact on comparative rates of self-harm.

Rates of assaults and self-harm in women particularly, have been attributed to the complex needs and difficulties presented by female offenders. Women enter the prison system with a range of complex problems, including addictions (legal and illegal substances), high levels of unemployment, existing self-harming, high levels of experiences of victimisation (sexual and physical), poverty, mental health issues, poor (or no) housing, high levels of social exclusion, low educational attainment, and low training or skills levels (Corston, 2007; Fawcett, 2004, 2009). Similar problems are also in evidence for many men in prison, though a lower proportion of men than women suffer from these problems. The solution called for is to treat women differently but the case for this is not proven.

To guarantee equality, however, we need to acknowledge that the pains of imprisonment may be greater for women – women being housed further from their homes and possibly suffering more punishment for breaches of prison discipline within prison. If punishment is to be equal, these factors need to be addressed and/or taken into account when sentencing. Furthermore, women respond differently to incarceration: they appear to suffer its effects more acutely, so that equal penal decisions result in greater levels of punishment for women. This last point is difficult to prove and has not yet been convincingly demonstrated but should not be totally ignored and, if true, again should be a mitigating factor for both men and women, one which would impact on a higher proportion of female offenders but one which would ensure equality of treatment through equality of outcome.

## People first, offenders second?

After fifty years of advances in our understanding of the role of gender on crime it is curious that current debates about the treatment of women have shifted again to justify differential treatment in sentencing decisions on the basis of an offender's gender. In many respects it seems that those reformers in government and other organisations are falling back on visions of causes of female crime that are closer to the long-discredited classical views of Lombroso and contemporaries than anyone would like to admit. Women are seen as victims (in the main of men) and their circumstance – coerced, mentally ill, vulnerable and socially disadvantaged. These characteristics, reformers suggest, warrant differential treatment in sentencing. These views clash, of course, with the fundamental notion of offenders as rights-bearing citizens, whose offending behaviour should be dealt with in strict accordance with the proportionality principle. It is important to acknowledge here that in relation to the characteristics of offenders, regardless of gender, age or ethnicity, we are only discussing the 'known knowns', those offenders who are caught up in the system. Given the large attrition in the criminal justice process, we cannot be certain that the attrition process does not work differently for different social groups (see discussion in relation to young people by Cooper and Roe, 2012: iii). Thus, we have no way of knowing how (un)representative those caught up in the system are of the dark figure of the offender population or whether and, if so exactly how, the situation is different for men and women. Additionally, many comparisons are based on prisoners, and it is important to remember that we are not comparing like with like when looking at the female and male prison population in terms of patterns of offending, demographic characteristics and other relevant factors. It would be more appropriate to compare men and women on remand and men serving short-term sentences for property crime with women offenders in the same position. This has not been possible for this chapter. However, we argue that this is unnecessary, as a better solution would be reached via a gender-neutral approach.

There are many good arguments for reducing the use of imprisonment for both men and women: the harm caused to already vulnerable members of society who often have committed only minor crimes; the harm caused to dependants of offenders sentenced to imprisonment;

the lack of rehabilitation or reduction in offending behaviour; and the costs to society.

   The costs to society of female imprisonment are great: it is expensive; more women offend after a prison sentence than after other forms of punishment, suggesting that other sentences rehabilitate more effectively; putting children into care is expensive and probably has a negative effect on juvenile offending (both male and female). For the sake of society there is therefore a need to address female criminality without the use of custody and to ensure effective socialisation through community sentences. However, similar claims could be made against the use of prison for many men, especially those who have committed offences similar in seriousness to those committed by women, in particular property offences (Ashworth, 2013). Therefore these arguments apply across the population and not just to one gender. We opened the paper with Frances Crook's call for the abolition of imprisonment for women, and she points out that she would like to see a general reduction in imprisonment. However, this call implies that any abolitionist movement needs to break down resistance to abolition of imprisonment by going for easy targets, for example women and children, and once this has been achieved, moving the argument on. There is, however, a significant risk of fragmenting the call for reform for adult offenders, which is unhelpful. Moreover, the arguments as they are applied – special considerations for those who are victims, primary carers, coerced should apply to everyone; and introducing simplistic claims of gender difference may prove counterproductive to calls for reform. Furthermore, what the earlier discussion has highlighted is that the system is already discriminatory. There are some ways in which the system appears to treat women differently – a higher proportion of both first-time female offenders and non-violent female offenders are sent to prison. If true, this suggests that the standards being applied are having a negative effect on women. This may be evidence that the present standards are themselves discriminatory. The present guidelines appear gender-neutral (equal treatment) but are, in effect, discriminatory, leading to differences in outcomes, and therefore leads to inequality. This outcome inequality needs to be addressed. What is needed is not different treatment for women but something more radical, more likely to deliver true equality – a truly gender-neutral approach to the whole process of punishment and dealing with offenders.

   In each section, we have suggested some changes that might be made. However, as Ashworth (2013) suggests, there are aspects of the whole system (for example sentencing for property offending) which need to be reconsidered, and the effect of sentencing rules on men and women certainly needs to be more carefully studied, to ensure that the rules are equal and fair for both men and women. Each of the measures outlined earlier would be non-discriminatory, improving sentencing decisions for both men and women, but would have a greater impact on women, serving to iron out present perceived discriminatory aspects of the system.

Finally, punishment as experienced needs to be more carefully explored – not to argue for different sentencing based on gender, but to ensure that the sentencing guidelines deliver both equality of treatment and of outcome. If guidelines do not deliver equality, it suggests either that the guidelines need to be revisited to be made genuinely gender-neutral and/or that changes can be made in the implementation of the punishment to deal with some of the issues, for example more very small prison units for women to ensure that they are closer to home. This approach both delivers the justice called for by the reformers and does so in a gender-neutral way – one which has real equality at its core.

## References

Adler, F. (1975) *Sisters in crime: The rise of the new female criminal*, NY: McGraw Hill.

Ashworth, A. (2010) *Sentencing and criminal justice* (5th edn), Cambridge: Cambridge University Press.

Ashworth, A. (2013) *What if imprisonment were abolished for property offences?*, London: Howard League for Penal Reform.

Berman, G. (2011) *Prison population statistics*, House of Commons Library.

Box, S. and Hale, C. (1983) Liberation and female criminality in England and Wales, *British Journal of Criminology*, 23 (1): 35.

Burke, R. H. (2005) *An introduction to criminological theory* (2nd edn), Cullompton: Willan.

Burman, M. (2012) Transforming punishment of women in Scotland?, www.sccjr.ac.uk/wp-content/uploads/2012/12/Clinks-Conference-Presentation-Dec-2012.pdf

Carlen, P. and Worrall, A. (2004) *Analysing women's imprisonment*, Devon: Willan Publishing.

Clinks (2012) *Breaking the cycle of women's offending: A system re-design*. RR3 Task & Finish Group on Women, www.clinks.org/publications/reports/rr3-women-tfg

Clinks (2014) *Breaking the cycle of women's offending: Where next*, London: Clinks, www.clinks.org/sites/default/files/basic/files-downloads/Clinks%20Women's%20Conference%20report.pdf

Cooper, C. and Roe, S. (2012) *An estimate of youth crime in England and Wales.* Research Report 64, London: Home Office, www.homeoffice. gov.uk/publications/science-research-statistics/research-statistics/ crime-research/horr64/

Corston Report (2007*) The Corston Report: A report by Baroness Jean Corston of a review of women with particular vulnerabilities in the criminal justice system*, London: Home Office.

Crook, F. (2014) I would give up... women's imprisonment, www.crimeandjustice.org.uk/resources/i-would-give-womens-imprisonment

Deakin, J. and Spencer, J. (2003) Women behind bars: Explanations and implications, *Howard Journal for Penal Reform*, 42: 123-36.

Easton, S. and Piper, C. (2012) *Sentencing and punishment: The quest for justice* (3rd edn), Oxford: Oxford University Press.

Fawcett Society (2004) *Women and the criminal justice system: A report of the Commission on Women and the Criminal Justice System*, London: Fawcett Group.

Fawcett Society (2009) *Engendering justice – from policy to practice: Final report of the Commission on Women and the Criminal Justice System*, London: Fawcett Group.

Gelsthorpe, L. and Morris, A (2002) Women's imprisonment in England and Wales: A penal paradox, *Criminal Justice*, 2 (3): 277-301.

Government Action to Reduce Women's Offending (2004) www. cjp.org.uk/news/archive/government-action-to-reduce-womens-offending-11-03-2004/ (Last Accessed May 2015).

Hedderman, C. (2004) Why are more women being sentenced to custody? in G. McIvor (ed.) *Women who offend*, London: Jessica Kingsley.

Heidensohn, F. and Silvestri, M. (2012) Gender and crime, in M. Maguire, R. Morgan and R. Reiner (eds) *The Oxford handbook of criminology* (5th edn), Oxford: Oxford University Press.

Home Office (2004) *Women's Offending Reduction Programme*, London: Home Office.

Home Office (2006) *Crime in England and Wales 2005/6*, Home Office Statistical Bulletin 12/06. London: Home Office.

Home Office (2009) *Crime statistics in England and Wales 2008/09 Volume 1: Findings from the British Crime Survey*, Home Office Statistical Bulletin 11/09, London: Home Office.

Jacobson, J. and Hough, M. (2007) *Mitigation: The role of personal factors in sentencing* London: Prison Reform Trust, www.prisonreformtrust. org.uk/Portals/0/Documents/mitigation%20-%20the%20role%20 of%20personal%20factors%20in%20sentencing.pdf

James-Hanman, D. (2014) *What's this got to do with violence against women?* www.crimeandjustice.org.uk/resources/whats-got-do-violence-against-women

Jones, S. (2008) Partners in crime: A study of the relationship between female offenders and their co-defendants, *Criminology and Criminal Justice*, 8 (2), 147-64.

Light, M., Grant, E., and Hopkins, K. (2013) *Gender differences in substance use and mental health amongst prisoners.* Ministry of Justice Analytical Series, London: MoJ, www.gov.uk/government/uploads/system/uploads/attachment_data/file/220060/gender-substance-misuse-mental-health-prisoners.pdf

Ministry of Justice (2012a) *Statistics on women and the criminal justice system 2011*, London: MoJ, www.gov.uk/government/uploads/system/uploads/attachment_data/file/220081/statistics-women-cjs-2011-v2.pdf

Ministry of Justice (2012b) *Safety in custody statistics quarterly update to June 2012*, London: MoJ, www.gov.uk/government/uploads/system/uploads/attachment_data/file/218386/safety-custody-june-2012.pdf

Player, E. (2014) Women in the criminal justice system: The triumph of inertia, *Criminology and Criminal Justice*, 14 (3), 276-97.

Pollak, O. (1950) *The criminality of women*, NY: Barnes.

Prison Reform Trust (2012a) *Reforming women's justice: Reducing the imprisonment of women*, www.prisonreformtrust.org.uk/Portals/0/Documents/Womenleaflet.pdf

Prison Reform Trust (2012b) *Women in prison*, www.prisonreformtrust.org.uk/Portals/0/Documents/WomenbriefingAug12small.pdf

Prison Reform Trust (2014) *Why focus on reducing women's imprisonment?*, www.prisonreformtrust.org.uk/Portals/0/Documents/why%20focus%20on%20reducing%20womens%20imprisonment.pdf

Rafter, N. (2009) *The origins of criminology*, Hoboken: Taylor and Francis.

Rawls, J. (1971) *A theory of justice*, Harvard, MA: Harvard University Press.

Roe, S. and Ashe, J. (2008) *Young people and crime: Findings from the 2006 Offending, Crime and Justice Survey.* HOSB09/08, London: Home Office.

Scottish Commission (2012) *Commission on Women Offenders: Final report*, www.scotland.gov.uk/About/Review/commissiononwomenoffenders/finalreport-2012

Sentencing Guidelines Council (2004) *Seriousness: Overarching principles*, http://sentencingcouncil.judiciary.gov.uk/docs/web_seriousness_guideline.pdf

Sentencing Guidelines Council (2011) *Assault – Definitive guideline*, http://sentencingcouncil.judiciary.gov.uk/docs/Assault_definitive_guideline_-_Crown_Court.pdf

Simon, R. J. (1975) *Women and crime*, Lexington, MA: Lexington Books.

Smart, C. (1979) The new female criminal: Reality or myth?, *British Journal of Criminology*, 19 (1): 50.

Stewart, D. (2008) *The Problems and Needs of Newly Sentenced Prisoners: Results from a National Survey*, Ministry of Justice Series 16/08, October 2008, London: Ministry of Justice.

UN (2010) United Nation Rules for the Treatment of Women Prisoners and Non-Custodial Measures for Women Offenders (Bangkok Rules). Resolution 2010/16, www.un.org/en/ecosoc/docs/2010/res%202010-16.pdf

United Nations Convention on the Rights of the Child (1989) www.unicef.org.uk/Documents/Publication-pdfs/UNCRC_PRESS200910web.pdf

Williams, K., Papadopoulou, V. and Booth, N. (2012) *Prisoners' childhood and family backgrounds*. Ministry of Justice Research Series 4/12, London: MoJ.

Women in Prison (2011) *Breaking the cycle for women*, London: Women in Prison, www.womeninprison.org.uk

# 'A very high price to pay?' Transforming Rehabilitation and short prison sentences for women

*Julie Trebilcock and Anita Dockley*

## Introduction

Significant increases to the prison population in England and Wales during the last twenty years have generated concerns about the overuse of imprisonment, particularly for women and those serving a short sentence. In 2010, major changes to the criminal justice system were proposed by the Coalition government, including the introduction of new community rehabilitation companies (CRCs) and a 'Payment by Results' (PbR) scheme whereby financial rewards are given for reducing levels of reoffending (Ministry of Justice (MoJ), 2010; MoJ, 2013h; MoJ, 2013i). Other significant developments in the new Transforming Rehabilitation (TR) agenda (MoJ, 2013h; MoJ, 2013i) include the introduction of resettlement prisons, 'through the gate' services and statutory supervision for short sentence prisoners after release. Drawing from the findings of an interview survey of 25 short sentence women prisoners and prison staff, this chapter provides an overview of the short-term imprisonment of women in England and Wales.[1] Key areas of the TR reforms are explored, and the chapter concludes by considering the risks and opportunities they may present for women sentenced to, or eligible for, a short prison sentence.

## The short-term imprisonment of women in England and Wales

Every year over 60,000 adults receive a short prison sentence of less than 12 months. Under the Offender Rehabilitation Act 2014, this group will be subject to statutory supervision after release. Historically this group usually served half their sentence in custody and the remainder in the community on licence, with no post-release supervision or intervention from probation (unless they were aged between 18 and 21 years). This is despite the fact that short sentence prisoners have the highest reconviction rates among adult prisoners (MoJ, 2013a), and the cost of crime committed following release from a short prison sentence is estimated to be between £7 billion and £10 billion each year (National Audit Office (NAO), 2010).

On 27 June 2014, a total of 3,935 women were in prison in England and Wales, 88 more than on the same day in 2013 (MoJ, 2014c) and 135 in excess of the highest projection for this date (MoJ, 2013d). While prosecution rates for men and young people have been falling since 2004, the numbers of women subject to prosecution have remained stable (MoJ, 2014a). Women are six times more likely to be convicted of a summary than an indictable offence and the vast majority (69.3%, n=2212) of women sentenced to immediate custody are convicted of non-violent offences (MoJ, 2014b). In 2014 more than half (51.8%, n=3,691) were sentenced to three months or less, a further 19.2% (n=1,365) for between three and six months and 5.9% (n=697) for between six and twelve months (MoJ, 2014a).

The challenges faced by women who come into contact with the criminal justice system have long been recognised (see, for example, Carlen, 1983; Carlen, 1990; Carlen and Worrall, 2004; Heidensohn, 1985). Previous research has identified high levels of physical, sexual and emotional abuse among women who offend (Morris et al, 1995; Rumgay, 2004). Women in prison are more likely than men to have been in care (Williams et al, 2012) and more than half report having been victim to domestic violence (Social Exclusion Unit, 2002). Approximately 70% of women in prison have no qualifications and more than a third are unemployed before being sent to prison (Social Exclusion Unit, 2002). Problems with substance misuse and psychological health tend to be more severe for prisoners who are adult, female and sentenced to less than 12 months (Stewart, 2008). Indeed, women account for a disproportionate number of self-harm incidents in prison (MoJ, 2014d), and 70% of women in prison have two or more mental health disorders (Social Exclusion Unit, 2002). On arrival at prison, a third of women report that they have drug problems and a fifth report problems with alcohol (Her Majesty's Inspectorate of Prisons (HMIP), 2010).

Such characteristics mean that women may find it harder to adapt to prison than men (Carlen, 1998) and find themselves particularly disadvantaged by a system 'conceived by, intended for and dominated by men' (Scott and Codd, 2010: 34). Women have often been overlooked or neglected in the development of 'what works' initiatives, and the evidence for how to best support this group and reduce their reoffending continues to be less developed (Gelsthorpe and Hedderman, 2012). The consequences are that prison 'frequently does not meet their needs, nor take account of their different life experiences' (Fawcett Society, 2004: 1).

These insights were supported by our research with short sentence women and prison staff (Howard League, in press). The women had a complex range of needs and often reported high levels of mental health problems and substance misuse prior to their imprisonment. Of particular concern was that these characteristics added to the challenges of adapting to the prison environment. One woman told us:

> 'I'm a fragile sort of person and I don't know what I'm doing. On the outside I had a carer. I had to have support. I had to be with someone at all times. And now since I've been in here ... prison is making me worse. I'm trying to do it but when I am behind the door I just break down.' (Gina; theft, 6-month sentence)

Many women were particularly anxious about what they had lost as a consequence of imprisonment. As a result of imprisonment a third of women prisoners lose their home (Social Exclusion Unit, 2002) and a third of women prisoners anticipate being homeless on release (Howard League, 2005). A key issue for the women in our sample was housing, which they viewed as something that could assist or hinder their rehabilitation. Those who were reliant on housing benefit were often concerned about losing their accommodation on the outside, and many expressed anxiety about being placed in hostels because of the characteristics and drug misuse of other residents. The detrimental consequences of losing housing (or other positive aspects of their lives such as children and employment) represented common themes. One woman told us:

> 'It is a very high price to pay if you are going to lose your kids and your house, all for shoplifting, or other petty little crimes ... The first time I come in here I lost my kids to social services because I wasn't able to look after them. And then I lost my home because the bill hadn't been paid. So I got out with nothing. So when you go back out, it is hard to like get all of that back. They just expect you to go back to normal. But how are you supposed to do that

when you are homeless and you've got no kids?' (Maddie; robbery, 12-month sentence)

This quote demonstrates how imprisonment can place additional strain on women because of their role as primary carers for children and other family members (Medlicott, 2007; Walker and Worrall, 2000). Women often struggle to maintain contact with their children while in prison (Sheehan and Flynn, 2007) and their children may experience emotional, social and material damage as a result (Howard League, 2011). The majority of women in our research expressed considerable regret and shame about the negative impact their imprisonment was having on their children and other family members. One woman told us:

'My mum is a bit rocky, well not rocky, but she can't deal with this, she can't get hurt anymore. She went all through it with my sister. My sister lost five kids to social services, and now I'm involved with social services, and she's like "no I can't deal with this" and so she has kind of shut the door. I think that is to protect herself kind of thing.' (Vicky; shoplifting, 4-month sentence)

In addition to feelings of loss and shame, many women indicated their imprisonment made it difficult to resolve the challenges they were experiencing in their lives. This highlights how there is often limited access to offending behaviour programmes, education and work (NAO, 2010) and that some short sentence prisoners do not have access to sentence planning assistance and offender supervisors (HMIP, 2012: 70). With limited opportunities to address their problems, many women were anxious about their release:

'I'm absolutely cacking myself. It's not flown by, but it's not dragged out. But yes it has gone too quickly for anything to have been done.' (Caroline; assault, 4-month sentence)

While staff highlighted many areas of good practice and clear attempts to help women serving short sentences, they also indicated that a short-term prison sentence was inadequate for supporting longer-term rehabilitation. Staff were generally negative about the utility of a short prison sentence, and many expressed concern about the destabilising impact that imprisonment could have on the lives of women and their children. Staff expressed concern that short sentence prisoners often received little practical support on release and frequently commented on the need for more intensive long-term support:

> 'Sometimes they don't know where to go or what to do ... That support that they had in prison is suddenly gone because they've left ... The minute they come up against a brick wall, they don't know who to turn to then. There's no support. So what do they do? They go back to what they know, and then they come back in.' (Paula, senior prison officer)

Staff also pointed to the difficulties involved with resourcing effective interventions with short sentence women prisoners. The resource-intensive nature of short prison sentences, coupled with the anticipated low success rate, added to the negative views that some staff held about short prison sentences. One member of staff commented:

> 'It can be disheartening with the churn and seeing the same faces over and over again. But the main thing is to try and keep them alive and try to educate them ... We do often have to put a lot of work into one individual and support their needs.' (Tara, drugs worker)

Many women appeared to lack confidence in their ability to avoid reoffending on their release. Various reasons were given, including ongoing drug and alcohol issues, homelessness or anxieties about returning to the same geographical area. Those who had served several prison sentences were particularly pessimistic about life on the outside, highlighting that the accounts of 'revolving door' prisoners are often characterised by fatalism because of concerns about homelessness and addiction (Howerton et al, 2009). Such findings lend further support to Armstrong and Weaver's (2010: 3) concerns, that it is 'the cumulative effect of doing many short sentences, more than the experience of any single sentence, which carries the largely negative impacts'. One woman reflected on the failure of numerous short prison sentences to provide the help she needed:

> 'I think I have got something like 38 convictions, all for shoplifting and that sort of thing. So there is a problem in there, and obviously, jail, it is not working ... They need to sort something out to help people on drugs. You just can't do a detox on a short sentence, you need a longer

time to do it. But then going out into the community is hard, because you are back where you was before.' (Vicky; shoplifting, 4-month sentence)

In contrast to our research with men serving short prison sentences (Trebilcock, 2011), the women in our study were generally more positive about community sentences and probation than they were about prison. While some (though significantly fewer than in the male sample) indicated that a short prison sentence had the benefit of allowing them 'time out', many pointed to the damage that their imprisonment had caused. Those who had previously served community penalties usually indicated that they had had supportive and constructive experiences of working with probation. One woman described her relationship with her previous probation officer as follows:

'I had an excellent relationship with my probation officer ... Really supportive and that ... She spent the time listening to my problems ... And it calmed me down and really helped me with certain issues.' (Lucy; assault, 6-month sentence)

While the women commonly described positive experiences of working with probation, the majority who had served community sentences also indicated that they had a history of breaching them. Many attributed this to ongoing substance misuse, although some also described situations where they felt they had been 'set up to fail', because appointments had been made at inconvenient times in relation to their childcare responsibilities. A small number of staff expressed similar concerns that it was sometimes too easy for women to fail to meet the requirements of their community sentence. One resettlement worker told us:

'We had someone the other day, and she missed probation twice, but in many ways it was through no fault of her own because the appointments were too early and she had to get her kids to school, didn't have a car, so by the time she dropped the kids off she was 15 minutes late. They breached her and sent her to prison.' (Helen, resettlement caseworker)

## Transforming Rehabilitation: key reforms

Many of the themes explored above will be familiar to those who work with women serving short prison sentences. Reforms to the criminal justice system brought about by the Coalition government (see MoJ, 2010; MoJ, 2011; MoJ, 2012; MoJ, 2013h; MoJ, 2013i) and under the Offender Rehabilitation Act 2014, have the potential to impact significantly on this group of women. In the remainder of this chapter we outline some of the key TR reforms, before reflecting on the possible consequences for women who are either eligible for, or sentenced to, a short prison sentence.

### Introduction of new community rehabilitation companies (CRCs)

A significant change being brought about by TR is the introduction of new CRCs. High-risk offenders, such as those subject to Multi-Agency Public Protection Arrangements, will continue to be managed by the National Probation Service, while newly created CRCs will be responsible for delivering probation services in the community to the majority of low- and medium-risk offenders. CRCs came into force on 1 June 2014 and may now enter into agreements with local authorities to provide services that would previously have been delivered by probation trusts. Commissioning is structured by a 'straw man' system of payments, where a fixed fee for service can be topped up by additional PbR payments to incentivise good performance (MoJ, 2013e).

### Introduction of statutory supervision for short sentenced prisoners

Section 2 of the Offender Rehabilitation Act 2014 requires that all offenders sentenced to one day or more in prison will be subject to at least 12 months' statutory supervision after release. Post-sentence supervision should usually involve eight requirements, although some can be omitted if the governor of the releasing prison agrees they are not suitable or not necessary to support rehabilitation. Standard requirements include living at a specified address, being of good behavior and keeping appointments. Two further supervision requirements, drug testing and drug appointments, can be requested by the supervisor, if deemed appropriate. Guidance (under PSI 31/2014 / PI 29/2014) lists the eight requirements in full and insists that they are 'more limited in type and number' than those attached to prisoners on licence, because post-sentence supervision should be primarily focused on rehabilitation (National Offender Management Service (NOMS), 2014).

*Introduction of resettlement prisons and 'through the gate' services*

Another key aim of TR has been to reconfigure the prison estate to create a network of resettlement prisons across the country, with service delivery based on a 'through the gate' model. Given the small number of women's prisons, all 12 will be reconfigured as resettlement prisons. Each resettlement prison will be aligned with one of 21 new contract package areas, and providers will be expected to work with people in custody and in the community following release.[2] It is proposed that short sentence prisoners spend their whole sentence in a resettlement prison, while longer sentence prisoners should move to a resettlement prison at least three months prior to release. Further details about proposed changes to the female prison estate and information about TR pilots, including a Through the Gate Substance Misuse Service and an open unit for 25 women at HMP Styal, were published in October 2013 (NOMS, 2013b).

## Transforming the rehabilitation of short sentence women?

Following the deaths of six women in a 12-month period at HMP Styal, the Corston Report was published (Corston, 2007). Corston argued for alternatives to prison for women to be developed, and expressed particular concern about the use of short prison sentences. Since publication of the report, government recognition of the different needs of women and the benefits of a different criminal justice response has developed (see Kendall, 2013 for a review). However, many of Corston's recommendations were not taken forward by government (Corcoran, 2010b) and the new TR reforms present both 'risks and opportunities for the Corston agenda' (Justice Select Committee, 2013: 5). Given current uncertainties about how TR will meet the needs of women or how the reforms will work in practice, we conclude our chapter by considering the possible implications of TR for women either sentenced to, or eligible for, a short prison sentence.

### Ensuring that services are gender-responsive

In March 2013, the government published its *Strategic objectives for female offenders* (MoJ, 2013f) and established a Ministerial Advisory Board for Female Offenders. These were followed in October 2013 by a response to the Justice Select Committee's report concerning women who offend (MoJ, 2013b), a review of the female custodial estate (NOMS, 2013b) and a stocktake of community services for women (NOMS, 2013a). An amendment was also made to the

Offender Rehabilitation Act 2014, to ensure that arrangements for the supervision and rehabilitation of offenders comply with the public sector duty under section 149 of the Equality Act 2010. Reflecting this, gender-specific requirements have been incorporated into the tendering process, which stipulate that providers should endeavour, where possible to: give women the option to have a female supervisor; allow women to attend appointments in a female-only environment; and ensure that women are not forced to undertake unpaid work in male-only environments (MoJ, 2014e). Supporting guidance has also been issued, to ensure that potential providers are sensitive to the need to accommodate women in their service delivery.

These developments lend credence to the MoJ's (2013i: 10) claim that they will 'develop provider contracts which ensure that appropriate services are provided, and that there is increased flexibility to tailor rehabilitation to the needs and characteristics of the individual'. However, as the contracts roll out,[3] how (and the extent to which) gender-specific requirements are addressed in practice, needs to be scrutinised. It will be important to assess the options actually offered to women and how these may differ across contract package areas, given the cost-sensitive environment in which new initiatives will emerge.

One area of practice championed by Corston has been the development of women's centres (for more information, see Joliffe et al, 2011; Radcliffe and Hunter, 2013). If gender-specific requirements are to be properly met, women's centres may have a key part to play in delivering services to women. Indeed, TR could be a driver to expanding or sustaining such provision. However, women–centred provision, and the manner in which it is delivered, is both complex and expensive. It is essential that these centres continue to have access to sufficient funding. Moreover, women's centres provide services that are available to all women in the community and the strength of this inclusive approach should not be lost. Care should be taken not to alienate non-offenders from using services, but this may be difficult in the context of an increasingly offender-focused funding stream. Equally, it is important to ensure that women in contact with the criminal justice system feel that women's centres are genuinely a *place for them*.

While some have found gender-responsive treatment to be effective (Saxena et al, 2014), others warn that gender-sensitive punishment can have unintended and possibly negative consequences for women (Kendall, 2013). Research has found that despite government funding, the development of women's centres has not led to increased diversion of women from custody (Joliffe et al, 2011). Others have observed how gender-responsive practices may frame women who offend as 'fundamentally flawed' and 'fixable', and by focusing on individual deficits, 'structural issues disappear from view and correctional practices gain legitimacy because it is claimed they can address women's needs' (Kendall, 2013: 45). This reminds us that reducing offending by women is not simply a matter for the criminal justice system (Carlen, 2013; Justice Select Committee, 2013), and structural inequalities experienced by women also need to be addressed elsewhere.

### Ensuring that the new 'criminal justice market' offers quality as well as value for money

Concerns about the introduction of a 'criminal justice market' and its implications for women are discussed more fully elsewhere (see Chapter Thirteen in this book; see also Corcoran, 2010a; Gelsthorpe and Hedderman, 2012). Providers who can demonstrate positive results will have resources directed towards them. However, the way in which results will be measured continues to be uncertain. Moreover, in the context of significant budgetary cuts across government and the inevitably cost-sensitive priorities of CRCs, it is difficult to envisage what services may be financially viable or desirable. It is also unclear what capacity the voluntary sector will have to flourish in an arena that will be cost-sensitive and structured by the ethos of PbR. There is a risk that small but effective voluntary organisations may be unable to compete, or may lose their original ethos as a result of the TR reforms.

Uncertainty around the funding of women's services has raised problems before (Hedderman, 2012) and has the potential to impact on staff morale and service user engagement. Concerns about staff-to-prisoner levels, lower pay and high staff turnover in the private sector management of prisons (Grimwood, 2014; Nathan, 2011), alongside estimates that the extra costs of statutory supervision could amount to £30 million per year (MoJ, 2013c; MoJ, 2013j), raise additional concerns about the quality, value and delivery of services under TR.

### Supporting the effective implementation of resettlement prisons and 'through the gate' services

While the aim of creating new resettlement prisons is to ensure that 'most offenders are given continuous support by one provider from custody into the community' (MoJ, 2013i: 6) it is difficult to see how this will work in the female estate. All 12 women's prisons will be designated resettlement prisons, but many women will inevitably find they are held in a prison that is outside their 'home' CRC, meaning the services they receive in prison and in the community will be delivered by different providers. If a woman is not directly supported by her 'home' CRC in prison, it appears that the 'home' CRC will be expected to buy in services from the host CRC.

This presents a number of challenges to the effective implementation of CRCs. Given that increasing prison numbers are currently higher than projected (MoJ, 2013d), the extent to which close to home constructive regime activities and staff support will be available 'through the gate' is unclear. There is a risk that the limited access that short sentence prisoners have to offending behaviour programmes (NAO, 2010), sentence planning assistance and offender supervisors (HMIP, 2012: 70) will continue or even worsen under the new CRC model, because of funding and budgetary concerns. Many resettlement initiatives, such as the Open Unit at HMP Styal, are likely to be reserved for women serving longer sentences, but it is essential that sufficient resources are also offered to the short sentence population. Effective management of transfers between different CRCs will also be crucial, given that an individual's relationship with their probation officer is significant in terms of their future offending (McNeill, 2005; Shapland et al, 2012; Wood et al, 2013).

Communication between different providers and the women in receipt of their services will need to be of a high quality. If services are to operate truly 'through the gate', the reconfiguration of the women's estate and new services need to be properly communicated to prisoners, outside agencies and the courts. Concerns have already been raised that the TR reforms have not been well communicated to many women in prison, which is heightening anxieties about where they will serve their sentence (Women in Prison, 2014).

### Avoiding disproportionate punishment and increases to the short sentence population

Perhaps the way short sentence women prisoners are most likely to benefit from TR is with the introduction of post-release statutory supervision. However, statutory supervision will disproportionately affect women, and concerns have been expressed that it may amount to 'disproportionate and unfair punishment' (Prison Reform Trust, 2013: 3). Others have questioned whether 12 months of supervision, irrespective of the length of imprisonment, is entirely necessary or appropriate (Annison et al, 2014).

Concerns have also been raised that statutory supervision may serve to increase the female prison population on the basis that short prison sentences come to be viewed more positively by the courts, which may find reassurance in the statutory obligation to supervise and support women after their release (Prison Reform Trust, 2013). Player (2005: 425) observes that 'the courts have tended to favour sentences that address the welfare needs of women rather than those that adopt a primarily retributive response'. However, under a 'welfare' approach, women may find that their sentence is 'up-tariffed' in an attempt to secure high levels of supervision and/or custody to help 'care' for women who come before the courts (Player, 2005). Research with sentencers has found that while they are sceptical about the extent to which imprisonment achieves what it should do, some nevertheless believe that prisons have the capacity to provide people with access to services that are not available in the community (Tombs and Jagger, 2006).

It is important that the courts are properly informed about TR and the provision of services in both custody and the community. There is a risk that, if unaware, the judiciary will continue to sentence women as they have done before, and may be averse to making decisions that could be perceived as either lenient or unsafe in the context of new and unknown services. Recent research suggests that sentencers' awareness of women's community services is low (Joliffe et al, 2011; Radcliffe and Hunter, 2013). Moreover, magistrates have expressed concerns about the uneven provision of women's community services across the country and how sustainable they are in the current economic climate (Radcliffe and Hunter, 2013). However, the MoJ has been undertaking educative work with sentencers in the Greater Manchester area, hopefully indicating an appreciation of the need to ensure that the judiciary are properly aware of the TR reforms and able to develop a clear understanding of what holistic provision may be available, and where.

The final area of concern is that statutory post-release supervision will increase the risk that women are returned to court, and possibly prison, for failure to comply with the requirements. In particular, the new optional drug testing supervision requirement, given the high proportion of short sentence women with substance misuse issues, may have significant consequences. Tough supervision requirements could have the unintended consequence of increasing the use of short spells in prison to manage low-risk and non-violent women. It is important that the requirements, and a woman's ability to meet them, are considered in a flexible and genuinely rehabilitative manner. Moreover, providers need to properly understand the needs – and sometimes chaotic lives – that many women in the criminal justice system may have. If supervision is to be genuinely rehabilitative, it should be measured by what Hough et al (2013: 17) have termed 'normative compliance', whereby people are encouraged to buy into desistance rather than being 'cajoled or supervised into doing so'.

## Conclusions

The privatisation of probation services and introduction of statutory supervision for all short sentence prisoners represent a significant departure from previous policies and will have a clear impact on women eligible for, or sentenced to, a short prison sentence. It is therefore essential that the reforms are subject to post-legislative scrutiny and that the impact on women is closely monitored. Our research generally lends support to the concern that 'prison is an expensive and ineffective way of dealing with many women offenders' (Justice Select Committee, 2013: 4). Locking women up for short periods of time has the potential to exacerbate many of the problems these women experience. Hence, it is important that services in the community continue to be developed and enabled to be sufficiently innovative and flexible in their delivery to women. Evidence suggests that community-based approaches, properly tailored to the gendered needs of women, are likely to be far more effective both in terms of reducing the likelihood of reoffending and for enabling women to feel supported to turn their lives around. Continuity of care, rather than an extension of punishment, needs to be achieved to break the cycle of women's offending. It is important that market-based priorities do not undermine attempts to provide women with individualised and appropriate services that help support them on a path to desistance. Finally, the introduction of statutory supervision must be closely monitored, to ensure that it does not lead to 'up-tariffing' at court or increasing the number of women being returned to prison for failing to meet the requirements. Should this happen, the TR reforms would be a very high price to pay, not only in financial terms but also in social and material terms for the increasing number of non-violent and low-risk women sent to prison.

### Notes
[1]  Pseudonyms are used to protect the identity of participants.

[2]  In February 2014, the MoJ published a revised list of resettlement prisons and their contract package areas, www.justice.gov.uk/downloads/rehab-prog/resettlement-prison-list.pdf

[3]  All CRC contracts are due to be in place and ready by the end of March 2015.

## References

Annison, J., Burke, L. and Senior, P. (2014) Transforming Rehabilitation: Another example of English 'exceptionalism' or a blueprint for the rest of Europe?, *European Journal of Probation*, 6 (1): 6-23.

Armstrong, S. and Weaver, B. (2010) *User views of punishment: The comparative experience of short prison sentences and community-based punishments*, Research Report 04/2010, Glasgow: The Scottish Centre for Crime and Justice Research.

Carlen, P. (1983) *Women's imprisonment: A study in social control*, London: Routledge & Kegan Paul.

Carlen, P. (1990) *Alternatives to women's imprisonment*, Milton Keynes: Open University Press.

Carlen, P. (1998) *Sledgehammer: Women's imprisonment at the millennium,* Basingstoke: Palgrave Macmillan.

Carlen, P. (2013) 'Preface' in B. Carlton and M. Segrave (eds) *Women exiting prison: Critical essays on gender, post release support and survival*, Abingdon: Routledge.

Carlen, P. and Worrall, A. (2004) *Analysing women's imprisonment*, Cullompton: Willan.

Corcoran, M. S. (2010a) Dilemmas of institutionalization in the penal voluntary sector, *Critical Social Policy*, 31 (1): 30-52.

Corcoran, M. S. (2010b) Snakes and ladders: Circuits of penal reform for women under New Labour, *Current Issues in Criminal Justice*, 22 (2): 233-51.

Corston, J. (2007) *The Corston report: A report by Baroness Jean Corston of a review of women with particular vulnerabilities in the criminal justice system*, London: Home Office.

Fawcett Society (2004) *Women and the criminal justice system. A report of the Fawcett Society's commission on women and the criminal justice system*, London: Fawcett Society.

Gelsthorpe, L. and Hedderman, C. (2012) Providing for women offenders: the risks of adopting a payment by results approach, *Probation Journal*, 59 (4): 374-90.

Grimwood, G. (2014) *Prisons: The role of the private sector*, House of Commons Standard Note SN/HA/6811, 30 January 2014.

Hedderman, C. (2012) *Empty cells or empty words? Government policy on reducing the number of women going to prison*, London: Criminal Justice Alliance.

Heidensohn, F. (1985) *Women and crime,* London: Macmillan Press.

Her Majesty's Inspectorate of Prisons (2010) *Alcohol services in prisons: An unmet need. Thematic report by HM Inspectorate of Prisons*, London: HMIP.

Her Majesty's Inspectorate of Prisons (2012) *HM Chief Inspector of Prisons for England and Wales Annual Report 2011-2012*, London: HMIP.

Hough, M., Farrall, S. and McNeill, F. (2013) *Intelligent justice: Balancing the effects of community sentences and custody*, London: The Howard League for Penal Reform.

Howard League (2005) *Women in prison in England and Wales: Paper submitted to the United Nations Eleventh Congress on Crime Prevention and Criminal Justice*, London: Howard League for Penal Reform.

Howard League (2011) *Voice of a child*, London: Howard League for Penal Reform.

Howard League (in press) *First timers and frequent flyers: The reality of short term prison sentences for women*, London: Howard League for Penal Reform.

Howerton, A., Burnett, R., Byng, R. and Campbell, J. (2009) The consolations of going back to prison: What 'revolving doors' prisoners think of their prospects, *Journal of Offender Rehabilitation*, 48 (5): 439-61.

Jolliffe, D., Hedderman, C., Palmer, E. and Hollin, C. (2011) *Re-offending analysis of women offenders referred to Together Women (TW) and the scope to divert from custody*, London: MoJ.

Justice Select Committee (2013) *Women offenders: After the Corston Report, Second Report of Session 2013-14*, London: The Stationery Office

Kendall, K. (2013) Post-release support for women in England and Wales: The big picture, in B. Carlton and M. Seagrave (eds) *Women exiting prison: Critical essays on gender, post-release support and survival*, London: Routledge.

McNeill, F. (2005) The place of the officer-offender relationship in assisting offenders to desist from crime, *Probation Journal*, 52 (3): 221-42.

Medlicott, D. (2007) Women in prison, in Y. Jewkes (ed.) *Handbook on prisons*, Cullompton: Willan.

Ministry of Justice (MoJ) (2010) *Breaking the cycle: Effective punishment, rehabilitation and sentencing of offenders*, London: The Stationery Office.

MoJ (2011) *Competition strategy for offender services*, London: MoJ.

MoJ (2012) *Punishment and reform: Effective probation services*, London: Stationery Office.

MoJ (2013a) *2013 Compendium of re-offending statistics and analysis*, London: MoJ.

MoJ (2013b) *Government response to the Justice Committee's Second Report of Session 2013-14 Female Offenders*, London: MoJ.

MoJ (2013c) *Offender Rehabilitation Bill impact assessment*, 9 May 2013, London: MoJ.

MoJ (2013d) *Prison population projections 2013–2019 England and Wales*, London: MoJ.

MoJ (2013e) *Rehabilitation programme – Payment mechanism Straw Man*, May 2013, London: MoJ.

MoJ (2013f) *Strategic objectives for female offenders*, London: MoJ.

MoJ (2013h) *Transforming Rehabilitation: A revolution in the way we manage offenders*, London: MoJ.

MoJ (2013i) *Transforming Rehabilitation: A strategy for reform. Response to consultation CP(R) 16/2013*, London: MoJ.

MoJ (2013j) *Updated impact assessment for the Offender Rehabilitation Bill*, 20 June 2013, London: MoJ.

MoJ (2014a) *Criminal justice statistics 2013 England and Wales*, London: MoJ.

MoJ (2014b) *Offender management annual tables*, London: MoJ.

MoJ (2014c) *Population bulletin: Weekly 27th June 2014*, London: MoJ.

MoJ (2014d) *Safety in custody statistics England and Wales. Update to December 2013*, London: MoJ.

MoJ (2014e) *Update on delivery of the Government's strategic objectives for female offenders*, London: MoJ.

Morris, A., Wilkinson, C., Tisi, A., Woodrow, J. and Rockley, A. (1995) *Managing the needs of female prisoners*, London: Home Office.

Nathan, S. (2011) 'Prison privatization in the United Kingdom', in A. Coyle, A. Campbell and G. Neufeld (eds) *Capitalist punishment: Prison privatization and human rights*, London: Zed Books.

National Audit Office (NAO) (2010) *Managing offenders on short custodial sentences*, London: The Stationery Office.

National Offender Management Service (NOMS) (2013a) *Stocktake of women's services for offenders in the community*, London: NOMS.

National Offender Management Service (2013b) *Women's custodial estate review*, London: NOMS.

National Offender Management Service (2014) *Post-sentence supervision requirements, PSI 31/2014, PI 29/2014*, London: NOMS.

Player, E. (2005) The reduction of women's imprisonment in England and Wales. Will the reform of short prison sentences help?, *Punishment and Society*, 7 (4): 419-39.

Prison Reform Trust (2013) *Prison Reform Trust briefing on the Offender Rehabilitation Bill, House of Commons Second Reading, 11 November 2013*, London: Prison Reform Trust.

Radcliffe, P. and Hunter, G. (2013) *The development and impact of community services for women offenders: An evaluation*, London: Institute of Criminal Policy Research, Birkbeck.

Rumgay, J. (2004) *When victims become offenders: In search of coherence in policy and practice*, London: Fawcett Society.

Saxena, P., Messina, N. P., Grella, C. E. (2014) Who benefits from gender-responsive treatment? Accounting for abuse history on longitudinal outcomes for women in prison, *Criminal Justice and Behavior*, 41 (4): 417-32.

Scott, D. and Codd, H. (2010) *Controversial issues in prisons*, Maidenhead: McGraw-Hill.

Shapland, J., Bottoms, A., Farrall, S., McNeill, F., Priede, C. and Robinson, G. (2012) *The quality of probation supervision – a literature review: Summary of key messages. Research Summary 2/12*, London: MoJ.

Sheehan, R. and Flynn, C. (2007) Women prisoners and their children, in R. Sheehan, G. McIvor and C. Trotter (eds) *What works with women offenders*, Cullompton: Willan.

Social Exclusion Unit (2002) *Reducing re-offending by ex-prisoners*, London: Office of the Deputy Prime Minister.

Stewart, D. (2008) *The problems and needs of newly sentenced prisoners: Results from a national survey*. Ministry of Justice Research Series 16/08, London: MoJ.

Tombs, J. and Jagger, E. (2006) Denying responsibility: Sentencers' accounts of their decisions to imprison, *British Journal of Criminology*, 46 (5): 803-21.

Trebilcock, J. (2011) *No winners: The reality of short term prison sentences*, London: Howard League for Penal Reform.

Walker, S. and Worrall, A. (2000) Life as a woman: The gendered pains of indeterminate imprisonment, in Y. Jewkes and H. Johnston (eds) *Prison readings*, Cullompton: Willan Publishing.

Williams, K., Papadopoulou, V. and Booth, N. (2012) *Prisoners' childhood and family backgrounds. Results from the Surveying Prisoner Crime Reduction (SPCR) longitudinal cohort study of prisoners*, Ministry of Justice Research Series 3/12, London: MoJ.

Women in Prison (2013) *Transforming Rehabilitation for women in the criminal justice system*, London: Women in Prison.

Wood, M., Cattell, J., Hales, G., Lord, C., Kenny, T. and Capes, T. (2013) *Reoffending by offenders on Community Orders: Preliminary findings from the Offender Management Community Cohort Study*, London: MoJ.

THIRTEEN

# The role of the media in women's penal reform[1]

*Gemma Birkett*

## Introduction

Baroness Corston, in her 2007 *Review of women with particular vulnerabilities in the criminal justice system*, believed that 'an integral part' (Corston, 2007: 11) of the women's reform agenda involved 'educating the public' on matters of women's offending and imprisonment. Calling on the then Labour government to assume this responsibility, Corston hoped that 'this may go some way to … encourage a reasoned and enlightened debate' (Corston, 2007: 11). Four years and a change in political administration later, Corston's response to the Coalition government's *Breaking the cycle*[2] consultation (its first official foray into criminal justice policy making) expressed frustration about the lack of penal progress for women, and argued that 'reducing the number of women in custody would be welcomed by the public and supported in the media' (Corston, 2011: 3). While it is beyond the scope of this chapter to document the extent to which the public may support a reduction in the female prison population,[3] it will drill deeper into the second part of this assertion. Based on empirical data gathered from interviews with directors of national penal reform organisations, former Justice Ministers and senior civil servants, social commentators and journalists from across the spectrum,[4] this chapter will critically explore the role of the national print news media in the development of women's penal policy. In investigating the viewpoints of journalists working on crime and home affairs, it will simultaneously explore the extent to which the news media is viewed as a policy-making 'tool' by those seeking to reform the penal system. With an overarching focus on the endeavours of penal reform campaigners, it will shed more light on this specialist network of policy actors.

Like others engaged in lobbying, making arguments perceived as having traction with the political elite is a key part of campaigners' work (Mills and Roberts, 2012: 8), and they do so through variously undertaking a combination of lobbying, media work, research and campaigning on criminal justice issues (Mills and Roberts, 2012: 8). While individual mission statements, ideologies and choice of rhetoric may differ, the overarching 'problem' as far as women's penal reform campaigners are concerned is the unnecessary overuse of imprisonment for non-violent female offenders (who make up the majority of the female prison population) and the lack of gender-specific policies in a criminal justice system dominated by men. Highlighting the peripheral status of penal reform on the policy agenda, this chapter will shine a spotlight on the relations between penal reform campaigners, policy makers and journalists, before considering some practical tips for those working in this area.

## Penal reform and the news media

While the exact role of the media in the policy process is a moot point (see McQuail, 1987; McCombs, 2014), it is mostly agreed that 'by highlighting particular aspects of the information stream, the media may help to set the tone for subsequent policy action' (Jones and Wolfe, 2010: 19). Although not always key agents, as 'focusing' partners in the course of agenda-building there can be an important role for the news media in determining which issues are important, both for the public and for policy makers (Soroka et al, 2012: 205). It is claimed that the press have become the primary source of crime knowledge for the public (Hobbs and Hamerton, 2014: 131; Marsh and Melville, 2014: 210), and while academics and other commentators continue to debate the exact level of influence on public opinion, it is clear that 'newspapers are ... powerful voices contributing to the public narratives within which societies make sense of crimes' (Peelo, 2006: 161 in Hobbs and Hamerton, 2014: 129). By constructing a (sometimes distorted) framework through which the general public are able to understand the greater 'crime problem' (Commission on English Prisons Today, 2008:1), journalists are able to 'define what we think about, what we see as "problems", and the solutions we consider' (Cavendar, 2004: 336; see also Ericson et al, 1991; Galtung and Ruge, 1973; Chibnall, 1977; Soroka et al, 2012). Acting as gatekeepers, journalists can ensure 'that large segments of the social world are systematically excluded from representation and discussion in the media, and thus public knowledge of those segments is effectively impoverished' (Chibnall, 1981: 87). A fundamental preoccupation for those working in this area is that 'penal reform does not instinctively strike a sympathetic chord with large numbers of the public' (Blom–Cooper, 1977: 7) and is considered as having little audience or readership appeal by journalists (Schlesinger and Tumber, 1994: 149). It is clear that operating in a 'field of struggle that is already structured by particular ways of seeing and thinking about, punishment' (Loader, 2010: 353) presents substantial challenges for those seeking to reform penal policy.

While there does, however, exist a broad political consensus about the unnecessary overuse of short custodial sentences for non-violent women (see the Coalition government's *Strategic objectives for female offenders* – Ministry of Justice (MoJ), 2013; updated in MoJ, 2014), a number of obstacles persist. In its 2012 inquiry on women offenders, the House of Commons Justice Select Committee concluded that the ongoing challenge for policy actors is to 'present to the public, and indeed the judiciary and the media that it is possible to construct alternative sentences for women that are more challenging and more likely to reduce reoffending than a short spell in prison' (House of Commons Justice Select Committee, 2013: 157). With the policy blueprint more or less agreed, the issue has largely become one of communication: to journalists (working for the agenda-setting, predominantly right-wing new media), to the public, and to those individuals considered unsympathetic to the reform agenda. Yet in order to successfully address the challenge outlined earlier, political actors must be afforded access to the market-driven 'fund of [public] ideas' (Price and Tewksbury, 1997: 177), by no means a straightforward task. Interviews with policy makers and campaigners highlighted two overarching obstacles: that the subject of penal reform is of limited interest to the majority of journalists, and that journalists' sense of sensationalist 'news values' (in certain sections of the popular press at least) often work in direct opposition to the messages about women offenders that they wish to pursue.

Those seeking to influence penal policy reform for women are faced with a *further* barrier, in that social attitudes to male and female offending differ (see Heidensohn, 1996). While political actors are able to pursue the rhetoric of vulnerability in relation to women offenders (a discourse rarely available for men), this remains in the face of entrenched social constructions of the 'ideal woman'. Women have traditionally been identified with 'home and hearth' and motherhood (Seal, 2011: 495), and while no longer sent to houses of correction, those that deviate from their feminine 'norm' are subject to widespread criticism and censure (see Carlen, 2002; Faith, 2011), particularly in right-leaning news publications. Feminists, in particular, have argued that media depictions typically provide binary classifications of female criminality, where the objects of speculation are labelled either 'bad' or 'mad' (Jewkes, 2004: 113), 'virgin' or 'vamp' (Benedict, 1992). Of ongoing concern to those working in this area is that some journalists continue to draw on stereotypical representations of high-profile women offenders (Jones and Wardle, 2010: 57), which act as 'templates' (Kitzinger, 2000) or 'mental pigeon-holes' (Dyer, 1993) for politicians and the public alike.

Interviews with journalists confirmed that while 'ordinary' cases of women's offending did not satisfy the news values of dramatisation, titillation and novelty (Chibnall, 1977), stories involving violent women's offending were considered to be at the other end of the spectrum. One journalist working for a right-leaning publication explained that: "it's fascinating when you get a woman who has committed a particularly violent crime like Fred West's wife, Rose". Interviews also revealed that some journalists (all working for right-leaning publications) did not view the female prison population as a problem that needed to be 'resolved'. One journalist believed that, "as a general view, I think people aren't generally interested, and are slightly turned off by it", while another questioned: "is anyone ever interested in penal reform?" Despite such viewpoints, there was a clear understanding among other journalists of the broader issues surrounding women's offending and punishment. One journalist working for a left-leaning publication saw "ambivalence in British society towards women offenders; on the one hand there is still an old fashioned sense of expecting a higher standard of behaviour from women ... [but] on the other hand there is a sense, post-feminism, that women should be treated with equal severity with men when they have offended". One former journalist admitted that: "there is some understanding that there are huge numbers of women in prison who shouldn't be there, but that kind of gets subsumed in this general obsession with public perception and hard-line penal policy". One journalist admitted that many stories about women offenders reverted to lazy and unhelpful "stereotyping shorthand", and that the tabloid press especially like "to deal with things that [they] can put in a box". While it is important to highlight that not all sections of the news media engage in such activity, it is clear that journalistic understandings of this subject are multifarious.

## Penal reform campaigners as news sources

Journalists working across the political spectrum described mixed relations with penal reformers. Those working for right-leaning publications did not tend to use the information provided by campaigners, deeming the subject to be of little interest to their newspapers' readership. One journalist working for a right-leaning publication confirmed that the information provided by campaigners "was [not] the sort ... that's going to be useful to me, really". One journalist recalled that he "sometimes" spoke to campaigners, but not in "vast numbers", while another admitted that he didn't "tend to deal with them very much". One journalist working for a right-leaning publication questioned the level of coverage that campaigners should naturally expect to receive, while another journalist working for a left-leaning publication did not view low coverage as "problematic, necessarily". Highlighting the existence of ideological obstacles, one journalist believed that low coverage was due in part to "a resistance among some in the media to the liberal ideas they have". Like other policy problems, it is clear that the subject of penal reform is political, moving in and out of ideological fashion depending on the government of the day. In highlighting the peripheral nature of media access for campaigners (see McCombs, 2014), one former journalist disputed that their "influence on the agenda has been anything other than marginal for a long time".

In addition to pockets of ideological resistance, all journalists believed that the majority of campaigners did not possess sufficient knowledge of the news production process. While some journalists were aware that campaigners operated with extremely limited resources, this was not viewed with universal sympathy. Highlighting the need for campaigners to be more proactive, one former journalist was clear that they needed to understand that "the national media are bombarded with stories every day, they're not just sitting there waiting for your particular issue to pop up on their desk ... you've got to work hard to get interest". Stories about women were critiqued for being "dull and dry" by one journalist, while another journalist admitted that campaigners needed to give their stories more "rah-rah skirt". Critique was also levelled at those who did not make themselves more readily available to the inevitable whims of the news cycle. Dismissing the regular sending of press releases as an ineffective strategy, all journalists believed that campaigners were "too slow moving". One journalist working for a right-leaning publication encapsulated such viewpoints, when he stated that "if they are organisations where you have to ring up and it takes forever, you think [I'm not going to] bother".

Campaigners were, however, acutely aware that when compared to other, more 'worthy' policy problems, reform of women's penal policy (catering for just 5% of the total prison population) was not considered important by the vast majority of journalists. In spite of the resolve of some to achieve "a sensible discussion" in the media, many campaigners felt pessimism at the likelihood of this occurring. One campaigner did not believe she had ever received "any positive coverage", while another admitted that the subject area was "not attractive, that's the bottom line. People don't want to know." Aware of their peripheral status, one campaigner concluded that: "you've really got to fight as a penal reformer to get something of your agenda into the public domain". Campaigners also recognised that journalists' news values often worked in direct opposition to their public messages. Highlighting an example of 'ignorant' journalism, one campaigner recalled a story that "Blackpool women's centre was running head massage classes for prisoners ... that's all they pick up and so it's a totally ignorant view". While some campaigners were keen to work with journalists to 'balance' such stories, others refused to engage in reactive media work. Having been 'burnt' by past experiences, one campaigner concluded that: "there's no point in talking to these people because it's not an avenue that you can use".

It is clear that operating on the periphery of the media agenda presents many challenges to those wishing to influence 'the fund of [public] ideas' (Price and Tewksbury, 1997: 177). It is consequently easy to see why many campaigners remain disillusioned about working in the media spotlight and are reticent to pursue closer relations with journalists. Providing the perspective from government, the following section will highlight that, despite having an institutional advantage, policy makers shared similar concerns about media engagement.

## Policy makers as news sources

While routinely criticised for being too 'media conscious' and relishing their public 'visibility' (see Rhodes, 2011: 106), those former Justice Ministers interviewed for this research (from across the political spectrum) did not operate in this manner. Consistent with the experiences of penal reform campaigners, policy makers described a picture of either extreme difficulty in achieving media coverage or strong feelings about the sensationalised distortion of facts when stories *were* reported, with seemingly little in the way of balanced reporting. The lack of ministerial interest stemmed from either a genuine belief that media coverage was of less importance than 'getting the job done', or that being on the receiving end of coverage was generally a negative experience, and therefore to be avoided in the main. In direct contrast to the aspirations of Baroness Corston, one former Justice Minister viewed media coverage for the women's agenda as 'secondary', while another agreed that it was 'not important'. One former Minister disliked the public aspect of the role and expressed a strong desire to "get on with the policy ... without having to worry about fighting off *the Sun* and *the Mail*". Highlighting difficulties in achieving the 'right' news coverage, one former Minister recalled that: "even if I tried to put in something positive, you'd never get it through the noise, so an ideal day is not to be in the media".

While Ministers had the relative autonomy to decide whether to pursue media strategies, their civil servants[5] (policy officials) did not. Operating under pressure from colleagues in the press office, one former civil servant admitted that the women's policy unit came under a "huge amount of pressure" to produce "good news" stories. With press officials adopting the role of journalists, policy officials (themselves concerned with research and implementation) were viewed as "a bit problematic", due to their resistance to publicise short-term policy successes. Describing similar experiences to both Ministers and campaigners, policy officials were highly sceptical of the (particularly right-wing) journalists operating in this area. One former civil servant believed that most coverage on women's penal policy was "voyeuristic" and "dramatic", and explained that "when we got [media] interest they weren't looking for solutions". Journalists, as far as she was concerned, had no real interest in alternatives to custody, and this provided an obstacle to the policy strategies that the department wished to publicise.

It would, however, be erroneous to paint an entirely negative picture of government–media relations. Interviews with former Ministers and policy officials revealed instances of media work, often in collaboration with penal reformers. 'Savvy' examples of joint campaigning involved reformers pursuing media coverage to 'lay the ground' for official announcements or forthcoming policy proposals. Yet despite such instances it would be fair to say that, similar to the position adopted by many campaigners, government media strategies were considered 'secondary' and of less importance to agenda-setting than contemporary policy analysts may predict.

It is possible at this stage to identify the existence of a clear barrier between the news imperatives of journalists and the messages that policy makers and campaigners wish to pursue. That the media can act as important sources to publicise the issues of pressure groups (Hobbs and Hamerton, 2014: 5) is widely recognised, but this is clearly subject dependant. Interviews revealed that penal reform is an issue of limited interest to media professionals (even those deemed sympathetic to the cause), and campaigners, reticent to frame their issues in more sensationalist, journalist-friendly packages, have consequently found it difficult to operate in the media sphere. Although it is important to recognise that not *all* media coverage of women offenders is sensationalist or trivialised, it is clear that media narratives are complex (see the analysis of the 'chivalry hypothesis' by Grabe et al, 2006, for example). While media representations can create the impression that crime is more violent and prevalent than it really is (Hobbs and Hamerton, 2014: 129; see also Hough and Roberts, 1995; Roberts et al, 2002), the reality is that women offenders constitute just 5% of the custodial estate, and are incarcerated for short periods of time[6] for mostly non-violent offences.[7] Those working on women's penal policy know only too well that the vast majority of women offenders are almost certainly *not* the people journalists are thinking of when they call for tougher sentencing (Hedderman, 2012: 11), yet how to effectively communicate this message?

## Strategies to improve coverage

Given the climate within which they work, it is easy to see why there is a tendency for some political actors to focus their efforts away from the media spotlight. The intensification of stealth strategies has been debated elsewhere (see Green, 2009; Loader, 2010; Birkett, 2014) and will not be revisited here, suffice to say that in our 21st-century, 24/7 'mass mediated reality' (Nimmo and Combs, 1983) total secrecy is no longer achievable or desirable. In order to confront the challenges highlighted throughout this chapter, those wishing to improve their media coverage may look to the literature on framing (see Snow et al, 1986; Entman, 1993; Terkildsen and Schnell, 1997), and seek to 'patrol the facts' (Ericson et al, 1989: 18) in ways that are most likely to resonate with journalists. Highlighting the need for such actors to improve their media strategies, Solomon argued that 'it is naïve to expect newspapers and broadcasters to be responsible conduits of information, and [that campaigners must] develop *more effective communication strategies*' (Solomon, 2005: 35, emphasis added).

Interviews with journalists revealed that campaigners could make more progress if they developed more sophisticated strategies of information management. One journalist-turned-campaigner was clear that: "using clever tactics, playing the game with journalists, being savvy, is part of getting your message out there and part of achieving the momentum for change". While several campaigners were keen to describe such media work, a haphazard picture of media relations emerged. Some campaigners clearly understood the concept of framing and were aware that they needed to stop saying 'the same old thing'. Although by no means a universal strategy, the right way for some meant framing their messages in ways that were more likely to resonate with those who were traditionally unsympathetic to the penal reform agenda. Appreciating the need to be opportune when it came to coverage meant that other campaigners gave less thought to the strategic messages that they wanted to pursue. Responding to 'anything and everything', some campaigners engaged in a confusing 'scatter gun' approach, which acted to blur the key point(s) that they worked to articulate.

The main critique from journalists was the need for newsworthy stories that would be more interesting to readers. While journalists were not particularly interested in policy proposals, they *were* interested in individual cases. All journalists believed that campaigners needed to make a greater use of case studies and be more prepared to give examples of 'women doing good'. One campaigner was aware that, "without the actual women, they don't want to know", but, in common with other campaigners, was reluctant to provide journalists with access to clients for ethical reasons. Journalists also described the need for campaigners to cultivate greater working relations within the industry. Those journalists working for right-leaning publications believed that campaigners needed to make far more effort in developing relations, and those working for the left-leaning press agreed this to be a judicious strategy. By simply targeting those they perceived to be 'ethical' (predominantly working for the left-leaning press), all journalists agreed that campaigners were simply preaching to the converted. The real skill, as one former journalist put it, was to "convince people who are naturally hostile". Most journalists were clear that campaigners needed to think more strategically about how they could work with agenda-setting news outlets such as the *Daily Mail*.

## Influencing penal discourse for women

As the issue of women's imprisonment arguably 'remain[s] outside or on the edge of public consciousness' (Hilgartner and Bosk, 1988: 57), it is clear that campaigners wishing to pursue media coverage must make important decisions about the mode of discourse that they adopt (see Schlesinger et al, 1991: 400). In so doing, a considered analysis of Rutherford's (1993) typology of competing penal ideologies (punitive, 'efficiency first' and reformative) would prove beneficial. Recent research by Mills and Roberts (2011; 2012) similarly identified the above typologies in relation to penal reform sector strategies (labelled 'crime fighting', 'managerialist' and 'humanitarian'). In short, punitive or 'crime fighting' rhetoric is framed within the 'tough on crime' agenda and argues that community punishments are a more robust alternative to custody; 'managerialist' or 'efficiency first' discourse focuses on dispassionate arguments about the financial wastage of sending so many people to prison; while 'humanitarian' or 'reformative' messages highlight the human costs of imprisonment (Mills and Roberts, 2011; 2012). Interviews with campaigners revealed the use of all three forms of rhetoric in relation to the punishment of women offenders. The above framework will be used to explore their utility as public messages.

One campaigner was clear that tough or 'crime fighting' strategies were the most effective with policy makers and the media, and that others needed to "stop this constant focus on women as victims. We know they're victims, but ... if you want to bring the government with you, and the media, there has to be a better balance." For those adopting 'crime fighting' discourse, being savvy meant employing "a messaging structure that doesn't just irritate and annoy the people you are actually trying to get on board". 'Tough' strategies required campaigners to address 'the values of middle England' and successfully articulate that community alternatives for women were challenging and by no means 'soft'. Other campaigners described a judicious way forward as one that focused on the financial wastage of sending large numbers of women to prison unnecessarily. Touting a 2008 report from the New Economics Foundation,[8] which provided an economic argument for the increased use of women's community alternatives, some campaigners felt that such arguments would resonate among those right-wing journalists and politicians who were not traditionally sympathetic to the agenda. In seeking to 'play the Treasury card' (Loader, 2010: 361), campaigners were supported by one journalist working for a left-leaning publication, who believed that they would have greater traction in the right-wing press if they "made the economic argument ... talk through their pockets".

Unlike the other messaging structures that aim to work *within* the dominant media–crime paradigm, 'humanitarian' or rehabilitative discourse adopts an inclusionary approach and seeks to explore the wider problems surrounding women's offending and imprisonment. Mills and Roberts concluded that such discourse was not considered a universally viable option by campaigners, due in large part to concerns about the current political climate (Mills and Roberts, 2012: 29). Consistent with Newburn and Jones' assertion that 'failure to talk tough on crime [has become] akin to political suicide (Newburn and

Jones, 2005: 74), such a viewpoint was confirmed by one campaigner, who explained that "the policymakers are frightened to death of what will come into the papers if they are seen to take an unequal approach or a soft approach".

Yet despite its perceived distance from the current political agenda, some campaigners were pursuing (or keen to pursue) overtly 'humanitarian' or social justice messages. Keen to move public debate from the current emphasis on *penal* solutions for *social* problems, one campaigner explained that: "if you take away the criminality it gets heard, it's a social justice issue". Highlighting empirical research that consistently finds people less punitive than the media or politicians maintain (see Roberts et al, 2002), and pointing to the results of a 2007 *SmartJustice* poll[9] that purported to demonstrate public backing for increased alternatives to custody for women, such campaigners believed there would be widespread support for this agenda.

## Conclusion

While a primary tool of contemporary lobbying is the use and manipulation of the media (Hobbs and Hamerton, 2014: 72), relations between journalists and penal reform campaigners are unsettled. As journalists (or certainly those working for right-leaning publications) are often unprepared to cover stories on this subject, the topic of women's penal policy exists on the fringes of the media agenda. This chapter has highlighted the series of challenges for campaigners wishing to sell their policies in the 'competitive market-place' of ideas (Schlesinger and Tumber, 1994: 7), and it is easy to see why some may prefer to work privately. Yet operating this way does little to dampen the 'hot' climate of public opinion on matters of crime and justice (see Loader, 2010) and gives little allowance for prevailing attitudes to be challenged, let alone improved (Green, 2009: 529). In order to successfully insert their claims into news publications and influence 'the fund of ideas' (Price and Tewksbury, 1997: 177), it is clear that campaigners must 'understand the conventions and values that drive journalists' (Wallack et al, 1999: 40).

There is a clear requirement for campaigners to understand the practical realities of news production, and how they choose to frame their messages is a crucial part of this process. In considering Rutherford's (1993) competing penal ideologies, the previous section of this chapter highlighted the dominant modes of discourse used by penal reformers in their arguments about women. While it is by no means the intention to pitch one strategy against another, it is widely documented that the most successful messages are those which are framed within the dominant ideology (Gramsci, 1971; Snow et al, 1986; Terkildsen and Schnell, 1997). With successive governments talking increasingly tough (and austere) on crime control, it could be argued that the messages most likely to be successfully inserted into media discourse are those that are framed through punitive or 'efficiency first' rhetoric. Yet that is not to state that 'humanitarian' or social justice discourse has little chance of campaign success. As we enter the unchartered territory of *Transforming Rehabilitation*, there is a hope that the rhetoric of rehabilitation will pervade official discourse to a greater extent than it has done since the election of the Conservative-led Coalition in 2010. The newly formed private community rehabilitation companies, tasked with the post-custodial care of the vast majority of women offenders (who commit non-violent, low-level crimes), will have the opportunity to work with the wider social justice and welfare sector in order to reduce recidivism, and it is in their financial interests to do so.

Of course, it is a regrettable acceptance among many in the sector that none of the strategies mentioned here are likely to be considered sufficiently newsworthy to warrant a sharp surge in media interest. While understandably viewed as a secondary strategy (to the more traditional and private types of lobbying), there is a clear requirement for campaigners to engage with the news media. While Baroness Corston has stated that reducing the female prison population would be supported by the public and the media (Corston, 2011: 3), this is a subject that warrants further investigation. What is apparent, however, is that those promoting 'what works best' for women's penal reform will require a deeper understanding of how the competing frames of discourse are interpreted by those traditionally unsympathetic to the agenda, regardless of whether they are journalists, politicians or members of the public.

## Notes

[1] The data in this chapter were previously published in Birkett, G. (2014) Penal reform discourse for women offenders: Campaigners, policy strategies and 'issue reframing', *Crime, Media, Culture: An International Journal*, 10 (2): 115-32, published by Sage. The editors would like to thank the journal and the publisher for their permission to publish these data.

[2] The *Breaking the cycle: Effective punishment, rehabilitation and sentencing of offenders* Green Paper of 2010 was based on Conservative party proposals developed during its latter years of opposition. Its stated aim was to initiate a 'rehabilitation revolution' (MoJ, 2010: 1).

[3] Many of the arguments regarding the state of public opinion on women offenders are framed using data gathered from the 2007 *SmartJustice* (ICM) poll conducted by the Prison Reform Trust. With just over 1,000 respondents, and one of the very few polls ever specifically conducted in public opinion and women offenders, the results determined that the majority of respondents (86%) supported community alternatives for women, along with an element of community payback. While this small-scale poll undoubtedly provides a useful indication of public opinion, there is a pressing need for further empirical research in this area.

[4] The data used in this chapter were gathered as part of doctoral fieldwork. Over 30 interviews were conducted with policy actors and journalists operating in the field of criminal justice, including: 10 interviews with crime and home affairs journalists (including two former journalists), four interviews with former Ministers, three interviews with former civil servants from the Women's Policy Unit at the MoJ, and 10 interviews with the directors and staff of penal reform campaign organisations.

[5] The former policy officials interviewed for this research had operated in the senior ranks of the MoJ. Unlike Ministers who are politically appointed, civil servants are permanent and anonymous, and are consequently able to accrue a great deal of specialist knowledge. A significant part of the advisory role is to provide Ministers with information, such as statistical evidence, the viewpoints elicited from consultations and the 'pros and cons' of particular policy options (Dorey, 2005: 71).

[6] Over half of the women entering prison in 2011-12 were to serve six months or less (MoJ (2012) *Offender management statistics quarterly bulletin*, April to June 2012, London: MoJ.)

[7] Over 80% of women entering custody in 2011-12 were for non-violent offences (MoJ (2012) *Offender management statistics quarterly bulletin*, April to June 2012, London: MoJ.)

[8] While viewed critically by some for its untransparent methodology, the New Economics Foundation (2008: 8) report argued that for every £1 invested in alternatives to prison, £14 worth of social value is generated to women and their children, victims and society over 10 years, and that the long-term value of these benefits is in excess of £100 million over a decade.

[9] http://tinyurl.com/po7a3gc

## References

Benedict, H. (1992) *Virgin or vamp: How the press covers sex crimes*, Oxford: Oxford University Press.

Birkett, G. (2014) Penal reform discourse for women offenders: Campaigners, policy strategies and 'issue reframing', *Crime, Media, Culture: An International Journal*, 10 (2): 115-32.

Blom-Cooper, L. (1977) The role of voluntary organisations as pressure groups in penal reform, in N. Walker (ed.) *Penal policy-making in England* (papers presented to the Copwood Round-Table Conference, December 1976), Cambridge: Institute of Criminology.

Carlen, P. (ed.) (2002) *Women and punishment: The struggle for justice*, Willan: Cullompton.

Cavendar, G. (2004) Media and crime policy, *Punishment and Society*, 6 (3): 335-48.

Chibnall, S. (1977) *Law-and-Order News: An analysis of crime reporting in the British press*, London: Tavistock.

Chibnall, S. (1981) The production of knowledge by crime reporters in S. Cohen and J. Young (eds) *The manufacture of news: Social problems, deviance, and the mass media*, Beverly Hills, CA: Sage.

Commission on English Prisons Today (2008) *The role of the media in shaping penal sentiment: Briefing paper*, www.prisoncommission.org.uk/fileadmin/howard_league/user/pdf/Commission/mediabriefing1.pdf

Corston, J. (2007) *The Corston report: A report by Baroness Jean Corston of a review of women with particular vulnerabilities in the criminal justice system*, London: Home Office.

Corston, J. (2011) *Breaking the cycle: Response of the APPG for Women in the Penal System*, www.howardleague.org/fileadmin/howard_league/user/pdf/Consultations/Corston_APPG_Submission.pdf

Dorey, P. (2005) *Policy making in Britain: An introduction*, London: Sage.

Dyer, R. (1993) *The matter of images: Essays on representations*, London: Routledge.

Entman, R. (1993) Framing: Toward clarification of a fractured paradigm, *Journal of Communication*, 43 (4): 51-8.

Ericson, R., Baranek, P. and Chan, J. (1989) *Negotiating control*, Toronto: University of Toronto Press.

Ericson, R., Baranek, P. and Chan, J. (1991) *Representing order*, Toronto: University of Toronto Press.

Faith, K. (2011) *Unruly women: The politics of confinement and resistance*, NY: Seven Stories Press.

Galtung, J. and Ruge, M. (1973) Structuring and selecting the news, in S. Cohen and J. Young (eds) *The manufacture of news: Deviance, social problems and the mass media*, London: Constable.

Grabe, M., Trager, K., Lear, M. and Rauch, J. (2006) Gender in crime news: A case study test of the chivalry hypothesis, *Mass Communication & Society*, 9 (2): 137-63.

Gramsci, A. (1971) *Selections from the prison notebooks*, NY: International Publishers.

Green, D. (2009) Feeding wolves: Punitiveness and culture, *European Journal of Criminology*, 6 (6): 517-36.

Hedderman, C. (2012) *Empty cells or empty words? Government policy on reducing the number of women going to prison*, London: Criminal Justice Alliance.

Heidensohn, F. (1996) *Women and crime*, London: Macmillan.

Hilgartner S. and Bosk, C. L. (1988) The rise and fall of social problems: A public arenas model, *The American Journal of Sociology*, 94 (1): 53-78.

Hobbs, S. and Hamerton, C. (2014) *The making of criminal justice policy*, Abingdon: Routledge.

Hough, M. and Roberts, J. V. (1995) *Understanding public attitudes to criminal justice*, Milton Keynes: Open University Press.

House of Commons Justice Select Committee (2013) *Women offenders: After the Corston Report*, Second Report of Session 2013-14 HC92, London: TSO.

Jewkes, Y. (2004) *Media and crime*, London: Sage.

Jones, B. D. and Wolfe, M. (2010) Public policy and the mass media: An information processing approach, in S. Koch-Baumgarten and K. Voltmer (eds) *Public policy and mass media: The interplay of mass communication and political decision making*, London: Routledge.

Jones, P. and Wardle, C. (2010) Hindley's ghost: The visual construction of Maxine Carr, in K. Hayward and M. Presdee (eds) *Framing crime: Cultural criminology and the image*, Abingdon: Routledge.

Kitzinger, J. (2000) Media templates: Patterns of association and the (re)construction of meaning over time, *Media, Culture and Society*, 22 (1): 61-84.

Loader, I. (2010) For penal moderation: Notes towards a public philosophy of punishment, *Theoretical Criminology*, 14 (3): 349-67.

Marsh, I. and Melville, G. (2014) *Crime, justice and the media*, 2nd edn, Abingdon: Routledge.

McCombs, M. E. (2014) *Setting the agenda: Mass media and public opinion*, Cambridge: Polity Press.

McQuail, D. (1987) *Mass communication theory*, London: Sage.

Mills, H. and Roberts, R. (2011) Is penal reform working? Community sentences and reform sector strategies, *Criminal Justice Matters*, 84 (1): 38–41.

Mills, H. and Roberts, R. (2012) *Reducing the numbers in custody: Looking beyond criminal justice solutions*, London: Centre for Crime and Justice Studies.

Ministry of Justice (MoJ) (2010) *Breaking the cycle: Effective punishment, rehabilitation and sentencing of offenders*, London: TSO.

MoJ (2013) *Strategic objectives for female offenders*, London: MoJ.

MoJ (2014) *Update on delivery of the government's strategic objectives for female offenders*, London: MoJ.

New Economics Foundation (2008) *Unlocking value: How we all benefit from investing in alternatives to prison for women offenders*, www.neweconomics.org/publications/entry/unlocking-value

Newburn, T. and Jones, T. (2005) Symbolic politics and penal populism: The long shadow of Willie Horton, *Crime, Media, Culture: An International Journal*, 1 (1): 72-87.

Nimmo, D. and Combs, J. (1983) *Mediated political realities*, NY: Longman.

Peelo, M. (2006) Framing homicide narratives in newspapers: Mediated witness and the construction of virtual victimhood, *Crime, Media, Culture: An International Journal*, 2 (2): 159-75.

Price, V. and Tewksbury, D. (1997) News values and public opinion: A theoretical account of media priming and framing, in G. A. Barnett and F. J. Boster (eds) *Progress in communication sciences: Advances in persuasion*, vol. 13, Greenwich, CT: Ablex.

Rhodes, R. A. W. (2011) *Everyday life in British government*, Oxford: Oxford University Press.

Roberts, J., Stalans, L., Indermaur, D. and Hough, M. (2002) *Penal populism and public opinion: Lessons from five countries*, Oxford: Oxford University Press.

Rutherford, A. (1993) *Criminal justice and the pursuit of decency*, Winchester: Waterside Press.

Schlesinger, P. and Tumber, H. (1994) *Reporting crime: The media politics of criminal justice*, Oxford: Oxford University Press.

Schlesinger, P., Tumber, H. and Murdock, G. (1991) The media politics of crime and criminal justice, *The British Journal of Sociology*, 42 (3): 397-420.

Seal, L. (2011) Ruth Ellis and public contestation of the death penalty, *The Howard Journal of Criminal Justice*, 50 (5): 492-504.

Snow, D. A, Burke Rochford Jr, E., Worden, S. K., and Benford, R. D. (1986) Frame alignment processes, micromobilization, and movement participation, *American Sociological Review*, 51 (4): 464-81.

Solomon, E. (2005) Is the press the real power behind punitivism?, *Criminal Justice Matters*, 59: 34-5.

Soroka, S., Lawlor, A., Farnsworth, S. and Young, L. (2012) Mass media and policymaking, in W. Xun, M. Ramesh, M. Howlett, S. Fritzen and E. Araral (eds) *Routledge Handbook of Public Policy*, Abingdon: Routledge.

Terkildsen, N. and Schnell, F. I. (1997) How media frames move public opinion: An analysis of the women's movement, *Political Research Quarterly*, 50: 879-900.

Wallack, L., Woodruff, K., Dorfman, L. and Diaz, I. (1999) *News for a change: An advocate's guide to working with the media*, Thousand Oaks, CA: Sage.

# FOURTEEN

# Conclusions

*Jill Annison, Jo Brayford and John Deering*

Preceding chapters have covered a wide range of topics and theories about female offenders and the criminal justice system. In drawing together some overall conclusions, this chapter will engage with issues arising from the Corston Report (2007) and the current Transforming Rehabilitation (TR) programme, and make some tentative observations about possible futures. Some of the impetus that drove the compilation of this book came from what is now regarded, at least among academics, practitioners and campaigning groups, as 'received wisdom': namely, that women's offending and their needs within the criminal justice system are different to those of males. It is thus concerning and somewhat perplexing that these aspects still do not seem to find resonance at central government level, with persisting conventional notions, or at least unquestioned assumptions, that a criminal justice system designed by men for men can provide equality, or that females can be slotted into 'male' approaches to justice. From the perspective adopted in this book these approaches are viewed as limited, both in their scope and in their effectiveness. Instead, our conceptualisation (in line with Corston) opens the door to exploring what women's needs are and what might 'work' in a holistic way to ameliorate problems and thus help reduce women's offending.

The publication of the Corston Report in 2007 drew attention to the many women serving sentences for minor or non-violent offences; such responses were felt to be both disproportionate and inappropriate. Corston clearly identified women's vulnerabilities, including domestic violence, childcare issues, being a single parent, mental illness, low self-esteem, eating disorders, substance misuse, poverty, isolation and unemployment (Corston, 2007: 2), and argued that these vulnerabilities are likely to result in crisis points, which ultimately may result in entry into the criminal justice process and, in many cases, into prison. She concluded that for most women (other than those committing the most serious crimes), it was more appropriate to address the range of issues connected with their offending before imprisonment became a serious option.

Moreover, Corston argued that when women were made subject to community sentences, these should be different in focus, content and style to those imposed on men. These arguments were based on the assertion that the reasons for women's and men's offending are often different, as are their routes towards desistance; that their needs differ and thus that measures introduced to address these issues need also to be different, in order to maximise the chances of successful outcomes. In other words, this was a principled stance and also an issue of 'fitness for purpose'.

As indicated in the various chapters in the book, although the Corston Report was welcomed by the then Labour government, it clearly presented two significant challenges, given the direction in which the criminal justice system had been moving over the previous 20 years.

The first challenge was about the 'punitive turn' that saw a general 'up-tariffing' of sentencing for women offenders, with the women's prison population in England and Wales more than doubling (from 1,979 to 4,267) between 1995 and 2010 (Prison Reform Trust, 2014). While this may have now reduced slightly and levelled out, it shows little sign of reversing to the previous significantly lower level: 'at 10th October, 2014 the women's prison population in England and Wales stood at 3,902, 50 less than a year previously' (Prison Reform Trust in conjunction with Soroptimist UKPAC, 2014: 13). The trend for the increasing use of custody in England and Wales can be traced back to the Criminal Justice Act 1993. This repealed important provisions of its 1991 predecessor, which had successfully begun to reduce the prison population. The reasons for this have been widely debated elsewhere (for example Bottoms, 1995; Garland, 2001; Pratt et al, 2005; McIvor and Burman, 2011) and will not be revisited here. However, it is of importance to note that Corston's recommendation to reduce the incarceration of women, on the basis that most women's offending was insufficiently serious to warrant custody, came up against the political and legislative shift away from an emphasis on keeping custody for the more serious offences, and a playing down of persistence, that had been central features of the Criminal Justice Act 1991 (see Ashworth, 2010).

The second challenge – and one that in many ways raised separate issues of methods and content – was provision for women on community orders. As noted earlier, it has long been argued that the criminal justice system has been designed for men and that only minor adjustments have ever been made for women, including in the provision of community supervision by the probation service. While there have been some notable exceptions, one of which is the subject of Chapter Five (by Asher and Annison), the prevailing tendency has been for standard processes to be applied: this overlooks 'gender variables, context and power dynamics' that have an impact on women offenders (Jordan, 2013: 3). Moreover, in line with the overarching arguments that run throughout this book, 'interventions must challenge the structural and cultural oppression that women face' (McDermott, 2014: 362).

As well as emphasising these wider considerations, Corston threw down a further challenge to the way in which the government had moved the practice of the probation service and hence community supervision. Over the previous 20 years, this had moved away from what might be regarded as 'traditional' practices aimed at 'rehabilitation', towards its agenda of offender management, risk assessment and punishment, while still retaining a residual commitment to rehabilitation (Vanstone, 2004; Raynor and Vanstone, 2002). In brief, Corston argued that supervision with women should be holistic and individual, needs-based and empowering, and conducted in a manner that women found unthreatening and engaging, rather than managing and confrontational (Corston, 2007: 2).

Within this context, the chapters in this book have reviewed the ways in which policy has changed since Corston, and have also considered how things might develop in the future. Each chapter draws its own conclusion and it is not our intention to revisit them in any detail, but to try to draw out some overall themes/conclusions.

The chapters within Part One and Part Two of this book emphasise the crucial importance of the structural, social and personal factors that impact on pathways into and out of the criminal justice system for female offenders. The various approaches endorse the integration of holistic approaches which, in line with Corston, are seen as best practice in this field, not least because they connect in a meaningful and ongoing way with the lived experiences of girls and women. What is striking throughout all these chapters is the impetus in this area of policy and practice that came from the Corston Report (2007) and the innovative developments across probation, youth justice and third sector settings, often in collaboration with each other. However, what is also apparent across all of these spheres is the small-scale nature of many of the projects and the lack of full organisational integration of these principles and approaches; this has left many of them vulnerable in the face of the TR changes. This, in turn, has led to particular concern that female offenders will yet again become a marginalised group in the criminal justice system, particularly given the political rhetoric of 'management' of offenders and where Payment by Results (in terms of reducing reoffending) will drive delivery of interventions, at least to some degree (see MoJ, 2013a). The prospect that female offenders will continue to be fitted into a system designed primarily by, and for, men is the key stumbling block that, despite Corston's visionary recommendations, has not been taken on board at central government level. Indeed, as noted in 2013 by the Justice Select Committee:

> The Government's proposals for Transforming Rehabilitation have clearly been designed to deal with male offenders. Funding arrangements for provision for women appear to be being shoehorned into the payment by results programme, resulting in the likelihood of a loss of funding for broader provision encompassing both women offenders and those with particular vulnerabilities that put them at risk of offending. (House of Commons Justice Select Committee, 2013: 86)

The crucial importance of holding onto distinctive provision for female offenders is reiterated throughout the chapters in Parts One and Two, and the perspectives provided from these different contexts lend support to the following recommendations:

> Leadership is needed to bridge the disconnect between policy and implementation; gender-specific approaches are the exception but should be the rule; uncertain funding of services working with women in trouble is counter-productive; attitudes to women in trouble are perceived as barriers to progress; and, there are clear opportunities to reduce the women's prison population. (Prison Reform Trust in conjunction with Soroptimist UKPAC, 2014)

This last point reiterates the interlinkage between these various elements of policy and practice in relation to the way that female offenders are dealt with both in community and custodial settings. When considering how issues around the imprisonment of women might have changed since Corston, it is clear that there has been formal concern about the rate of female imprisonment for almost 20 years. As Burman, Malloch and McIvor argue in Chapter Four, the growth in the female prison population (at least in the case of Scotland) can more likely be attributed to the increasing use of custodial sentences by courts than to any changes in the pattern of female offending (see also McIvor and Burman, 2011). The failure of the government to curtail magistrates' powers to remand in custody and to pass short prison sentences for minor offences could have addressed some of these issues, but to date this has not happened. It would appear that judicial independence is not the issue at stake; rather it is a continuing preference for wanting to be seen as being 'tough on crime'.

Moreover, contrary to Corston's strictures, it would seem that some women are sent to prison to 'help' them with criminogenic needs, as a 'place of safety' or 'for their own good'. However misguided we might regard this – and Corston explicitly spoke out against this practice (Corston, 2007: 9) – it is the case that some initiatives in the form of prison programmes have been set up to help women deal with needs and problems associated with offending. These programmes have been designed to help reduce the pain and damaging effects of the prison environment (Carlen, 2002: 222). Unfortunately, such initiatives have often helped to justify more women being locked up, and improvements of this nature may inadvertently help legitimate the sending of increasing numbers of women to prison in the future. It is depressing in the extreme that Carlen's cautionary words from 2002 are still of such relevance in the current circumstances:

> Most of the cosmetically-new policies currently reinvigorating the power of carceral clawback in the English women's prisons have been powered by the common-sense ideologies of optimistic campaigners (and prison-illiterate therapeutic experts) who have failed to remember (or who never have realised) that prison is for punishment by incarceration. (Carlen, 2002: 221)

However, reducing the number of women in custody is not a straightforward issue. One of the key arguments set out by reformers is that, because of women's vulnerabilities, there should be differential treatment in sentencing. This would help to reduce the number of women sent to custody and as a solution to the problem this may seem like a sensible way forward. However, as Feilzer and Williams argue in Chapter Eleven, there is a better solution; one that may be reached via a gender-neutral approach. While there are many very good reasons for reducing the number of women being sent to prison, Feilzer and Williams argue that those reasons are also applicable to men, especially those who have committed offences similar in seriousness to those committed by women. Thus, any special considerations should apply to all. It is pointed out in their chapter that the criminal justice system is already discriminatory; and as noted earlier, it is a system designed by men to deal with male offending. Feilzer and Williams argue for a more radical approach to delivering true equality. This involves revisiting sentencing; an improvement in sentencing decisions for both women and men would have a greater impact on women, which would iron out the present discriminatory aspects of the system while reducing the number of females being sentenced to custody.

Furthermore, Trebilcock and Dockley in Chapter Twelve point out that while the TR proposals to introduce post-custody supervision for all short-term prisoners may make access to services easier for some women, the attendant dangers are that resources may turn this supervision into a reporting process that increases the chances of women coming into further conflict with the criminal justice system via breach. The point is made that whatever changes come into being, these need to be closely monitored by government to assess their impact. Moreover, although in some ways provision for women prisoners may have improved and be more targeted and appropriate (see Annison and Hageman, Chapter Eight, and Stevens, Chapter Ten), there remain considerable concerns about women in custody. Ultimately, however, our argument goes back to one of the central points of Corston: that too many women are being sentenced to custody in the first place and that prison needs to be displaced as a main sentencing option for most women offenders (Corston, 2007: 9).

In terms of future developments, it seems reasonable to conclude that the TR changes have indeed 'transformed' the entire agenda of criminal justice both for women and for men. Taking the first of Corston's challenges, that of the reduction in the use of custody, there seems nothing to suggest that government thinking is changing in this regard, either in terms of a reduction in overall incarceration, or in terms of viewing women's offending as different to men's, as it continued to assert the need for 'one criminal justice system' (MoJ, 2013b: 5). The 2013 document *Transforming Rehabilitation* noted the considerable cost of prison sentences (£3 billion a year) and regarded reconviction rates as too high (MoJ, 2013a: 6), but its solution was not to reconsider the continued high rates of imprisonment, but rather to increase overall costs for the system by the introduction of compulsory post-sentence supervision for short-term prisoners. While the document did claim that its changes would be 'cost neutral' via the 'competing of services' (MoJ, 2013a: 11), it clearly remains committed to current rates of custody. It is the case that government can legislate, and has in the past legislated, in order to limit the use of custody, as in the case of young offenders with the Criminal Justice Act 1982 and the Criminal Justice Act 1988 and for adults with the Criminal Justice

Act 1991. Current prospects do not seem good. For the foreseeable future, the government seems committed to the overuse of custody for women (and men), rather than the limiting of its use to those who have committed serious offences and/or who pose a significant risk of harm to the public.

In terms of community supervision, the creation of the community rehabilitation companies (CRCs) in June 2014 has thrown open to considerable doubt all current provision for women and the shape in which this might develop in the future. In Chapter Two, we concluded that since Corston (and despite some notable exceptions), community supervision had not routinely emerged as different to that provided for men, nor, when provided by usually small, third sector organisations, had it obtained secure funding across England and Wales (Clinks, 2013). With the privatisation of the CRCs occurring in February 2015, the involvement of those third sector organisations that have been most successful in providing the type of flexible, needs-based approach that is argued within this book as most appropriate for women must be in considerable doubt. Indeed, in publishing its list of successful bidders for the CRCs, the MoJ displayed a preference for a limited number of larger third sector organisations as 'secondary' bidders alongside the 'primes', which are, with one or two exceptions, private sector organisations (MoJ, 2014).

All of this raises the question of what might be done, as it is one thing to analyse current arrangements and offer a critique; it is quite another to change the status quo. Of course, the relevance and success of academic criminology in changing government policy has been called into question, particularly the paradoxical situation of the discipline's expansion in popularity but allegedly declining political influence (Loader and Sparks, 2011). It is beyond the scope of this book to enter into this debate, or to consider in any detail the success (or otherwise) of campaigning and of political groups in achieving change. As Birkett points out in Chapter Thirteen, one of the main problems for campaigners is the low profile of penal reform on the wider political agenda, despite crime and punishment being almost perpetual 'hot topics' in sections of the media and politics. Perhaps it is the heat of the topic that is one of the fundamental problems, in that it makes reasoned debate about these issues very difficult to promote and achieve.

The Corston Report (2007) was transformative in its scope and in its vision: the chapters in this book provide positive testaments, alongside critical critiques, regarding developments in recent years. However, the revolutionary extent of change advocated by Corston was ultimately constrained by the continuing entrenchment of prison as a sentencing sanction for women – a pivot around which policy and practice continue to revolve. While campaigning groups hold onto the spirit of change advocated by Corston (for example, the 'Justice Matters for Women' call to action from the Centre for Crime and Justice in collaboration with Women in Prison, 2014), the strictures of contestability and Payment by Results enshrined within the neoliberal TR political project seem likely to change the criminal justice landscape in a way that can only be of concern in relation to female offenders. The lack of cohesion – and a 'one size fits all' approach for offenders – is the complete antithesis of the holistic and women-centred concept advocated by Corston. The chapters in this book point to alternative visions of policy and practice for and with women offenders, and encourage an informed debate in this area. Much has been gained over recent years, but much stands to be lost. Corston's clarion call for 'a distinct, radically different, visibly-led, strategic, proportionate, holistic, women-centred, integrated approach' (Corston, 2007: 1) should not be lost in the onslaught of ideological change.

### References

Ashworth, A. (2010) *Sentencing and criminal justice* (5th edn), Cambridge: Cambridge University Press.

Bottoms, A. (1995) The philosophy and politics of punishment and sentencing, in C. Clarkson and R. Morgan (eds) *The politics of sentencing reform*, Oxford: Clarendon Press.

Carlen, P. (2002) New discourses of justification and reform for women's imprisonment in England, in P. Carlen (ed.) *Women and punishment: The struggle for justice*, Cullompton: Willan.

Centre for Crime and Justice in collaboration with Women in Prison (2014) *Justice matters for women*, www.crimeandjustice.org.uk/justice-matters-women

Clinks (2013) *Run ragged: The current experience of projects providing community based female offender support services. Interim headlines*, London: Clinks.

Corston, J. (2007) *The Corston report: A report by Baroness Jean Corston of a review of women with particular vulnerabilities in the criminal justice system*, London: Home Office.

Garland, D. (2001) *The culture of control*, Oxford: Oxford University Press.

House of Commons Justice Select Committee (2013) *Women Offenders – after the Corston Report, 2nd report of 2013-14 session*, London: TSO

Jordan, S. (2013) *Missing voices: Why women engage with, or withdraw from, community sentences*, Research paper 2013/01, London: The Griffins Society.

Loader, I. and Sparks, R. (2011) *Public criminology?*, London: Routledge.

McDermott, S.-A. (2014) You empower us and then what? A practitioner reflection on work with women offenders: Why this must go beyond the probation interview room, *Probation Journal*, 61 (4): 358-64.

McIvor, G. and Burman, M. (2011) *Understanding the drivers of female imprisonment in Scotland, Research Report 02/2011*, Scottish Centre for Crime & Justice Research, www.sccjr.ac.uk/publications/understanding-the-drivers-of-female-imprisonment-in-scotland/

MoJ (2013a) *Transforming Rehabilitation: A strategy for reform*, May, London: TSO.

MoJ (2013b) *Government response to the Justice Committee's 2nd Report of session 2013-14, Female Offenders*, London: TSO.

MoJ (2014) *The Transforming Rehabilitation Programme: The new owners of the CRCs*, www.gov.uk/government/uploads/system/uploads/attachment_data/file/389727/table-of-new-owners-of-crcs.pdf

Pratt, J., Brown, D., Brown, M., Hallsworth, S. and Morrison, W. (eds) (2005) *The new punitiveness: Trends, theories, perspectives*, Cullompton: Willan.

Prison Reform Trust (2014) *Why focus on reducing women's imprisonment? A Prison Reform Trust briefing*, www.prisonreformtrust.org.uk/Portals/0/Documents/why%20focus%20on%20reducing%20womens%20imprisonment.pdf

Prison Reform Trust in conjunction with Soroptimist UKPAC (2014) *Transforming lives: Reducing women's imprisonment*, www.prisonreformtrust.org.uk/PressPolicy/News/vw/1/ItemID/254

Raynor, P. and Vanstone, M. (2002) *Understanding community penalties: Probation, policy and social change*, Buckingham: Open University Press.

Vanstone, M. (2004) *Supervising offenders in the community: A history of probation theory and practice*, Aldershot: Ashgate.

# Index

9 781447 319313